Losing Eden

The Western History Series

Conquests and Consequences: The American West from Frontier to Region
Carol L. Higham and William H. Katerberg

Choices and Chances: A History of Women in the U.S. West
Sheila McManus

Expectations of Equality: A History of Black Westerners
Albert S. Broussard

Innovation and Inspiration: Religion in the American West
Todd M. Kerstetter

Losing Eden: An Environmental History of the American West
Sara Dant

Losing Eden

*An Environmental History
of the American West*

Sara Dant

WILEY Blackwell

This edition first published 2017
© 2017 John Wiley & Sons, Inc

Registered Office
John Wiley & Sons, Ltd, The Atrium, Southern Gate, Chichester, West Sussex, PO19 8SQ, UK

Editorial Offices
350 Main Street, Malden, MA 02148-5020, USA
9600 Garsington Road, Oxford, OX4 2DQ, UK
The Atrium, Southern Gate, Chichester, West Sussex, PO19 8SQ, UK

For details of our global editorial offices, for customer services, and for information about
how to apply for permission to reuse the copyright material in this book please see our website at
www.wiley.com/wiley-blackwell.

Library of Congress Cataloging-in-Publication Data

Names: Dant, Sara, 1967– author.
Title: Losing Eden : an environmental history of the American West / Sara Dant.
Other titles: Western history series.
Description: Chichester, UK ; Malden, MA : John Wiley & Sons, 2016. | Series: Western history series |
    Includes bibliographical references and index.
Identifiers: LCCN 2016012198| ISBN 9781118934289 (cloth) | ISBN 9781118934296 (pbk.) |
    ISBN 9781118934302 (epdf) | ISBN 9781118934319 (epub)
Subjects: LCSH: West (U.S.)–Environmental conditions–History. | Human ecology–
    United States–History.
Classification: LCC F591 . D258 2016 | DDC 978–dc23 LC record available at
    https://lccn.loc.gov/2016012198

A catalogue record for this book is available from the British Library.

Cover image: Shutterstock/Tu Le

Set in 10/12pt Minion by SPi Global, Pondicherry, India

1   2017

For Dan and Claire.

Contents

List of Figures

Acknowledgments

Losing Eden is my valentine to the American West, land that I love, and proof that writing a book takes a village; I have been fortunate to live in a heavily populated one. First, thanks to Carol Higham and Will Katerberg, whose editorial skills and patience have guided this long project to its final conclusion. Their care and consideration have been above and beyond, and this book is much stronger because of them. Thanks, too, to Andrew Davidson, who first signed on for this book with Harlan Davidson and carried it with him when he made the jump to Wiley – I appreciate the ride. Thanks also to Camille Bramall for her careful copyediting and to Denisha Sahadevan and Nivetha Udayakumar for managing the book's production.

The list of colleagues and friends who have influenced this endeavor is long, but a special thanks to: Bill Allison, LeRoy Ashby, Lisa Brady, Lincoln Bramwell, Karl Brooks, Mike Childers, Jeff Crane, Bill deBuys, Michael Egan, Eric Ewert, Dale Goble, Greg Gordon, Frank Harrold, Mark Harvey, Molly Holz, Kathryn MacKay, Kevin Marsh, Susan Matt, Jennifer Ross-Nazzal, Richard Sadler, Gene Sessions, John Sillito, Sarah Singh, Adam Sowards, Louis Warren, Don Worster, and David Wrobel. Thanks also to Brett Badley for his maps, Joyce Dant for her original artwork, Weber State University's College of Social and Behavioral Sciences and the History Department for funding support, and the Southern Utah Wilderness Alliance, Buffalo Bill Center of the West, Boise State University Library, NASA, and the US Forest Service for images.

I can hardly believe that Hal Rothman is no longer here to point out my errors and chide me for not citing him more. His energy still inspires me and

I will always be grateful for his friendship. I am also in debt to countless students over the years who've helped shape this narrative. No, I will not raise your grade.

Thanks to my parents Joyce and Michael Dant and sister Jill Schlessinger for unwavering support and encouragement – navigating through life is much easier when you know for certain there's a safety net.

Losing Eden is dedicated to the two loves of my life. I wrote this book as an act of hope that my daughter Claire might live Thoreau's dream "to know an entire heaven and an entire earth." It would take more words than stars, however, to count the ways that Dan Flores enhances and enriches my life, so I will simply say, thank you for everything, babe.

Introduction

The Nature of the West

"Order is the dream of man," writer Wallace Stegner concluded, encapsulating the environmental history of the American West in just six simple words.

Environmental history is a relatively new discipline that emerged in the 1960s and 1970s during the heyday of the environmental movement. As "history," it is the study of change over time, but instead of focusing on traditional topics like presidents and wars, environmental history examines the evolving relationship between people and nature – it is rooted in place. From this perspective humans exist *within* nature, not apart from it, and like all animal species, our survival depends upon the health of the habitat in which we live. We both shape and are shaped by the world around us.

There are perhaps as many different definitions of "the West" as there are westerners, but in this text, the term describes the contiguous, continental region lying west of the 100th meridian (see Figure 0.1). This longitudinal divide separates the more arid West from the more lush East, effectively delimiting an ecological as well as geographical distinction that has affected the human/nature interaction over time. Beyond these cartographic boundaries, the West's exceptionalism derives from its unique environment. It is a land of extremes. The highest and lowest temperatures ever recorded in the United States occurred in the West; in the lower 48, the West has the tallest peaks and the lowest valleys; the West also holds national snow records, hail-size records, no-rain records, and even fastest temperature rise and drop records. For Stegner, the West's aridity is essential: "[it] gives the western

Losing Eden: An Environmental History of the American West, First Edition. Sara Dant.
© 2017 John Wiley & Sons, Inc. Published 2017 by John Wiley & Sons, Inc.

Figure 0.1 The American West. Source: Map drawn by Brett Badley and reproduced with permission.

landscape its character … the air its special dry clarity … [aridity] puts brilliance in the light and polishes and enlarges the stars … exposes the pigmentation of the raw earth … limits, almost eliminates, the color of chlorophyll … [and] erodes the earth in cliffs and badlands." There is no way to comprehend the past or present West, and by extension the nation, without understanding the pervasive influence of these powerful natural forces. As the region's greatest asset and challenge, the natural West has constantly forced residents to rethink and reconfigure their relationship with the land.

Far from the "wilderness" described in earlier histories, the West was never an undiscovered "Eden," but instead an ancient homeland with landscapes that humans have inhabited, modified, and managed for thousands of years. Native peoples generally lived lightly on the land, but sometimes pressed it beyond its carrying capacity. When Europeans and later Americans arrived, then, they were engaging not with undisturbed nature, as so many argued until the 1990s, but these immigrants nevertheless portrayed the West as an "Eden" or Promised Land destined for them. By definition, "Eden" is synonymous with unspoiled paradise, a pristine utopia of bounty and abundance. For some, the West fulfilled this divine "land of milk and honey" vision, but for many, the region constituted a harsh and unforgiving desert of aridity and struggle, while others envisioned it as a vast expanse of material wealth to exploit and plunder. This fusion of Edenic myth and environmental and economic reality shapes both the past and present, and the title, *Losing Eden*, underscores this complicated relationship, encourages readers to lose this conceit of a "virgin continent," and provides a central theme for this book.

The following chapters synthesize the West's complex history and illuminate several key sub-themes designed to challenge readers to think critically and deeply about the past. First, as a consequence of the European introduction of a capitalist market system, tension soon developed between economy and environment, between promoting economic success and development, and preventing ecological destruction. As Stegner, who wrote about the West better than anyone, explained: "for at least three millennia we have been engaged in a cumulative and ambitious race to modify and gain control of our environment." Many historians have argued that the East's early relationship with the West was colonial and exploitive: extractive industries funneled western raw materials to eastern factories, larger and wealthier eastern financial institutions plundered the West for their own material gain, and eastern lawmakers dictated land policy to largely powerless westerners. Even former Secretary of Interior Bruce Babbitt, a westerner, observed that "traditionally, the American West has been something of a third-world economy based on resource extraction." While there is certainly much truth in these generalizations, the reality is more complicated. Easterners did plunder the West, but so, too, did many westerners. The natural resources of the West did flow to eastern factories, but they also built western cities and fueled trade across the Pacific. Ultimately, the West has enjoyed a disproportionate flow of federal largesse in the form of railroads, water projects, roads, and public lands, and some of the earliest efforts to conserve and preserve nature in the region came from the East. The West-as-Colony stereotype persists, however, for two essential reasons: first, it has significant foundation in fact, which this text will explore; and second, it is a story that westerners want to hear about themselves because it absolves them and places plundering blame squarely on eastern shoulders. But rather than ask "Whose fault?," this book encourages readers to consider a far more important question: "At what cost?" Americans have long celebrated "progress," material wealth, and technological advancements without considering their true environmental price. This exploit versus protect riddle remains a challenge even into the twenty-first century.

A second common thread running through much of the West's environmental history and this book is the "tragedy of the commons," a cautionary idea popularized by ecologist Garrett Hardin. Hardin argued that individuals acting in their own self-interest will ignore the best interests of larger society and deplete "common" resources. To illustrate his point, he used the example of a local community grazing "commons," "open to all," where each resident could sustainably graze one cow. An individual herdsman could easily rationalize that the addition of one more cow to the pasture would have no appreciable negative effect on the "commons," but would bring appreciably greater profit to the herdsman himself. So long as he is the only herdsman who thinks and acts this way, the "commons" remains unharmed and stable. But the "tragedy" arises when each herdsman in the community reaches this same conclusion and each adds another cow to the "commons." The individual's contribution does not measurably degrade the "commons" but the *collective* additions result in overgrazing. Even though the individual's intent is not malicious, the effect is nevertheless tragic. As Hardin writes, "Freedom in a commons brings ruin to all."

Hardin's example is oversimplified and abstract, as not all people or groups utilizing community-managed resources ("commons") have careened headlong toward "tragedy." In this text, the "tragedy of the commons" predicament is most useful for explaining the exploitation of open-access resources such as forests, water, air, and grazing lands, rather than the more narrow, legal definition of "commons" Hardin outlined. Uniquely in the West, public lands, such as national parks, forests, and reserves, endeavor to counter Hardin's predictions of environmental "ruin" through federally regulated natural resources. Utilizing the "tragedy of the commons" idea to examine the long-term environmental consequences of the transition from local to national and international economies acts as a powerful metaphor for understanding the environmental problems that arose in the American West, returning again to the "at what cost" question.

Finally, the goal of achieving sustainability, and avoiding the "tragedy of the commons," provides a unifying purpose to this environmental history of the American West. Sustainability's objective is the creation of environmental stability and ecological health within the framework of economic development and political systems. It is essential to our survival. Ecologists and scientists have coined the term "Anthropocene" to describe the time period, roughly since the Industrial Revolution circa 1800, when human activities have increasingly defined the physical environments of the earth. Stegner has called us "the most efficient and ruthless environment-busters in history." As we move into the twenty-first century and confront the effects of our long-term exploitation of nature and the challenges of global climate change – undeniable in the West – we must learn the environmental lessons of the past or suffer the consequences.

In the end, we care about what we know. This environmental history of the American West endeavors to connect readers with this place, whether the West is "home," a vacation destination, or merely a source of curiosity. No matter where we live, we all need clean air, clean water, and a healthy environment, which makes all of us "environmentalists." Stegner believed that "if I had not been able periodically to renew myself in the mountains and deserts of western America I would be very nearly bughouse." Indeed, he called the wild places of the West the nation's "geography of hope." Understanding the whole of the West's environmental history can help and perhaps motivate us to move forward and sustainably create and maintain the conditions under which humans and nature can co-exist in productive harmony. To realize the hope, sustainability, not Edenic myth, must become the dream and reality of the West.

Note on content and structure:

To enhance readability and avoid repetition, this text uses the terms "Indian," "Native American," and "Native" interchangeably. When new expressions or specific terms appear, a short definition or description follows immediately. The suggested reading at the end of each chapter expands upon the ideas presented in the chapter, allows readers to pursue more in-depth analysis of certain topics, and connects historical interpretations with individual writers and thinkers. A book of this length makes no claim to being comprehensive, but instead provides a new perspective for examining the arc of history – it aspires to inspire. The hope is that readers will come away not only with a heightened curiosity about the world around them, but also a more complete understanding of the past, how that past connects to the present, and how we might move forward into the future.

Suggested Reading

Alfred W. Crosby, "The Past and Present of Environmental History," *American Historical Review*, 100 (October 1995), 1177–1189.

Mark Fiege, "The Nature of the West and the World," *Western Historical Quarterly*, Vol. 42, No. 3 (Fall 2011), 305–312.

Garrett Hardin, "The Tragedy of the Commons," *Science*, Vol. 162, No. 3859 (December 13, 1968), 1243–1248.

Journal of American History Round Table Discussion on Environmental History, 76 (March 1990), including Donald Worster, "Transformations of the Earth: Toward an Agroecological Perspective in History"; Alfred W. Crosby, "An Enthusiastic Second"; Richard White, "Environmental History, Ecology, and Meaning"; Carolyn Merchant, "Gender and Environmental History"; William Cronon, "Modes of Prophecy and Production: Placing Nature in History"; Stephen J. Pyne, "Firestick History"; and Donald Worster, "Seeing beyond Culture."

Walter Nugent, "Where is the American West? Report on a Survey," *Montana: The Magazine of Western History*, Vol. 42, No. 3 (Summer 1992), 2–23.

Wallace Stegner, *Where the Bluebird Sings to the Lemonade Springs: Living and Writing in the West* (New York: The Modern Library, 2002).

Wallace Stegner, "Wilderness Letter," Wallace Stegner to David E. Pesonen, December 3, 1960. http://web.stanford.edu/~cbross/Ecospeak/wildernessletter.html (accessed February 2, 2016)

Paul S. Sutter, "The World with Us: The State of American Environmental History," *Journal of American History*, Vol. 100, No. 1 (June 2013), 94–119. http://jah. oxfordjournals.org/content/100/1/94.full.pdf+html (accessed February 2, 2016)

Louis S. Warren, "Going West: Wildlife, Frontier, and the Commons," in *The Hunter's Game: Poachers and Conservationists in Twentieth-Century America* (New Haven: Yale University Press, 1997), 1–20.

1

Losing "Eden"

"We are a biological species arising from Earth's biosphere as one adapted species among many." As one of the foremost naturalists in the world, E.O. Wilson has long argued that humans and nature share a deep, almost symbiotic relationship – they each shape and in turn are shaped by the other. This instinctive bond between people and other living systems, the product of biological evolution, he calls "biophilia" – literally "love of life." Yet of all earth's species, humans harbor the greatest capacity to inflict damage on and ultimately destabilize and destroy the very environments that sustain them. "Darwin's dice have rolled badly for earth," Wilson writes. Over time, evolution singled out our highly intelligent carnivorous primate as the dominant species in the food chain, and the traits that ultimately ensured human success fell heavily on the natural world. Wilson hopes, however, that the same big brains that enabled us to learn myriad languages, develop increasingly effective technologies, and create vibrant cultures, can also help us prevent catastrophe and collapse. "We are human in good part because of the particular way we affiliate with other organisms," he argues, and we must "save the natural world in order to save ourselves."

A close examination of the "deep history" of the environment in the American West, this evolutionary work in progress, illustrates Wilson's biophilia hypothesis, revealing how the unique geographies of the West have exerted such a powerful influence on the peoples of this region and how those people, in turn, have shaped and altered this largely arid region over time. As the first people to set foot on the North American continent, westerners

Losing Eden: An Environmental History of the American West, First Edition. Sara Dant.
© 2017 John Wiley & Sons, Inc. Published 2017 by John Wiley & Sons, Inc.

constantly innovated. New tools, the advent of agriculture, fire- and irrigation-managed environments, and the development of extensive trade routes were essential to early survival and success in the West and belie the myth of a "pristine" "Edenic" America "discovered" by Europeans.

Christopher Columbus was not first. He did not "discover America" in 1492. In fact, he was very, very late. Instead, the discovery story begins much, much further back in time and on the *western* side of North America, not the eastern. In the beginning, earth's land masses were consolidated into one super-continent that scientists have called Pangaea. About 180 to 200 million years ago, Pangaea began to break apart as a result of plate tectonics. As the continents separated, the plants and animals on each began to evolve and adapt to their unique environmental circumstances. Over the ensuing millennia, this evolutionary divergence produced myriad species, including our own human ancestors, who first separated from the progenitors of chimps and apes in Africa between 6 and 10 million years ago. By about 4 million years ago, these forebears had evolved the unique trait of walking upright, and by 2.5 million years ago, protohumans had begun to use crude stone tools to hunt large game. Armed with this primitive weaponry, these early hunters effectively exploited the changing environments around them to become the most widely distributed large land animals on the planet. These protohuman precursors to our own species (*Homo sapiens*) included *Homo erectus* and *Homo neanderthalensis* (Neanderthals). Their migration out of Africa began about 1 million years ago and slowly diffused into Asia and eventually, by about 500 000 years ago, Europe. *Homo sapiens*, distinguished by their modern skeletons and larger brain sizes, emerged in Africa approximately 180 000 years ago. As *Homo sapiens* began to leave Africa for other destinations between 55 000 and 70 000 years ago, arriving in southeast Asia about 55 000 years ago and Europe and Australia about 45 000 years ago, their big brains enabled them to cope with colder climates, use fire to shape their environment, hunt larger game animals, and facilitated what some scholars have called the "Great Leap Forward" – a sudden burst of sophistication that led to greater social organization. By 30 000–40 000 years ago, *Homo sapiens* were capable of storing vast amounts of information, crafting more sophisticated hunting tools (e.g. flint flaking, spears), and transmitting this knowledge via spoken and then ultimately written language from generation to generation, in effect compressing the entirety of human experience and wisdom collected over thousands of years into the brains of the most current generation. All of this enhanced human adaptability. While paleoanthropologists, those who study early humans, hotly contest the nature of the interaction between *Homo sapiens* and Neanderthals, *Homo sapiens* eventually became the sole surviving species from this once-diverse family tree.

Although scientists still debate their precise arrival date in the Americas, archeological and paleontological evidence shows that modern humans first came from the Old World to the New World during the last Ice Age, at least 15 000 to 30 000 years ago (see Figure 1.1). During this time frame, the earth's climate was much colder and much of its surface water was locked up in sea ice and glaciers. As a result, sea levels dropped significantly and many previously flooded or submerged areas became dry. One of these places was the Bering Strait, which lies between today's Alaska and Siberia. While the Bering Strait normally cradles the Bering Sea, during the Ice Age this relatively narrow waterway became a land "bridge" called Beringia, perhaps 1000 miles wide north-to-south at times, across which large game animals (megafauna) slowly migrated and human hunter/gatherers followed in pursuit. Over time, both animals and humans followed ice-free corridors southward, eventually populating all of North, Central, and South America. Some archeologists have also argued that in addition to these inland migrants, other Old World humans may have followed the coastline along Alaska and then continued southward along the West Coast, using small boats to propel them to new destinations in the Americas. Tantalizing new scholarship also suggests the possibility of transoceanic immigrant travel to South America from Australia around 15 000 years ago. Regardless of how they arrived, these first Americans adapted to the diverse environments of the continents and developed hundreds of distinct cultures and languages long before Columbus and the Europeans eventually arrived thousands of years later.

Anthropologists and historians have identified and classified three basic phases of human history in the Americas prior to European contact. The term "Paleoindian" refers to the earliest inhabitants and their culture, which dominated from at least 15 000 years ago until approximately 9000 years ago. As these highly nomadic first Americans diffused across the continents, they engaged in intensive hunting and gathering, utilized stone tools, and lived in bands of between 20 and 60 individuals. By about 11 500 years ago, this included the Clovis Culture, characterized by their fluted-stone spear points and named after the site in today's New Mexico where archeologists first discovered their artifacts. Clovis (and later Folsom) peoples ranged across much of the West and incorporated a rich variety of plants and big game animals into their diet.

Approximately 10 000 years ago, global environmental changes that featured a gradual warming trend and the end of the Ice Age, also brought to a close the long Pleistocene Epoch (2.6 million years ago until 11 700 years ago). This profound environmental transformation was one of the causes of the disappearance of most of the Americas' megafauna and ushered in the "Archaic" period. During this phase, which predominated until about 4000–5000 years ago, Native peoples augmented big game hunting with seasonal fruit and vegetable gathering, fish, and small game. Many Natives continued to employ

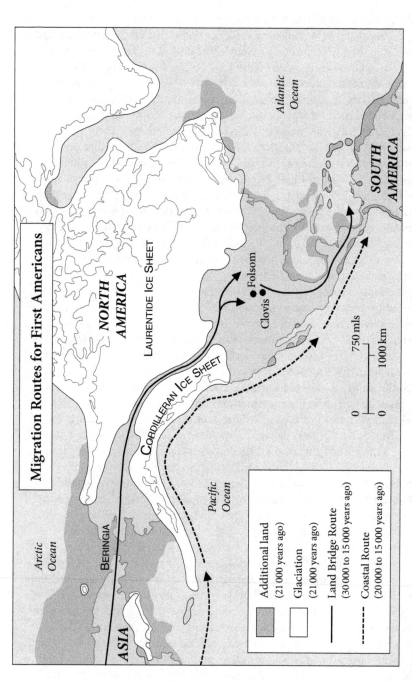

Figure 1.1 Archeological, geological, and anthropological evidence indicates that Eurasian inhabitants migrated to the Americas at least 15 000 years ago.

this subsistence strategy even after European contact, but others embraced agriculture and animal domestication beginning approximately 5000 years ago. This last phase of pre-contact history is known as the Neolithic Revolution.

Long before Columbus and the Europeans "discovered" the New World, Paleoindians and Archaic peoples had to learn to adapt and thrive in the Americas, and their interactions with the land profoundly shaped their cosmology. In sharp contrast to the Judeo-Christian creation story, which Europeans interpreted to mean that their [white male] God created the earth for humans to subdue and dominate, Native American origin stories depict a much closer bond between humans and nature, although most reject the basic premise that Paleoindians migrated from Asia to the Americas. The Kiowas believe they emerged into this world through a hollow log; the Pawnees arrived via whirlwind; Old Man Coyote created the Crows; and Southwestern Pueblos emerged from a dark underground womb-like portal called a *sipapu*. Regardless of their genesis, all Native creation stories are deeply rooted in nature and centered around bringing order out of chaos. Many accounts also involve the establishment of kinship ties between humans and animals, reinforcing their shared connection – their biophilia – with the natural world.

Whatever their point of origin, Paleo- and Archaic Indians relied directly upon their immediate environment to sustain them as hunters and gatherers, and the world these first Americans occupied was a floral and faunal cornucopia. As recently as 15 000 years ago, the primeval American West rivaled Africa's Serengeti Plains. A safari across that western landscape would have encountered camels and sloths and saber-toothed cats, herds of elephant-like mammoths and mastodons, giant early bison, horses, as well as lions and dire wolves and short-faced bears. According to many paleoanthropologists, once the Clovis hunters arrived around 13 000 years ago, they quickly helped drive the vast majority of these easy-target giants to extinction. Since many of these beasts were not prime hunter prey, however, some scientists have also argued that these massive extinctions resulted from climate change in the wake of the last Ice Age. Whatever the cause, and it is likely a convergence of both, the massive Pleistocene die-off permanently wiped out mammoths and mastodons, gigantic beavers and condors, and even a 6.5-foot saber-toothed Pacific Northwest salmon, in addition to the animals listed above. Indeed, with the exception of native pronghorn antelope, only those species that had migrated across Beringia with humans and had evolved earlier survival and co-existence strategies, such as elk, deer, and bighorn sheep, avoided this grim fate. This great ecological simplification meant the West lost much of the wildlife diversity that Africa still retains.

Among the most puzzling extinctions of the great Pleistocene die-off was that of North American horses. Historians and anthropologists have offered numerous explanations for their disappearance, but none seems quite adequate. Archeological evidence supports the combination of over-hunting and climate change as the major culprits for the extinction of mammoths and saber-toothed cats, whose small numbers and long gestational periods limited their populations anyway, yet little evidence exists regarding the disappearance of horses. Scientists believe that until about 10 000 years ago, ancestors of the modern horse dominated the natural environment of North America, constituting as much as one-third of the continent's faunal population. From their American base, these wildly successful inhabitants spread around the world (reverse Beringia migration) and became, over time, the zebras and wild Asian steppe ponies of the modern era. So, what happened here? How did this obviously successful, stable, significant population crash? Completely? Especially when their habitat, the vast grasslands of the western Plains, remained intact?

The usual suspects provide no answers. Paleontologists have found no evidence of horse jumps, for example, the mass-death kill sites used by early human inhabitants to harvest bison, nor have they found arrow points or hunting implements preserved with fossilized horse remains to indicate hunting as they have with, say, mastodons. Furthermore, if as some have posited, horses were so susceptible to human predation, why did they live on in other parts of the world? At this point, there seems to be no definitive answer to these vexing questions. But the consequences of the Pleistocene die-off were definitive. In combination with the slow development of agriculture in the Americas, the absence of big game animals with domestication potential further handicapped Archaic Indians in the coming Neolithic/Agricultural Revolution. When pastoral Europeans finally did arrive, they encountered Native Americans who had domesticated only one large mammal, the South American llama (and related alpaca), a few fowl, and dogs. American Indians utilized no other beasts of burden and their agricultural development lagged behind that of Europe's as a result.

Interestingly, of all the habitable continents colonized by migrant human populations, the Americas were the last to experience the "Neolithic Revolution" (Australia never experienced it). Literally "new stone age," the Neolithic Revolution was the grand human experiment in living with domesticated plants and animals that also included grinding stone tools and smelting metals. So why were the Americas late and with what consequences? The Fertile Crescent of the Middle East (present-day Iraq, Syria, Lebanon, Egypt) occupies the vanguard of the Neolithic Revolution, the most critical period of human development. Historians argue that this sweeping geographic arc encompassing the Tigris and Euphrates rivers of ancient Mesopotamia and the Nile River Delta of ancient Egypt formed the cradle of human civilization. It was here, at least 8000–12 000 years ago, that humans first learned to farm and raise livestock, and later to irrigate agricultural fields. Archeological evidence indicates that this Agricultural Revolution would also evolve independently at later dates in several other locations around the world. Everywhere the Neolithic Revolution occurred, it profoundly transformed the relationship between people and the natural world: human populations became less nomadic and more sedentary, produced food more efficiently and in greater quantities, and used the escape from daily hunting/gathering responsibilities to further develop art, culture, math, science, religion, and government. In essence, agriculture allowed humans to appropriate the energy of the sun for their own gain and accelerated cultural advancement.

In the Americas, however, the Neolithic Revolution began slowly and "accelerated tardily," according to environmental historian Alfred Crosby, leaving Native Americans at a distinct disadvantage when iron- and steel-wielding Europeans finally did arrive. Corn offers one explanation, he believes. Because this eventual staple evolved from a grass to a food source so slowly, the populations of the Americas, as well as their innovations, fell further and further behind those of wheat-growing Europe.

Europeans aggressively embraced sedentary agriculture, domesticated animals, and cultivated their farmlands far more rapidly than their Native American counterparts. Why? Population pressure. As human numbers increase and their demand for food rises correspondingly, people face a choice: control population or produce more food. They must "become either celibate or clever," Crosby humorously concludes. Celibacy has never been popular and population control was usually brutal, including instances in prehistory where Native peoples killed up to 40% of their female infants. Faced with such horrible prospects, humans usually chose plan B, a more reliable food supply, which farming readily addressed. But the shift from hunting and gathering to agriculture, which fundamentally altered their relationship with the natural world, usually did not occur until population densities outstripped the carrying capacity of the surrounding environment. In other words, only when people could no longer sustain their communities through subsistence hunting and gathering did they turn to the innovation of domestication. The limits of nature, in essence, forced steadily expanding human societies to make the leap. And because people settled in Europe far earlier than in the Americas, the population densities there reached critical mass earlier. The interconnectedness of the Old World – Eurasia and Africa – further facilitated the transmission of innovation through migration and trade, thereby giving Europeans a head-start in the Neolithic race. The Americas, by contrast, were disconnected from the rest of the world; as global temperatures gradually began warming approximately 15 000 years ago, signaling the end of the Ice Age, glaciers retreated and Beringia re-flooded. Paleoindians and later Archaic peoples, geographically isolated in the New World, would pay a heavy price in the long run for their Neolithic tardiness.

Despite an extensive scientific record of human habitation and alteration of the natural environment, the myth of a virginal American wilderness prior to the arrival of Europeans persists. Historians have challenged this Edenic vision, arguing that nineteenth-century writers and painters such as Henry David Thoreau and George Catlin created the "pristine myth" by overlooking the extensive habitat alteration that Indians had imposed and depicting them instead as rare and benign occupants simply waiting for "real" (European) history to begin. Nothing could be further from the truth. This mythology of a hemisphere "untrammeled by man" (to use the words of the 1964 Wilderness Act) is problematic for several reasons. First, it drastically underestimates the size and sophistication of Native populations. Prior to the arrival of Europeans, New World Indians probably numbered around 54 million, with 3.8 million living north of Mexico. Thus the Americas were far from "empty" and hadn't been for 15 000 years.

Second, the pristine "Eden" myth ignores the influence these millions exerted over the lands on which they lived. Environmental historians and anthropologists know that Indian use of fire throughout the West dramatically altered forest composition, expanded grasslands essential for game animal grazing, and dispatched pesky parasites such as lice. Burning favored fire-tolerant tree, shrub, and grass species and created more open park-like forest patterns in places like California. Regular seasonal burning also preserved open grasslands by halting tree and shrub growth and expansion; ecologists believe, for example, that the modern sagebrush landscape of the interior West only assumed that aspect by the 1800s, when non-Indian fire suppression replaced historic burning regimens. These ecological changes, in turn, created ideal habitats for large game animals, limiting Native need for domesticated livestock, and opened up suitable swaths for agricultural cultivation. In the Southwest, extensive canal systems irrigated fire-cleared gardens and fields and enabled sizable populations to live in otherwise arid environments. Deforestation, burning, and cultivation all also exposed soils to erosion.

The final problem with the pristine myth is that it reduces all early Indians to primitive terms and disregards their social and cultural sophistication, further obscuring the environmental impact of their urban settlements. Large populations took a heavy toll on local ecosystems necessitating long-range trade for goods and resources. These trade routes connected Native peoples throughout the continent and led to the establishment of extensive road systems, some of which remain in use to the present. In 1492, then, Columbus and arriving Europeans "discovered" not a pristine wilderness devoid of human influence, but a thoroughly Indianized natural environment and populations that had significantly altered and managed the American landscape for thousands of years. Far from being "benign," Archaic and Neolithic

Indians in fact exerted a disproportionate influence over the natural world and its major components. Perhaps nowhere was this influence more dramatic than in the evolution of maize/corn.

In the Americas, the shift from Archaic hunting and gathering to Neolithic agriculture occurred relatively recently, just 5000–7000 years ago in Mexico and about 4500 years ago in what is now the United States. Despite its recent appearance, agriculture was nevertheless transformative, and while the earliest domesticated plant in the Americas was squash, corn became the staple that allowed some New World Indians to flourish and expand. Humans and corn formed a powerful symbiotic relationship and the plant's evolution profoundly shaped the lives of Indians. Indeed some Mexico Natives still refer to themselves as "the corn people" and many western Indian creation stories revere the Corn Mother as the origin of their people – homage to the grain that sustained and sustains them.

Corn's caloric value derives from its ability to efficiently capture and store energy, but its modern cob-and-husk design renders it utterly dependent upon human beings for seed dispersal and reproduction. Simply put: without people to de-husk and plant it, corn would become extinct; husked cobs can't grow. Historically, there were no wild maize plants, no corn forebears so to speak, but Neolithic Indians quickly embraced hybridization to improve both the size and quantity of weedy grasses that eventually became corn. Corn, however, is terribly inefficient compared to wheat and other grains (grown by Europeans). It not only requires intensive human attention during all parts of its lifecycle – manual planting rather than simple scattering, individual hand-harvesting rather than sickle-swath mowing, and physical seed removal – but it is also lower in vitamin and protein content than wheat and more rapidly depletes the soil. Thus, corn farmers in the Americas had to expend far more energy to produce their staple than did their European wheat-growing counterparts.

Furthermore, while this "new" food sustained larger and larger populations, particularly in the arid American Southwest where it flourished, it also rendered Indians fundamentally less healthy. Paleopathologists, who study disease in early human populations, have discovered that corn consumption caused a dramatic increase in cavities and tooth decay, osteoporosis, increased the frequency of disease, and led to a *rise* in mortality at every age. The reasons are fairly simple: hunters and gatherers enjoyed a much more varied and rich diet of proteins, vegetation, and vitamins and minerals, while malnourished (especially in iron and calcium) agriculturalists relied heavily on this central starchy corn crop. Such a single or "monocrop" reliance also increased the potential for starvation among agriculturalists. If the one crop failed, so too did the Indians who cultivated it. Hunters and gatherers' dietary variety at least ensured the availability of *something* to eat. Finally, the sedentary life of

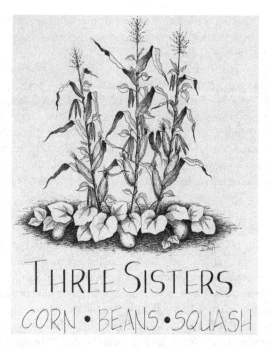

Figure 1.2 The "three sisters" constituted the primary agricultural crops of various Native American groups and were grown as a sustainable trio: beans vined up sturdy corn stalks and restored corn-depleted nitrogen to the soil, while ground-trailing squash acted as a weed barrier and conserved soil moisture. Source: Original artwork by Joyce Dant and reproduced with permission.

agriculturalists proved a fertile breeding ground for diseases and parasites, a fate nomadic hunters and gatherers nimbly avoided.

Corn, along with squash and beans, formed the "three sisters" trinity of Neolithic Native American domesticated agriculture (see Figure 1.2). Cultivation of squash, in the form of pumpkins and various gourds, predated that of maize, while the origins of bean cultivation are less clear. The combination of the three, however, creates a perfect and sustainable planting symmetry: cornstalks support vining bean plants; beans restore vital soil nitrogen depleted by corn; and squash plants provide a water-saving ground cover that shades the roots of all three. And compared to corn alone, the "three sisters" provided a more balanced suite of essential vitamins and complete proteins to Neolithic farmers as far north as the Dakotas.

The environmental shift to domesticated farming not only altered the diets and settlement patterns of Native American communities that adopted it, but also led to profound social changes. As Indians embraced agriculture, they also introduced class divisions into their societies. Unlike relatively egalitarian hunters and gatherers, agriculturalists developed social hierarchies to distribute food surpluses and manage lands. Not surprisingly, the elites thrived. Their control over and ability to "afford" to store food enabled them to survive during lean times while the working masses paid the ultimate price. Women's work also expanded as they added corn planting, weeding, harvesting, and grinding to their continued responsibilities for gathering, cooking, fuel collection, and child care. These responsibilities could convey influence, too; control over food carried power. These myriad challenges of corn evolution and cultivation have led many historians, like Crosby, and anthropologists to conclude that corn lies at the heart of the dramatic disparity between Old World and New World development and achievement. It certainly destroys the "pristine myth"; as the evidence above demonstrates, the West was no "Eden." Native peoples brought about their own substantial and significant environmental changes. In combination with their origin stories, these environmental relationships reinforced the first Americans' connection to the land.

As early as 8000 years ago, diversified cultures across the American West began developing technologies and lifestyles ranging from Archaic hunting and gathering to Neolithic agriculture specifically adapted to their particular location. Native people in this area occupied four geographic/topographic regions: the Pacific Coast, the Great Basin, the Rocky Mountains, and the Great Plains. And they did so in surprising numbers. Although a precise census count is impossible to achieve, as mentioned earlier, historians and anthropologists estimate that prior to the arrival of Europeans, Native populations north of Mexico probably numbered around 3.8 million. Of these, approximately 800 000 lived along the coast, just over 1 million lived in the Great Basin and Rocky Mountain regions, 908 000 lived in the Southwestern farming regions, and another 378 000 lived on the Great Plains. Again, these numbers hardly constitute a pristine or "virgin" wilderness, or the "Eden" that later European arrivals would mythologize.

The Sierra Nevada and Cascade ranges form the eastern boundary of the Pacific Coast region and enclose a diversified set of ecosystems ranging from the golden grasslands of California's interior to the lush and bountiful seashores that stretch from Baja to the Gulf of Alaska. In the Pacific Northwest and Columbia River Plateau, Archaic Indians diverged from their Southwestern corn-growing cousins and derived both their culture and their calories from salmon. Plateau peoples adhered to a more traditional hunting and gathering strategy that also utilized fire to manage their local environment, all of which centered around the great salmon runs. Salmon are anadromous fish, which means that they are born in freshwater rivers and streams and then make their way to the ocean where they live their lives in open waters before returning to the exact beds of their origin to spawn and die. Estimates of these annual prehistoric runs vary between 8 and 25 million fish. Native peoples gathered at sites along rivers such as the Columbia in places like the Dalles (about 65 miles east of present-day Portland), and harvested this rich bounty in staggering numbers. As a result, the Dalles became a major trading center with links extending south to California and ultimately across the continent. Not surprisingly, for people so dependent upon a fish, salmon became not only a source of calories but also of cosmology; the Chinookan-speaking people of the Pacific Northwest viewed their lives and fate as intimately intertwined with their primary food source. In addition to salmon, Pacific Coast Indians also fished for cod and halibut, harpooned whales, collected shellfish, hunted deer and elk, and gathered huckleberries, wild strawberries, and roots.

Farther south along the California coastline, cultural sophistication proliferated in the absence of corn-based agriculture but the presence of the sea. Shellfish, sea mammals, and a now-extinct flightless duck, in addition to gathered harvests of acorns, helped sustain nearly 10% of the total pre-Columbian population north of Mexico. These skilled, trade-based, class-organized settlements defy the traditional logic that only agriculture communities possessed social sophistication and sedentary villages. They were also far from the "heathen savages" described by early European explorers. As historian Colin Calloway has shown, "coastal peoples were hunters and gatherers, fishers and foragers, not farmers, yet they lived in sedentary villages, owned property, practiced economic and craft specialization, developed an elaborate material culture, built monumental architecture, held slaves, and measured rank by wealth and heredity."

East from the Pacific Coast, the Great Basin region between the Sierra Nevadas and Rocky Mountains displays a striking geographical diversity and demanded unique adaptations from its inhabitants. The glacial retreat that came about at the end of the last Ice Age left some 400 000 square miles of the formerly lush Basin arid and austere. The Great Basin is home to the largest desert in the northern hemisphere, the Sonoran, and sagebrush-speckled steppes provide the other significant vegetation pattern across this topography. These sere, harsh conditions usually meant that population densities were very low, following the ecological principle known as "Liebig's Law," which argues that the minimum amount of food available during the scarcest period limits population. Species, including humans, that fail to keep their numbers in check find that nature will do the dirty deed for them. Without food, "surplus" populations – of people or animals – die off, reducing them to more sustainable numbers, which in turn contributes to the overall stability of the ecosystem. In this region, piñon nuts provided valuable nutrition to

Archaic hunting and gathering bands, and everywhere, as Calloway notes, "Great Basin peoples pursued subsistence strategies that required intimate knowledge of the land and its animals, regular movement to take advantage of seasonal diversity and changing conditions, and careful exploitation of the environment." Traditional hunting and gathering also supported small bands of "Digger Indians," ancestors of modern Paiutes, as nomadic interior desert dwellers.

As the climate of the southwestern Great Basin continued to dry out and heat up, Indians there adapted by vigorously embracing agriculture, which allowed them to be more efficient consumers of calories by eating lower on the food chain. Successful Neolithic Indian populations switched from hunting big game to farming small plants. For Fremont culture groups living in Utah and parts of Idaho, Colorado, and Nevada, corn was critical. These part-time farming cultures lived in smaller family groups and supplemented their diets with hunting and foraging. In the desert Southwest, knowledge of corn cultivation flowed north out of Mexico and arrived in the Four Corners region of today's Utah/Arizona/New Mexico/Colorado approximately 3000 years ago. Across a relatively short span of time – perhaps 25 generations – corn, along with beans and squash, fueled population growth by providing efficient and storable calories that could sustain growing numbers through the unpredictable weather and precipitation cycles that marked this period. It also led to the development of pottery and basketry for storage and more permanent villages in the form of multi-storied pueblos. Near present-day Phoenix, Arizona, for example, the Hohokam people, forebears of modern Pimas, engineered their survival through the construction of the largest and most sophisticated irrigation network in the Americas, channeling scarce water from the Salt and Gila rivers through more than 1000 miles of canals to support populations in excess of 50 000.

This primary reliance upon agriculture, supplemented by more efficient foraging, proved remarkably successful, and also led to the coalescence of large pueblo settlements like those of the Chaco Canyon Anasazi in modern-day New Mexico (see Figure 1.3). Characterized now by its spectacular ruins, Chaco served as the center of ancestral Pueblo Indian culture. Massive, multi-storied, ceremonial great houses utilized sophisticated architectural and construction techniques and precisely aligned with solar, lunar, and cardinal directions. At its peak in 1050, Chaco's large sphere of influence sustained a population perhaps numbering as many as 15 000 in this harsh and arid environment of short growing seasons and long winters. Like the Hohokam, Chacoans built irrigation works to make their agricultural fields bloom.

Life here was not easy, however. Historian David Stuart's analysis of human remains at Chaco reveals that "broken bones, overwork, bad teeth, and seasonal hunger were common." Like so many successful cultures, the

Figure 1.3 Between 850 and 1150, ancestral Puebloan peoples built this four-story, 350 + -room Pueblo Bonito, Spanish for "beautiful town," which served as the center of the far-flung Southwestern Chacoan Culture that flourished for more than 300 years.

Anasazi eventually overreached the carrying capacity of their lands. By 1000 CE, foraging resources, especially meat, were already beginning to disappear, thus intensifying reliance on agricultural production, which itself relied on relatively predictable rainfall patterns. Despite the claims and promises of Anasazi elites, however, the weather did not fall under their purview. They could not make the sky rain. In the 1090s, severe drought devastated Chacoan corn and food reserves and, before long, the greatest society in ancient North America unraveled, just as Liebig's Law predicts. Anasazi farmers buried their dead, abandoned their homes, and dispersed to wetter climates, such as Mesa Verde in Colorado and the pueblos along the Rio Grande in New Mexico. The vast regional trade networks this ambitious society established, which included Pacific Coast shells, Plains bison hides, Idaho obsidian, Mexican macaws, and local turquoise, also disintegrated. Nature had taught a powerful lesson about the costs of environmental overreach – that human populations ignore natural parameters at their own peril. Native descendants of the Anasazi would not make the same mistakes again. New World European immigrants would.

To the east of this extensive Great Basin region lies the Rocky Mountain range, which bisects the northern hemisphere and, at its fullest extension from present-day New Mexico through Colorado, Utah, Wyoming, Idaho, and Montana into Canada, is one of the world's longest. Sculpted by water in its many forms, this craggy, undulating spine claims more than 50 peaks above 14 000 feet and supports a mosaic of vegetative zones ranging from mixed and short-grass prairie through broad-leafed deciduous forests; piñon, juniper, and ponderosa woodlands, fir, spruce, and lodgepole pines; to alpine tundra. This iconic range provides the headwaters for many of the West's mighty rivers – the Rio Grande, Platte, Arkansas, Colorado, Green, Columbia, Salmon, Missouri – and her towering heights act as the last major continental cloud obstacle for east-bound storms, scraping moisture from the sky and leaving a thirsty Great Plains grassland in their wake. The difficulties of life in these steep terrains dissuaded Paleo- and Archaic Indians from large-scale settlements here. Yet prior to European arrival, various groups did find ways to live on these slopes. Ancestors of the Crows, Shoshonis, Utes, and Salish peoples combined nomadic foothill hunting of mountain sheep, deer, and elk, with Plains forays for mammoths and ancient bison, and the gathering of roots and berries to forge long-term survival strategies. Archeological evidence also indicates that these early inhabitants made rock walls to herd and drive game animals and deliberately altered floral and faunal conditions to their advantage with fire.

Sprawling east from the Rockies lie the Great Plains, a seemingly endless expanse of grass lapping against the ephemeral "line of aridity" along the 100th meridian, where less than 20 inches of rain falls annually (the "magic" number needed to sustain non-irrigated agriculture). This vast savannah experiences periodic droughts as the aridity line fluctuates, which in turn has dramatic impacts on its flora and fauna. In this environment, agriculture and buffalo hunting formed the foundation of early Plains Indian subsistence. By 1000 CE, groups such as the Mandans, Pawnees, Wichitas, and Osages cultivated the "three sisters" in farming villages established along Plains river corridors. Postglacial climate conditions also favored the smaller modern American bison (*Bison bison*) – a dwarfed evolutionary survivor that emerged approximately 5000–10 000 years ago, and early Blackfeet and pre-horse Apache hunters effectively adapted their technology to this thick-hided animal. Plano-pointed weapons lacked the fluting found in Clovis and Folsom projectiles, but around 7500 years ago, Plains peoples invented the atlatl, a wickedly effective spear/dart-throwing device that used a lever action to increase the velocity of the projectile at a range of more than 100 yards. By about 100 CE, these hunters replaced the atlatl with even more efficient bows and arrows. Despite this hunting pressure, the great shaggy bison herds quickly multiplied in the vast expanses of the continent's plains, especially in the absence of horses, sustaining larger human populations and becoming central to the grasslands ecosystem that lured Native hunters and gathers for centuries.

Historians have argued that the expansiveness of the Plains encouraged herd evolution among the bison and that the Pleistocene disappearance of predators allowed their numbers to multiply. But the presence of proficient human hunters also contributed to the efflorescence of this Plains icon; as Archaic Indians shaped both the animal's population size and distribution, the Plains became a vast Bison Belt. Hunters who understood the seasonal patterns and habits of bison found an almost limitless bounty and thus a predictable and reliable food source that supported population expansion. Archaic Indians used fire to improve and expand bison-favored grasslands, direct herd movement, and drive them toward pre-selected kill sites. Communal hunters also utilized dead-end canyons and corrals to herd large groups of bison into a mass slaughter. But the most sensational form of buffalo hunting was surely the buffalo jump, where well-coordinated and timed maneuvers drove entire herds off a cliff to plummet to their death. Folsom-era jumps in Alberta and Texas date this practice as far back as 10 000 years. Carnage at this scale led to huge food surpluses, such that food drying and preservation became essential, and also to some waste. Not surprisingly, bison were central to the religious lives of Plains people. Strict spiritual guidelines and rituals governed all aspects of the hunt, preparation, and consumption of bison, sometimes blurring the distinctions between humans and animals. On the northern Plains, for example, the buffalo-calling ceremony transmitted the animal's power and maintained the close bond between the species through highly ritualized sexual intercourse between tribal women and men dressed as bison.

As this deep history demonstrates, it is time to lose the myth of "Eden." By the time Europeans finally arrived, Native peoples had flourished in the New World for tens of thousands of years, evolving societies ranging from relatively primitive hunting and gathering bands to sophisticated, agricultural, urban metropolises. In the American West, they had wrested a living from sometimes harsh and formidable environments that arriving Europeans shunned as inhospitable, through careful management of scarce natural resources. Native peoples also paid attention to changes in climate and rainfall and reacted accordingly. Approximately 5500 years ago, following the relatively wet and abundant Pleistocene Epoch, the West experienced a profoundly dry and hot interval geologists call the Altithermal. Native peoples responded by moving away from the areas that could no longer sustain them. As global warming transforms the American West of the twenty-first century in much the same way, the adaptive patterns established by these first westerners offer a useful cautionary tale and provide important insights into the central role of the environment in human history. As Wilson concludes, "expansion and stewardship may appear at first to be conflicting goals, but they are not." In 1492, however, newly arriving Old World Europeans were only interested in "expansion."

Suggested Reading

Mark Nathan Cohen, *The Food Crisis in Prehistory: Overpopulation and the Origins of Agriculture* (New Haven: Yale University Press, 1977).

William M. Denevan, "The Pristine Myth: The Landscape of the Americas in 1492," *Annals of the Association of American Geographers*, Vol. 82, No. 3 (September 1992), 369–385.

Jared M. Diamond, *The Third Chimpanzee: The Evolution and Future of the Human Animal* (New York: Harper Perennial, 2006).

Tim Flannery, *The Eternal Frontier: An Ecological History of North America and Its Peoples* (New York: Atlantic Monthly Press, 2002).

Dan Flores, "Introduction" and "Empires of the Sun: Big History and the Great Plains," in *American Serengeti: The Last Big Animals of the Great Plains* (Lawrence: University of Kansas Press, 2016), 1–28.

Glenn Hodges, "First Americans," *National Geographic*, Vol. 227, No. 1 (January 2015), 124–137.

Peter Iverson, "Taking Care of Earth and Sky," in Alvin M. Josephy, Jr, ed., *America in 1492: The World of the Indian Peoples before the Arrival of Columbus* (New York: Vintage, 1993), 85–118.

Shepard Krech, III, "Paleoindians and the Great Pleistocene Die-Off," *Nature Transformed*, TeacherServe, National Humanities Center, June 2008. http://nationalhumanitiescenter.org/tserve/nattrans/ntecoindian/essays/pleistocene.htm (accessed April 16, 2016).

Charles C. Mann, "1491," *The Atlantic*, March 1, 2002, 41–53.

Curtis W. Marean, "The Most Invasive Species of All," *Scientific American*, August 2015, 32–39.

Michael Pollan, "The Plant: Corn's Conquest," in *The Omnivore's Dilemma: A Natural History of Four Meals* (New York: Penguin, 2007), 15–31.

Clive Ponting, "The Spread of European Settlement," in *A New Green History of the World: The Environment and the Collapse of Great Civilizations* (New York: Penguin, 2007), 117–141.

David E. Stuart, "The Fall of Chacoan Society," in *Anasazi America* (Albuquerque: University of New Mexico Press, 2000), 107–124.

Edward O. Wilson, *Biophilia* (New Haven: Harvard University Press, 1986).

Carl Zimmer, "DNA of 11,500-Year-Old Children in Alaska Yields Clues about the First Americans," *The New York Times*, October 27, 2015. www.nytimes.com/2015/10/27/science/dna-of-ancient-children-offers-clues-on-how-people-settled-the-americas.html?_r=0 (accessed February 2, 2016).

2

The West Transformed

Saynday, the Kiowa trickster figure, was coming along, and before him stretched the wide Plains. Off in the distant east, he saw a dark, mounted figure riding slowly and deliberately. As the stranger drew closer, Saynday observed that the mysterious rider was clad all in black and that his face, although obscured by shadow and dust, was deeply scarred. "Who are you?" asked the stranger. "I am Saynday," he replied, "the Kiowas are my people. And who are you?" "I am Smallpox," the man in black answered. "I am one with the white man – they are my people as the Kiowas are yours. Sometimes I travel ahead of them, and sometimes I lurk behind. But I am always their companion and you will find me in their camps and in their houses." "What do you do?" Saynday inquired. "I bring death," Smallpox replied. "My breath causes children to wither like young plants in spring snow. I bring destruction. No matter how beautiful a woman is, once she has looked at me she becomes as ugly as death. And to men I bring not death alone, but the destruction of their children and the blighting of their wives. The strongest warriors go down before me. No people who have looked on me will ever be the same." Saynday shuddered at the prophesy and the death stench that encircled Smallpox.

Thinking quickly, Saynday told Smallpox that "my Kiowa people are few and poor already. We're not like the Pawnees [bitter enemies of the Kiowas]. They have great houses, half underground, in big villages by the river, and every house is full of people." Smallpox grew interested, "I like that,"

Losing Eden: An Environmental History of the American West, First Edition. Sara Dant.
© 2017 John Wiley & Sons, Inc. Published 2017 by John Wiley & Sons, Inc.

he said. "I can do my best work when people are crowded together." "Then you'll like the Pawnees," Saynday promised. "I think I'll go and visit the Pawnees first," Smallpox decided. "Later on, perhaps, I can get back to the Kiowas." As he reined his weary black death horse to the north, Smallpox warned Saynday, "Tell your people when I come to be ready for me. Tell them to put out all their fires. Fire is the only thing in the whole world that I'm afraid of." But as Saynday watched Smallpox ride away from the Kiowas, he set fire to the prairie grasses at his feet. Carried by the winds, the flames soon encircled Kiowa camps and kept them safe from Smallpox. Saynday congratulated himself and that's the way it was.

(Adapted from Marriott and Rachlin)

Unfortunately for the Kiowas and other Native peoples of the American West, no amount of trickster cleverness could save them from the impending disasters and transformation that exploring Europeans inadvertently unleashed. Disease may have been the most obvious and devastating consequence, even holocaust, of contact, but European introduction of exotic plants and animals, new social and cultural mores, and a global market economy irrevocably transformed the environment. That, in turn, altered human responses and meant that by 1800, Native Americans could no longer live in the West as they had traditionally. European market-based economies and Indian subsistence were simply incompatible, and the environmental changes wrought by the newcomers only reinforced their ultimate success.

Almost every school child learns the discovery ditty: In fourteen-hundred and ninety-two, Columbus sailed the ocean blue. The story usually continues that in this year, Christopher Columbus and his crew "discovered" America, with the implication that this allowed "real" history to begin. But Columbus was almost assuredly not the first Old World explorer to "discover" the Americas. Instead, perhaps as many as 500 years earlier, Norse sailors had begun prowling the shores along Newfoundland and Labrador in search of fertile fishing grounds. They had almost certainly made landfall and some contact with Native American peoples, but they neither arrived in significant numbers nor stayed for any duration, so their effect on the American environment was fleeting and ephemeral. Thus, Columbus' voyage retains its seminal place in American history not because he was first but because the Old World–New World connection he forged would last.

Sizable European colonization efforts emerged by the late fifteenth century for several key reasons. First, ambitious kings and queens consolidated their powers into nation states and their desire for greater wealth and territory led them to support and promote exploration and colonization beyond Europe. Second, expanding domestic populations, which began to recover from earlier disease epidemics, fueled a demand for broader trade both by generating a larger labor force capable of producing more trade goods to sell abroad and by stimulating a growing demand for consumer items at home. Third, the Reformations of the sixteenth and seventeenth centuries inspired European Christians, especially in the Roman Catholic Church, to save heathen souls across the globe. Portuguese mariners first led the way out onto the Atlantic, also known as "the sea of darkness," and by 1500, Portugal had captured control of the lucrative West African gold trade (which would later turn into an even more profitable slave-trade venture) and translated this new-found wealth into real power. It was a seductive model. Spain entered the exploration game with the hope of tapping into the other major known source of wealth at the time, the "Indies" (as Europeans called China, Japan, and India) with its alluring and lucrative spices, silks, drugs, and perfumes. These precious commodities fetched stunning prices in Europe because the primary routes for acquiring them – by land through Constantinople across bandit-riddled overland trade routes or by sea via the pirate-infested Indian Ocean – made them rare in Europe. Therefore, an efficient trade route would bring untold riches and power to whichever country could get there first. This was Columbus' basic proposal to Spain: to utilize the roundness of the earth and sail *west* to get to the East. His miscalculation regarding the size of the earth (he significantly underestimated it), however, left just enough room for the Americas. Columbus never acknowledged that he had discovered a "New World" (he maintained until his death that what he had encountered were the outer islands of the Indies). Nonetheless, his four voyages, which began in 1492, established Spanish precedence and dominance in the western hemisphere.

Historians label the period between Columbus' 1492 voyage and approximately 1520 the "Age of Exploration," and in these early years, most of Spain's efforts in the Americas focused on assembling reliable maps of new lands, sticking flags in beaches to proclaim Spanish sovereignty, and identifying resources for export and exploitation. By 1520, however, the Age of Exploration gave way to the "Age of Conquest," as Spain sought to claim and tame its new possessions. The next three decades witnessed some of the bloodiest chapters in all of recorded human history, as the Spanish exerted their dominance over a vast region extending from present-day California across to Florida and south through the Caribbean to the southern tip of South America (with the exception of Brazil, which was Portuguese). When Columbus and his men stepped ashore in the Bahamas on that fateful October 12th day, probably on present-day San Salvador Island, he and his men set this process in motion, transforming the Atlantic Ocean from an Old World–New World barrier into a two-way bridge that would, in time, transform the Americas and the world.

Columbus' voyages commenced a global redistribution of people, plants, animals, and diseases known as the "Columbian Exchange" (see Figure 2.1). As a

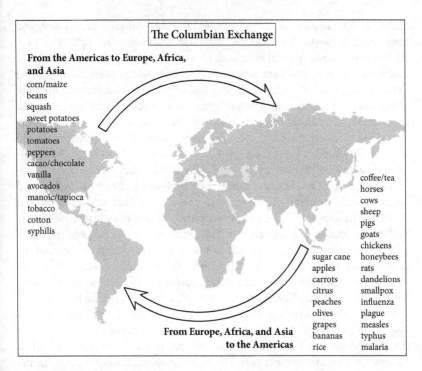

Figure 2.1 Columbus' 1492 arrival in the New World set in motion a transformative movement of peoples, plants, animals, and diseases between the Old World and the New World, which historians call the Columbian Exchange.

result of the re-flooding of Beringia approximately 10 000–15 000 years ago, the Americas' isolation from the rest of the world had led to the evolution of unique flora and fauna. Europeans had never seen fish with whiskers, snakes that rattled, or shaggy bison; they had never tasted blueberries or vanilla or tomatoes or chocolate. The three main staples that would soon form the foundation of the modern European diet – beans, corn, and potatoes (both white and sweet) – also came from the Americas via the Columbian Exchange. Manioc (an edible root that became an African staple) and peppers, peanuts and pineapples all traveled east across the Atlantic and west across the Pacific to feed growing European, Asian, and African populations. So, too, did tobacco, to which Europeans quickly became addicted, and cotton, which transformed European clothing.

Europeans also provided their own unique contributions to this environmental revolution in the Americas. Prior to Columbus, Native peoples throughout the Americas had only limited experiences with domesticated animals – llamas, alpacas, and guinea pigs in South America and turkeys and some dogs in North America. But European immigrants brought their prolific livestock across the Atlantic with them: cows, pigs, goats, sheep, rabbits, and horses, which would transform the lives of Native peoples in the coming century. By 1650, for example, Navajos actively shepherded growing flocks of sheep and goats, and incorporated these "new" animals into their diet and their material culture through trade goods such as rugs and clothing. Honeybees crossed the Atlantic, too, and were so prolific that Indians referred to them as "English flies." The introduction of these domesticated animals caused cascading changes to the land such as introduced exotic feed crops, fenced-in ranges, and wars on predators like mountain lions and wolves and bears. The Columbian Exchange also introduced Native peoples of the Americas to large-scale plantation crops such as wheat and sugarcane, rice, barley, and oats, and to entirely new foods such as onions and peaches, olives and peas, apples and okra, as well as coffee and tea. Accidental exchanges occurred as well. Old World dandelions, for example, readily re-seeded themselves in the Americas after sailing across the Atlantic in the guts and feed of livestock, and European rats successfully stowed themselves away on ships until they could escape onto a new continent, displacing the smaller, less aggressive rats of the Americas, and spreading unintentional exchanges like disease and famine. Even the lowly earthworm was a Columbian hitchhiker. Having gone extinct in most of North America during the last Ice Age, earthworms successfully recolonized continental soils following European immigration and began composting fallen foliage, aerating the land, and facilitating the establishment of exotic European plants in the Americas. Many historians have argued that one of the main reasons that Europeans successfully colonized the Americas was because many of their plants and animals thrived there, too. In essence, these immigrants could easily and readily replicate parts of their former lives and landscapes in this new place without having to learn new life-ways.

However, the other major factor in European settlement success in the Americas was the deadly array of diseases the immigrants carried with them across the Atlantic. Scientists classify diseases as either contact diseases (smallpox, influenza, common cold, measles), which spread via "contact" with bodily fluids, or vector diseases (plague, malaria, West Nile fever, Zika), which require a living organism "vector" such as a mosquito, tick, or flea. For several centuries prior to Columbus' New World arrival, almost every major contact *and* vector epidemic that wipes out human populations had ravaged Europe: smallpox, plague, measles, typhus, influenza, etc. Trade with Africa and the Indies brought these killers home to the continent and between roughly 1200 and 1500, Europe's population stagnated. Predictably, huge numbers of people died, but some did not. For a variety of reasons, their bodies successfully fought off the diseases and gave them immunity, which they then passed along to their children. Europe's population had begun to recover by the late fifteenth century as more people were born with immunity to these diseases. But possessing disease immunity also means a person can carry a disease without contracting it. Thus, when European explorers and settlers arrived in the Americas and encountered Native populations that had been geographically isolated from these diseases for thousands of years, the results were catastrophic ... for the Indians. Furthermore, where Europeans had historically only had to fight off one disease at a time, Native Americans got a panoply in just a short period of time. Often the first disease did not kill people but just weakened their immunity so that the second or third one finished them off.

The collapse of the Native populations in the Americas was stunning and helped pave the way for European conquest. Indians constituted a "virgin soil" genetic population, one that had never encountered these diseases because of their extreme geographic isolation from the rest of the infected world in the millennia after their migration across Beringia. Within just a few years of Columbus' arrival, however, disease rendered the Native peoples of the Caribbean nearly extinct. The once-mighty and far-flung Aztec Empire of Mexico, whose numbers reached as high as 25 million on the eve of contact, crumpled to 2 million within 50 years after smallpox raged through their cities and towns. The vast scope of the human toll is impossible to calculate since there was no precise census, but historians have estimated that no fewer than three out of every four Indians (and perhaps as many as 90%) died of European diseases and their aftermath within a few generations of Columbus' arrival. In the American West alone, that translates to approximately 1.6 million deaths. Disease struck hardest in areas of concentrated contact between Europeans and Native peoples, but as the opening story in this chapter illustrates, after devastating the coastal regions, smallpox and other killers made their way relentlessly into the interior of the continent. Thousands of Indians died without ever making contact with Europeans as terrified Natives, unaware that they were already contaminated, unwittingly became disease vectors (agents) for these slow and steady pathogens, either by fleeing their infected villages or by engaging in warfare with other Native groups. Imported European rats also helped spread European diseases via flea bites, creating a perfect symbiosis from which biologically defenseless Indians had no escape.

To add insult to injury, history suggests that there was no reciprocal population poisoning. With the exception of (rarely fatal) syphilis, Indians gave no deadly diseases to Europeans. Why not? Surely over several thousand years of human habitation in North America, viruses had mutated into something malignant? Two critical differences existed between European and

Native American societies at the time of contact. The first was population density. At the time of Columbus' "discovery," Europe's population roughly equaled that of the Americas, all of the Americas. Because of their much more limited geographic distribution, Europeans and other "Old World" peoples lived in much closer proximity to one another, which enhanced the likelihood of transmitting infectious disease. By contrast, Native Americans lived in widely scattered settlements across two vast continents, so that even if a virus did mutate and become deadly, it lacked the vectors necessary to spread and so died out and disappeared.

Second, Europeans not only lived in close proximity to one another, but also to their livestock, which provided a constant source of viral attack. Cattle, sheep, pigs, goats, poultry, rats, mice, dogs, and cats are all capable of infecting and/or transmitting a wide variety of viral and bacterial horrors to human hosts – the 2009 "swine flu" pandemic is a modern example. Except for the few examples mentioned above, Indians kept no domesticated animals. The deadly result of Indians' splendid isolation was that while Natives of the Americas had (temporarily) escaped the plagues and poxes that had ravaged European populations for centuries, they ultimately lacked the protective immunities that disease-exposed populations build up over generations. In the end, the germs of the European invaders proved far mightier than their guns.

Old World–New World contact proved contentious for many other reasons, too. The differences between Europeans and Native Americans derived not so much from the way they acquired food or sheltered themselves, but in their relationship to their natural environment and their social and economic organization. In these areas, the gaps generally proved profound and problematic, primarily for Indians, and in the long run destroyed the natural and social ecologies that shaped Native American ways of life.

European explorers and colonizers believed that God had commanded humanity to subdue the earth and granted human dominion over all living things. As a result, Europeans viewed themselves as existing outside of nature, above and removed, and believed the natural world was theirs for the taking, a gift from God to his chosen species. By contrast, Native Americans saw themselves as an extension of the natural world, intimately bound by the great cycles of life and death that affected the flora and fauna around them. This worldview does not mean that Indians did not exploit their natural environment; they did. It does not mean that Indians did not alter their natural environment through the use of fire and agriculture; they did. Generally, though, the Indian relationship to the natural world emphasized the interconnectedness of all living things, including people, and human abuse of the environment, instead of reverence and respect, came at the risk of spiritual retaliation.

Religious differences aggravated European–Native conflict in other ways as well. European colonizers, whether Catholic or Protestant, brought with them a devout belief in one god (monotheism), whose visage was that of a white man. They worshiped their god in a highly ritualized manner in formal churches according to written scripture. Native spiritual practices and beliefs varied widely, although most practiced a nature-based polytheism (belief in many gods) that invested the natural world with spiritual power and envisioned gods as animals, trees, celestial objects, or forces of nature. Because there was no alphabet-based writing present in the Americas prior to the arrival of Europeans, Indians primarily transmitted their rituals, stories, songs, and beliefs orally, making them situational, dynamic, and constantly evolving. From the European perspective, Indian spiritual life amounted to heathenish blasphemy, and the colonizers would spend the next several hundred years attempting to eradicate Native religious practices. The twin "gifts" of Christianity and civilization (order, government, culture, clothing), Europeans believed, were more than adequate compensation for what they would take from the land that God had provided for his chosen people, meaning the Europeans, of course.

Cultural ideas about property reinforced these religious differences. While both Native Americans and Europeans engaged in land ownership, their practices differed greatly. Europeans brought with them an understanding of the landscape itself as a private property commodity, a concept essentially unknown in the Americas prior to contact. Private property as a commodity, defined as exclusive access to and use of land such that an individual owner can *exclude* all others, arose naturally from European ideals of taming the land. But this legal definition clashed fundamentally with Indian practices of collective use and access, known as usufruct rights in European law. In a usufruct system, individuals or groups can obtain the right to use the land or resource of another provided they do not destroy or degrade the original resource: legal sharing. To Native Americans, the belief that an individual could actually own a piece of ground as a private, exclusive commodity seemed absurd; the land had been here long before and would exist long after any individual life. Indians did believe in and vigorously defended tribal territories, hunting grounds, personal possessions, homes, etc., and most Indian cultures *did* recognize private (which usually meant family) ownership of berry patches, fishing locations, and the sometimes extensive garden plots managed by women in agricultural tribes. But here, too, they protected only collective use of and access to resources *on* the land, not private possession of the land itself – a use view as opposed to a commodity view. These fundamentally incompatible ways of "owning" land led to serious initial conflicts. When early Europeans entered into land negotiations, for example, they believed they were buying exclusive private property (both the land and its resources as commodities), and began erecting fences and accosting "trespassers." Indians, however, believed they had sold only use and access, which the original seller could convey to numerous parties and still retain for themselves. In the long run, Native user rights proved no match for European private property laws and irate colonists with firearms. As environmental historian William Cronon has written, "a people who loved property little had been overwhelmed by a people who loved it much." Interestingly, this conflict between individual possession and communal access presaged later land struggles between conservation and preservation advocates.

In addition to their discordant attitudes about the natural world, Europeans and Indians also disagreed on social and cultural issues. As evidenced by their love of private property (land as a means to an end: wealth), Europeans generally valued the success of individuals over that of the community. Wealth determined one's status and social class, and individual upward mobility was the universal ambition. The global expansion of European trade in the 1500s and 1600s, and the evolution of commerce-oriented capitalism, only amplified this goal. By contrast, Native American societies generally elevated the good of the group above that of the individual. While Indians did strive to perform well in battle or ceremonies, their motivation was not usually for individual glory but for the well-being of the larger community, and status derived not from wealth but from service. The Potlatch Ceremony, practiced by the coastal Salish and other Pacific Northwest peoples, provides an excellent example. The ritual served as a means of redistributing tribal wealth and encouraging reciprocity among and between families. At the potlatch, families or individuals gave away valuable possessions – food, household items, and even dances and songs – often during lean winter months. As they enriched their neighbors while impoverishing themselves, they helped thwart Liebig's Law and thus the family's or individual's status rose within the clan, tribe, or village.

Europeans also flinched at the matrilineal and matrilocal organization of many Indian tribes such as Crows and Hopis, where individuals trace their identity and heritage through the mother's line and married couples reside with the female head of the household. At the time of contact, Europe was not only strongly patrilineal (heritage traced through the father's line) but also thoroughly male-dominated. Women held almost no legal rights; they could not own property (except under Spanish law), vote, hold political office, etc., and with the exception of a few queens, they were at the legal mercy of their fathers, husbands, or brothers. By contrast, many Native American societies, especially agricultural tribes, accorded women significant power, both political and economic. As mentioned in the previous chapter, the Agricultural Revolution had resulted in a gendered division of labor: women farmed while men hunted. In agricultural societies, then, since women contributed the bulk of the calories that sustained the community, they retained significant authority. To Europeans, allowing women to cultivate agriculture, divorce their husbands (by kicking the man out of *their* house), determine whether a tribe would go to war or not (they will feed the warriors ... or not), and actively participate in the political process (including chief selection) seemed the height of barbarism.

The Spanish, who arrived first and moved northward out of present-day Mexico by the late sixteenth century, dominated European settlement and colonization of the American West. One *raison d'etre* for New Spain – what the Spanish called their American colonies – was wealth generation. The mother country's search for merchantable commodities – natural resources with recognized monetary value – led her to establish a territorial hierarchy in her New World possessions. For Spain, the most lucrative resources, and thus her primary focus, consisted of the gold and silver flowing out of the former Aztec and Incan empires in Mexico and Peru, respectively. The crown's agricultural holdings in the Caribbean comprised a secondary, but still valuable resource. Distinctly third in the pecking order, primarily because they lacked anything of commercial value, were the lands north of Mexico. Northern New Spain – California across to Florida – seemed to hold no known merchantable commodities, only Indian labor and souls, and thus its value lay primarily in Spain's ability to claim the land and use it as a buffer to keep other European rivals at bay. To secure her more valuable territories, like Peru and Mexico, Spain had dispatched the troops; but to the future American West, the crown dispatched the padres, and the Catholic mission system became the primary fortifying institution of Spain's not-so-valuable northern territories.

Other European nations soon challenged the primacy of the Spanish. By the late eighteenth century, the Russians had begun edging southward from Alaska along the Pacific Coast, and the French had colonized along the Mississippi and fortified New Orleans, which pressed hard on New Spain. The Spanish occupation of both Texas and California was part of the crown's attempt to block the expansion of her French and Russian rivals, and soon missions stretched across Texas, headquartered around San Antonio, and reached northward along the California coast from San Diego to Sonoma. The Spanish sent mostly men to settle and minister these outposts and their liaisons with Native women soon manifested as a growing *mestizo* or mixed-race population.

The arrival of the padres proved deadly to the West's Native inhabitants, however, as Spain's missionizing efforts brought European diseases into the region. This intimate contact predictably facilitated disease transmission, and death followed the colonizers as they migrated northward. In 1690, for example, the first winter of contact with the Spanish devastated the Caddo population in what is now eastern Texas, and as the missions spread westward and northward, diseases like smallpox ravaged Native societies. By the end of the next century, this deadly killer had visited the Shoshones of present-day Idaho, causing the extinction of entire bands, and decimated the Native peoples of California by more than two-thirds (from a peak of nearly 325 000 in the 1760s to fewer than 100 000 by 1850). The pathogens were relentless and even the most clever Indian trickster figures like Saynday proved no match. As the story at the beginning of the chapter so clearly illustrates, Indians fully recognized that smallpox and other diseases arrived with whites … and not just the Spanish. In 1836, for example, the arrival of American Presbyterian missionaries Marcus and Narcissa Whitman in Oregon Country brought measles-infested death to the local Cayuse tribe, whose survivors finally responded by massacring the missionary couple and 10 others in 1847.

The Spanish Crown and mission system also profoundly shaped the lives of sixteenth-century Pueblo Indians, the diverse and culturally advanced peoples of the Rio Grande basin in present-day New Mexico, by altering the region's established Native power structure, introducing horse culture to the Indians of the West, and ushering in a market economy. Earlier contact with the 1540 expedition of Francisco Vásquez de Coronado, who was fruitlessly searching for the Seven Cities of Cibola (gold), and other conquistadors had alerted the Pueblos to the value of Spanish horses and metal implements as well as the power of Spanish weaponry. The Indians also initially saw the potential benefit of adding Franciscan friars and their powerful god to the Pueblo religious pantheon.

Thus in the summer of 1598, when Juan de Oñate arrived with a caravan of 500 settlers and 9 Franciscans to begin the process of claiming and taming New Mexico by establishing missions in the name of Spain, the potential for friendly relations existed. The king had even ordered that this process be "apostolic and Christian, and not a butchery," but Oñate was an entrepreneur not an ecclesiastic and his purpose was profit not "pacification." In 1598, Oñate founded the mission and surrounding Provence of Santa Fe in Nuevo Mexico, but his brutal leadership fell hard on the indigenous people. The following year in 1599, for example, after the people of nearby Acoma Pueblo refused to pay excessive food tributes (taxes), Oñate and his men launched a punitive attack that killed 800 men, women, and children, enslaved several hundred survivors, and chopped off the right foot of surviving warriors. Oñate's desperate search for wealth not only devastated the entire Pueblo region by exacting exorbitant tributes in food and hides, but also wrecked the New Mexico mission and settlement he founded. By 1601, most of the conscientious colonists had fled back to their Spanish homeland with tales of Oñate's savagery. Over the next few years, this grasping, so-called "Last Conquistador" extended his influence out onto the Great Plains and west to California, but he failed to strike it rich, and eventually returned to Spain after the courts convicted him of cruelty to both colonists and Natives and banished him from Nuevo Mexico. The Acomas never forgot Oñate, however. On a moonless night in January of 1998, as the state embarked on a year-long celebration of its 400th anniversary, several Acomas crept up to the imposing 12-foot-high statue at Oñate Monument near Espanola and carefully sawed off its right foot.

Despite Oñate's barbarism, Spain managed to retain control of the region primarily due to emerging inter-tribal warfare between Pueblos and Apaches, triggered by the arrival of the Spanish. The arid high deserts of New Mexico lacked the natural resources to sustain large human populations. For nearly a century, however, the largely nomadic Apaches had traded, and occasionally raided, with the sedentary Pueblos in a mostly mutually fulfilling relationship that exchanged Pueblo food for Apache protection and ensured the subsistence of both groups. The Spanish, however, tipped the fragile ecological balance by not only extorting resources such as corn and blankets from the Pueblos, leaving them bereft of trade goods when the Apaches arrived, but also by bringing alluring new resources, such as metal and horses into the region. In order to pursue their own subsistence, both Pueblos and Apaches soon needed European trade – to participate in this emerging market economy – more than each other and that strained an already fragile environment to provide more food and shattered the tenuous reciprocal trade relationships between these Native societies. As historian Elizabeth John has written, "Spain had unwittingly sparked among Apaches an equestrian revolution that would spread among Indian peoples far into the interior, transforming Native economies and upsetting balances of power for centuries to come." Interestingly, the Pueblo–Apache conflict also spawned mass Pueblo conversions to Catholicism, in the hope that the Franciscans' faith and Spanish might would provide salvation from devastating Apache raids. Thus, despite Oñate's blundering, this "soul" responsibility caused Spain to reconfigure her presence in New Mexico into a royal colony headquartered around the city of Santa Fe, founded in 1610 (the first permanent European settlement west of the Mississippi), with the purpose of teaching and ministering to the Pueblos.

Although the mission system may have dictated settlement patterns in northern New Spain, the desire for wealth still motivated Spanish colonists to move to the territory and exploit the land and labor of Nuevo Mexico for profit. In the end, however, this greed would have dire consequences. Under the *encomienda* system, which rewarded loyal Spaniards with land grants and limited rights to Native labor, the crown extended its control over the region, provided for the protection of the Pueblos against their Apache enemies, and promised greater food security with the introduction of Spanish livestock, wheat, and barley. But as prosperity returned, so, too, did Apache raiders.

Encomendero exploitation of the Pueblos also increased since the watchful eye of Spain was on the far side of the Atlantic. Starting in 1650, successive drought years combined with Apache attacks made Spanish corn and labor tributes unbearable for the Pueblos. By the 1670s, the specter of starvation hovered over the region and led to the abandonment of some Indian pueblos, among them Humanas Pueblo (aka Gran Quivira), the first settlement Oñate had encountered. Drought not only withered corn, wheat, and peppers but also the wild grasses essential for horses and cattle. Spanish atrocities, including Franciscan attempts to eradicate Pueblo religious practices by hanging, whipping, and jailing Pueblo medicine men, finally provoked an Indian uprising. In 1680, desperate Pueblos, pushed to the brink of social collapse by a decade of aridity and Spanish economic and spiritual abuse, rose up in rebellion. The 1680 Pueblo Revolt drove the crown and its minions out of the region for more than a decade. In 1692, when the Pueblos finally allowed the Spanish to return to Santa Fe, it was on Pueblo terms, which included an end to the *encomienda* system, the legal right to practice their Native religion, and the assimilation of Spanish crops, trade goods, and livestock into the emerging market economy.

One important environmental consequence of the 1680 Revolt was the spread of horses and horse culture (the herding and breeding of horses) throughout the American West. As discussed in the previous chapter, horses had disappeared from the Americas as a consequence of the great Pleistocene die-off that also wiped out mastodons and saber-toothed cats. Unlike the latter two, however, horses were fated to return, and when they did, they flourished, re-occupying their ancestral environmental niche with remarkable vigor. The Spanish first reintroduced the horse to its ancient homeland in the sixteenth century. While the aforementioned Apaches learned horse culture from the Pueblos by the 1650s, and some southern tribes such as the Caddos of East Texas and the Rio Grande-dwelling Jumanos had horses as early as the 1660s, it was the 1680 Pueblo Revolt that effectively diffused *Equus caballus* throughout the American West (see Figure 2.2). As the padres and other Spanish survivors fled the Pueblos' fury, they left behind their horses in numbers far greater than the local Indians could effectively utilize or absorb. Turned loose on the Plains or escaped from corrals, these adapted equines flourished in their ancient "native wild," and horse populations soared. Estimates suggest that by 1800, present-day Texas and New Mexico alone were home to more than 2 million of these animals, while the missions of California, which did not even receive horses until the 1770s, slaughtered horses as nuisances by the early 1800s.

Following the 1680 Pueblo Revolt, horse culture rapidly spread from tribe to tribe across the West through trade and theft, and transformed Native relations with the natural world. Great Basin Utes acquired horses directly

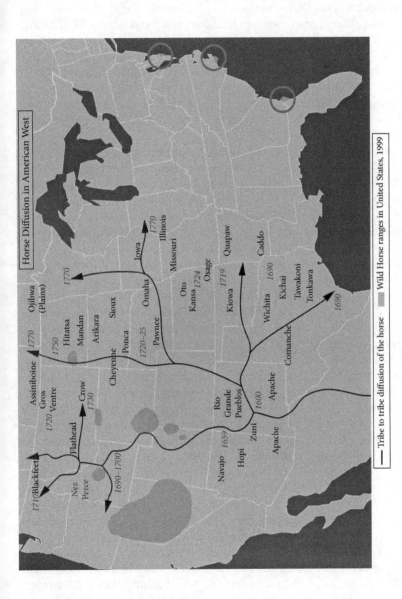

Figure 2.2 Diffusion of horse culture across North America following the 1680 Pueblo Revolt. Source: Reproduced with permission of Dan Flores.

from the eastern Pueblos. Historical evidence suggests that from there, horses dispersed north to Idaho Shoshone bands and east to Texas Comanches, both linguistic kin of the Utes, who were mounted as early as 1690. The Comanches then drove horses northward into the Kiowa and Pawnee tribes by 1720. The Shoshones and affiliated Bannocks quickly became middleman horse traders in the Pacific Northwest, where they supplied tribes such as the Nez Perces and Cayuses with mounts by the beginning of the eighteenth century. Horse culture continued at a full gallop eastward to the Blackfeet and Crows of present-day Montana and Wyoming and throughout the Missouri and Yellowstone river valleys, incorporating the Mandans, Assiniboines, and various bands of Sioux by mid-century.

The arrival of the horse was transformative. Horses not only conveyed riders farther and faster, which in turn allowed tribes to claim larger territories and participate in raids for material goods and ever more horses, but they also allowed Indians to expand northward and eastward onto the Great Plains. As historian Pekka Hämäläinen humorously observes, "horses also made nomadism infinitely more agreeable." Mounted riders could more effectively and efficiently hunt and exploit the great shaggy bison wealth (as many as 30 million) that had bloomed across the Great Plains during the earlier equine absence. The result was the emergence of a complex Indian–horse–bison economy.

By the early 1700s, horse-mounted Indians such the Comanches and the Sioux streamed out across the Great Plains, taking advantage of the great expanses of grass that nourished the horses and bison that, in turn, became the foundations of their subsistence for the next 150 years. According to Hämäläinen, "the Plains Indian horse culture represents the ultimate anomaly – [European] ecological imperialism working to Indians' advantage." At least for a while. In these flush times, estimates indicate that the Plains could have sustained nearly 200 000 subsistence (but not market) hunters, and horses conveyed authority, prestige, and might to the tribes that possessed them. Throughout the American West, Native groups quickly, voluntarily, and eagerly embraced horse trading. In an emerging economy, analogous in many ways to the American fur trade, Indians conveyed captured animals north and east via trade fairs and bartering in what environmental historian Dan Flores has called the "great horse funnel." The Comanches further refined this system by augmenting their captive herds with careful breeding and selective raiding. As a result, their influence eventually extended along a broad north–south band from the Dakotas south into New Mexico and Texas. As Flores concludes, "to a significant degree, [Indians] *created* the western horse trade, built their own internal status systems around it, and for a century used it to manipulate the geopolitical designs of competing Euroamericans anxious for profits and alliances with them."

Full-blown equestrianism may have catapulted the Comanches to the pinnacle of Plains power, but it also proved to be their and other tribes' ultimate undoing. Their ever-expanding horse herds competed directly with bison for grass and water, the two foundational resources of Plains ecology. Not surprisingly, the stunning success of Comanche Empire hunters and warriors attracted other tribes onto the Plains. This surging indigenous population's intense horse grazing, combined with their over-use of the relatively rare riparian zones along rivers and streams so essential to the survival of the Indian–horse–bison triad, soon stretched the carrying capacity of the natural environment. Too little grass for all of the hungry mouths and year-round exploitation of waterways that never had a chance to recover, rejuvenate, and re-grow their plant and animal biotic wealth meant that bison populations began declining by the late eighteenth century. The land simply could not supply this insatiable floral and faunal demand. Indians' hunting also pressed hard on the bison herds because hides served as *the* medium of Plains exchange – cash with horns – and so Indians killed the great shaggies in numbers far in excess of subsistence. Thus the rapid adoption of horse culture by Native peoples bound them into the emerging market economy of Euro-Americans. It was an unsustainable shift. Horses were the means to effectively capitalize on the wealth of the Plains and so they became, in effect, merchantable commodities. But at what cost? Horses and bison hunting meant that some Plains Indians abandoned more predictable subsistence agriculture and returned to a hunting/gathering lifestyle. It also meant embracing trade relations with whites in order to acquire the guns and metals necessary for warfare, efficient game pursuit, and hide processing, as well as trade goods and the food staples that these former agriculturalists no longer produced. Bison hides were the "cash" of the Plains market. This subsistence shift, combined with the Spanish introduction of livestock, horses, and agricultural grains, along with the devastation of Native populations due to disease, resulted in new Indian alliances and commercial relationships with the Spanish and other European powers that ultimately transformed traditional Native ways of life.

Over time Plains Indians became less of an "ecosystem people" and more of a "market people." For example, the Comanches' shift from agriculture back to hunting not only greatly diminished their knowledge of medicinal and subsistence plants, but also resulted in a redistribution of power within the tribes as the status of men, now the primary calorie providers, rose while agriculturalist women's influence declined. In many cases, the shift to horse culture and bison hunting ultimately led Plains Indians into polygyny (multiple wives), since women processed the buffalo hides their husbands killed and one wife often could not keep pace with her husband's harvest.

In the face of these remarkable ecological and cultural changes, it became impossible for Indians to continue to live as they had lived in the American

West prior to contact. The short-term effect of the horse–bison economy produced a cultural flourishing of Plains tribes such as the Comanches and Sioux, and power enough to shake the Spanish empire and later Mexico. But the long-term consequence was a gradual descent from subsistence into what historian Richard White has labeled "dependency," a situation where a competing dominant economy eliminates the ability of an existent economy to sustain itself and ultimately renders Native society and Native peoples "superfluous." It was not simply the military might of the Europeans that ensured their eventual dominance in the West, but rather the perfect storm of consequences that arose from their arrival in the Americas. "Guns, germs, and steel," as writer Jared Diamond has termed it, were certainly critical elements, but so too was the evolution of a market economy, which inexorably drew in Native Americans, sometimes eagerly. Neither disease nor the introduction of the market alone was enough to deliver a knock-out blow to Native cultures and societies, but in combination, the long-term social, cultural, and political effects were devastating to Indian ways of life.

Unlike a subsistence economy, a capitalist or market economy dictates not only the value of and means by which goods are traded but the very goods themselves – the merchantable commodities. The range of these commodities is notably far narrower than in a subsistence economy, where *any* item that sustains life has value, because merchantable commodities must possess a value mutually agreed upon by both seller and consumer. As anthropologist Marshall Sahlins argues, "wants may be 'easily satisfied' either by producing much or desiring little." Commercial economies emphasize the "producing much" gambit and by definition involve inter-dependence, which undermines independence, particularly when one market participant significantly outnumbers and out-produces all others.

A commercial economy and the desires it creates also has significant environmental implications. The fundamental goal of subsistence societies is survival, not the maximizing of production or profit. The ecological limits of their immediate surroundings and the demands they place on their local natural environment are limited and usually sustainable. In order to succeed, many subsistence societies practice mobility, through seasonal migrations, and periodicity, harvesting certain plants and animals only during certain times of year and leaving them to regenerate during others. Liebig's Law argues that the minimum number of resources available during the scarcest season further limits population sizes. Thus, subsistence economies, such as the pre-contact Pueblos, usually live sustainably within their natural environment because population does not exceed the carrying capacity of the ecosystem.

A market economy bypasses these environmental checks and balances. The laws of supply and demand not of a local population, but of a world market govern a capitalist system, and world markets generate potentially infinite demand for a narrow range of products. In addition, the profit incentive present in capitalism, and absent in subsistence, drives production increases in an attempt to sate what are ultimately insatiable demands. "Markets," writes Sahlins, erect "a shrine to the Unattainable: *Infinite Needs.*" Sometimes consumers desire certain commodities purely for the status that they convey. In the long run, this is unsustainable.

In the American West, Indians willingly entered into the European-introduced market system because it brought them horses and superior materials – knives, farming tools, guns, food, clothing, etc. But their participation drew them steadily away from traditional, more subsistence-oriented and ultimately more sustainable life ways. Capitalism and the market also undermined tribal cohesion by shifting Native focus away from the collective group and toward the individual, as "monetary wealth" in the form of shell and glass beads, horse herds, bison hides, and other forms of "cash," rather than community service, became the measure of social status. The histories of the Choctaws, Pawnees, and Navajos also reveal that within a relatively short time, Europeans introduced alcohol into the market, a shrewd move indeed, since this addictive addition could generate potentially infinite demand.

In order to acquire the European trade items upon which they had become increasingly reliant, Indians spent more and more of their time acquiring furs and hides for the market, which contributed to the over-hunting and even disappearance of many fur-bearing animals such as the beaver, but also resulted in an increased reliance on Euro-Americans for basic food and shelter requirements. This cycle of "dependency" borne of Indian agency (choice) meant that over time, Indians were no longer able to ignore the market; they *had to* participate in order to survive.

In the long run, the market system replaced traditional tribal authority as the determining agent for Indian land use, introducing the infinite and insatiable demands of a consumer economy to environments that had long provided sustenance and security to local economies. When, for example, the Pawnees of Nebraska turned to sedentary agriculture as bison numbers dwindled, and Southwestern Navajos eliminated native game to herd more sheep, they each shifted their modes of production away from subsistence and further integrated themselves into the market. These changes in tribal society were inextricably intertwined with changes in the environment, a bio-cultural process. Both groups abandoned diverse sources of subsistence to cater to the narrow demands of the market. In doing so, they overtaxed their soils, which soon became depleted and eroded, leaving them ever more dependent on European trade. It was a vicious cycle.

Indian participation in the market accelerated European dominance over and control of the American West. It also fundamentally altered human perception of the land itself, from one of nearly infinite resources capable of ensuring survival to one of limited commodities that could produce profit in an exterior-defined market. In a way, then, the natural environment proved to be the Europeans' most powerful colonizing ally and weapon. As Cronon put it, "economic and ecological imperialisms reinforced each other." In the short-to-medium term, Indians eagerly embraced economic and technological innovations, and proved remarkably resilient and adaptive to all the European changes in the land. But in the long term, the immigrants' diseases, trade goods, domestic livestock, and commodification of natural resources fundamentally undermined Indian subsistence, altered the natural environment, and ensured Native trade dependence.

Suggested Reading

William Cronon, "Bounding the Land," in *Changes in the Land: Indians, Colonists, and the Ecology of New England* (New York: Hill and Wang, 1983), 54–81.

Dan Flores, "Bringing Home All the Pretty Horses: The Horse Trade and the Early American West, 1775–1825," *Montana: The Magazine of Western History*, Summer 2008, 3–21.

Megan Gambino, "Alfred W. Crosby on the Columbian Exchange: The Historian Discusses the Ecological Impact of Columbus' Landing in 1492 on Both the Old World and the New World," *Smithsonian Magazine*, October 2011. www.smithsonianmag. com/history/alfred-w-crosby-on-the-columbian-exchange-98116477 (accessed February 2, 2016).

Pekka Hämäläinen, "The Rise and Fall of Plains Indian Horse Cultures," *Journal of American History*, December 2003, 833–862.

Adam R. Hodge, "'In Want of Nourishment for to Keep Them Alive': Climate Fluctuations, Bison Scarcity, and the Smallpox Epidemic of 1780–82 on the Northern Great Plains," *Environmental History*, Vol. 17, No. 2 (April 2012), 365–403.

Elizabeth A.H. John, "Indians in the Spanish Southwest," in Clyde A. Milner II, ed. *Major Problems in the History of the American West* (Lexington: D.C. Heath and Company, 1989), 49–63.

Margot Liberty, "Hell Came with Horses: Plains Indian Women in the Equestrian Era," *Montana: The Magazine of Western History*, Vol. 32, No. 3 (Summer 1982), 10–19.

Robert MacCameron, "Environmental Change in Colonial New Mexico," *Environmental History Review*, Vol. 18, No. 2 (Summer 1994), 17–39.

Charles C. Mann, *1493: Uncovering the New World Columbus Created* (New York: Vintage Books, 2012).

Alice Marriott and Carol K. Rachlin, *American Indian Mythology* (New York: Thomas Y. Crowell, 1968), 173–177.

Edmund S. Morgan, "Columbus' Confusion About the New World: The European Discovery of America Opened Possibilities for Those with Eyes to See. But Columbus Was Not One of Them," *Smithsonian Magazine*, October 2009. www.smithsonianmag.com/people-places/columbus-confusion-about-the-new-world-140132422 (accessed February 2, 2016).

Marshall Sahlins, "The Original Affluent Society," in *Stone Age Economics* (New York: Routledge, 1972).

Richard White, *The Roots of Dependency: Subsistence, Environment, and Social Change among the Choctaws, Pawnees, and Navajos* (Lincoln: University of Nebraska Press, 1983).

Sam White, "Cold, Drought, and Disaster: The Little Ice Age and the Spanish Conquest of New Mexico," *New Mexico Historical Review*, Vol. 89, No. 4 (Fall 2014), 425–458.

3

Claiming and Taming the Land

On July 24, 1847, a sick and weary Brigham Young peered down out of his covered wagon at the sprawling Salt Lake Valley of future Utah receding away into the west and reportedly proclaimed "this is the right place." Seeking refuge from persecution, the Lion of the Lord had led the Latter-Day Saints on a long and arduous journey from their adopted home in Nauvoo, Illinois, to the Great Basin, hoping that the splendid isolation of this desert environ would allow them to practice their religion in peace. But soon, tens of thousands would come to and through the Mormon state of Deseret. Just six months after Young descended to the shores of the Great Salt Lake, another cry of western discovery echoed across the continent and the globe. In January of 1848, James Marshall gleefully confided to a friend, "I have found it!" "It" was gold. Marshall and his friend were lousy secret-keepers, however, and news of Marshall's shiny discovery in the American River of California (northeast of today's Sacramento) touched off a gold rush frenzy in 1849 as hordes of prospectors poured into the region hoping to strike it rich.

In the period between the 1780s and the 1850s, the West enticed all manner of settlers from the United States, from religious refugees to fur traders, farmers, and gold seekers – it was "the land of milk and honey," "the Promised Land," "Eden," "Zion." The region's natural resource wealth made it an obvious prize and seemed to offer tantalizing opportunities to anyone adventurous enough to take the risk. It also almost inevitably led to warfare for control over the "best" and most valuable places, as both Native Americans and Mexicans had

Losing Eden: An Environmental History of the American West, First Edition. Sara Dant.
© 2017 John Wiley & Sons, Inc. Published 2017 by John Wiley & Sons, Inc.

drawn the same conclusions. In all cases, the environment fundamentally shaped western settlement and history during this period, but Euro-American settlers soon pushed back against these natural limits.

The realities of place dictated the course of westward migration for Euro-Americans. Lack of trees and water on the Great Plains, for example, propelled overland pioneers on to lusher California and Oregon, while the aridity of the interior West confined colonizers to settlements along reliable water sources such as rivers and streams. Yet even at this early juncture, white Americans, unlike their Native American, Spanish, and Mexican predecessors, were determined to bend nature to their farming, mining, or other extractive will, rather than live within nature's boundaries, confined by her carrying capacity. At what cost, then, did this conquest of the American West come? Perhaps fur trapper and trader Richens Wootton summed it up best: "the whole country has thrown off its wildness … outside of its rugged mountain peaks, its thickly wooded cañons and its natural scenery, the Wild West is no longer wild."

In 1783, the new American nation possessed the one key ingredient that nearly guaranteed her future economic, social, and political success: location. At the Revolutionary War's end, England had conceded generous boundaries to its former colonies: the Atlantic on the east, the Mississippi River on the west, British Canada to the north, and Spanish Florida to the south. And while the geopolitical challenges of being sandwiched in-between two powerful European rivals would prove daunting, the country also sat astride some of the most lucrative real estate on the planet, with the potential to expand. The United States, both in its original outline and its current configuration (with the exception of the northern portion of Alaska), lies completely within the "temperate zone," a term geographers use to describe the regions of the globe lying between the tropics and the polar circles. Although this zone has striking variations, it generally encompasses milder climates that contain the ideal balance of seasons, water supply, vegetation, and soil conditions that had enabled human civilizations to flourish for thousands of years. It is no accident that the majority of the world's population resides within these temperate borders. In the American West, this zone's natural bounty included bison and beavers, redwoods and white pines, gold and silver, mighty rivers and fertile soils – the natural resources that could fuel an empire.

After the American Revolution, white settlers eagerly pushed westward into, for them, new and unknown territories, west of the original 13 states but east of the Mississippi River, and the country needed a way to "make sense" of the land it now owned. The result was the Land Ordinance of 1785, a little-known but very powerful law that stands as one of the significant, and rare, accomplishments of the nation's first government, the Articles of Confederation Congress (see Figure 3.1). The Land Ordinance not only shaped the physical structure of the West but also Americans' perception of the land itself.

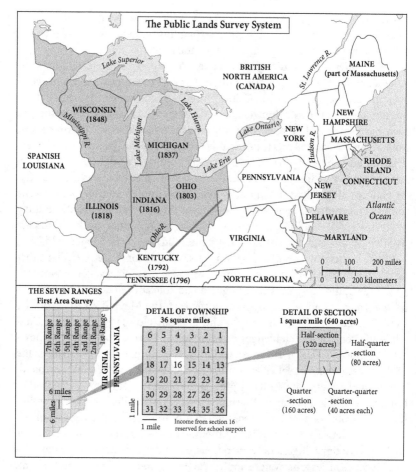

Figure 3.1 The Public Lands Survey System, created by the Land Ordinance of 1785, imposes this township and range grid system, originating in eastern Ohio, on the real property added to the United States by the 1783 Treaty of Paris and most subsequent land acquisitions. Designed primarily to subdivide and describe public lands, the system facilitated the transformation of nature into a commercial commodity.

The Land Ordinance confronted the vexing problem of property boundaries, which had been a fundamental source of conflict between colonizers and Native peoples since contact. Congress's solution to organizing the public domain, however, would have profound implications. On its surface, the Ordinance seemed simple and straightforward, providing for the survey and sale of then western lands (like Ohio, Michigan, and Tennessee) through the creation of the Public Lands Survey System. Still in use today, this system describes land (property) using the terms of "range," "township," and "section." Starting in eastern Ohio and extending at first to the nation's western boundary at the Mississippi River and eventually across the whole of the continent, government surveyors platted out public lands on a master grid. Each 6-mile-square "township" was and is subdivided into 1-mile-square "sections" (so 36 in each township), and each section contains 640 acres. The "range" was the number assigned to each township, in order, measured from a north–south principal meridian. While it sounds complicated, this squares-within-squares system simplified property identification. Prior to the law, property descriptions used natural features, and so it was not uncommon for deeds to include boundary descriptions such as: "from the junction of Rock Creek and Dry Gulch east one mile to the top of Pea Ridge, then north to the big pine in the rock outcrop, then west to Rock Creek, then south down the center of the creek to the point of origin." But as streams changed their course and trees died, property boundaries became murky. The new system changed all of that. In the whole of the world, there was only one Section 16 Township 46 North Range 10 East of the Third Principal meridian.

Thus, the Public Lands Survey System created real estate order out of wilderness chaos, but at a cost. These new boundary descriptions were completely devoid of environmental considerations. Their arbitrary lines bisected rivers, ignored mountain ranges, and paid no heed to soil conditions, swamps, or suitable browse (edible vegetation for livestock). Stripped of its natural identity, land itself became yet another commodity in the market economy, subject to the same exploitation and abuse as all other products forced to conform to the iron laws of supply and demand. In many ways, this imposition of a "rational" grid that ignored all environmental features typified the modern American approach to nature: it brought order out of chaos and altered the land to suit human needs instead of encouraging settlers to adapt their livelihoods to the environments in which they lived. Nature may abhor the square, but government surveyors and land speculators loved it.

Not surprisingly, the nation's appetite for this newest commodity was insatiable, and in a relatively brief and remarkable spurt of acquisition – 1783 to 1853 – the United States came to possess all lands from the 49th parallel (the US–Canadian border in the West) south to Mexico and from the Atlantic to the Pacific. The first major addition came in 1803. The Louisiana Purchase, which the United States acquired for a mere $15 million from France, instantly more than doubled the size of the country, adding more than a half-billion acres to the nation with the stroke of President Thomas Jefferson's pen. Expanding the land base of the republic made perfect sense to Jefferson, whose ideal citizen was the "yeoman farmer." Secure in his possessions, independent, civic, resourceful, democratic, and enterprising, the yeoman farmer embodied all the characteristics that would preserve and protect "life, liberty, and the pursuit of happiness," to be sure. But for Jefferson, a nation of farmers would also avoid the crushing poverty and class stratification that had emerged along with the factory system in England. When Jefferson took office in 1801, the United States was economically undeveloped, rural, agrarian, and boasted a total population of just over 5 million people. Industrialization might be inevitable, but if Jefferson could help it, not at the expense of family farms. For the third president, the Louisiana Purchase operated like a gigantic safety valve, ensuring that virtuous, independent farmers could always escape from the throes of eastern poverty to free lands in the West. And as the farmer's plow furrowed westward, Jefferson believed, the agrarian republic would flourish as it brought new lands under cultivation, added new resources to the market, and perfected nature by bringing "progress" through development. Order out of chaos, and liberty and prosperity for free Americans.

The key question behind the great Louisiana land grab, however, was quite simply, what had the nation acquired? The trans-Mississippi West was, in many ways, a great mystery to most Americans including Jefferson, but it had been sustaining a remarkable diversity of human existence for hundreds of generations. Government-sponsored exploration was the natural starting point and the goals of various federal expeditions reflected the extractive resource focus of the nation. While earlier French, Spanish, and even Russian explorers had preceded the Americans into the region, also looking for extractable wealth like beaver pelts, it was the systematic forays organized in the nation's capital that began to illuminate the real treasure the country had acquired. Jefferson, steeped in the intellectual rationalism of the Enlightenment, sought to bring order (and the township and range grid) to the chaotic West by dispatching "armies" of mapmakers, biologists, geographers, ethnographers, botanists, and zoologists. Jefferson's own 1785 *Notes on the State of Virginia* had detailed his home-state's natural history and now provided the framework for inventorying the Louisiana Purchase.

In 1803, Jefferson organized the Corps of Discovery under the capable leadership of Meriwether Lewis and William Clark, as one of the earliest official US probes into the West (see Figure 3.2). The primacy of the natural environment was evident. In addition to mapping the region, Jefferson instructed the expedition to locate the elusive (and non-existent) Northwest Passage, educate the Natives about their new "Great White Father," and collect scientific information regarding the flora and fauna, climate and terrain, all with an eye for potential development. Imploring Lewis to take "great pains" in the accuracy of his observations, Jefferson further instructed the Corps to become acquainted with "the soil and face of the country, its growth and vegetable production ... the animals of the country generally ... the mineral productions of every kind ... climate ... [and] the dates at which particular plants put forth, or lose their flower or leaf."

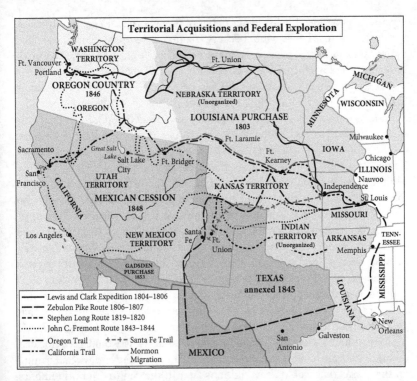

Territorial Acquisitions and Federal Exploration

Lewis and Clark Expedition 1804–1806
Zebulon Pike Route 1806–1807
Stephen Long Route 1819–1820
John C. Fremont Route 1843–1844
Oregon Trail + – + – Santa Fe Trail
California Trail Mormon Migration

Figure 3.2 The contiguous United States expanded geographically in an impressive burst of territorial acquisition: 1803 Louisiana Purchase, 1846 Oregon Treaty, 1848 Treaty of Guadalupe-Hidalgo, 1853 Gadsden Purchase. To encourage and promote American settlement and sovereignty, the federal government sponsored numerous exploratory expeditions.

Unlike the previous explorations of competing nations, Jefferson designed Lewis and Clark's broad reconnaissance mission to produce a thorough understanding of the market potential of the Louisiana Territory. Lewis, in particular, received extensive instruction in botanical collection techniques, Indian diplomacy, anthropological and ethnographic observation, mapmaking and instrument use, and the natural sciences during the summer prior to the expedition. From 1804 to 1806, the roughly 30-man Corps, armed with this environmental vision for exploration (as opposed to, say, a military purpose), navigated *up* the Missouri River, spent the winter with the Mandans in South Dakota, crossed the Rocky Mountains, descended the mighty Columbia, and returned to St. Louis after covering nearly 8000 miles. On the Great Plains alone, they collected specimens that represented at least 20 new animal species and 22 new plant species, and provided the first descriptions of pronghorn antelope, grizzly bears, trumpeter swans, Lewis' woodpeckers (named after the explorer), western rattlesnakes, cutthroat trout, and channel catfish, as well as far more thorough observations of bison, gray wolves, coyotes, and bullsnakes.

The development potential of this extensive field survey was immediately manifest. The information the Corps brought back to Washington fueled an American vision of harvestable riches and set a tone for subsequent expeditions to explore and document the West's vast commercial potential. In April of 1806, before the Corps' return, Jefferson had also dispatched a *second* Louisiana probe, the ill-fated southern counterpart to the Corps, led by Thomas Freeman and Peter Custis, to explore the origins of the Red River. But the so-called "Grand Expedition" only made it 650 miles before the Spanish firmly rebuffed them near the present-day southeastern border of Oklahoma. Despite this geopolitical checkmate, Custis nevertheless cataloged more than 260 species, including new discoveries such as the Mississippi kite (a bird species) and the bois d'arc tree, in his abbreviated three-month journey. Zebulon Pike's expedition in 1806–1807 and Stephen Long's in 1820 continued to advance American trade into the West, although their descriptions of the arid Great Plains as "The Great American Desert" ensured that generations of westward migrants would leap-frog over it for greener lands in Oregon and California (and that Native Americans would get relocated there). Explorers had yet to see the potential for ranching and wheat farming on the Plains that would draw millions later in the century. John Fremont's three western forays in the 1840s also mapped out much of the westward route to Oregon. And collectively, these expeditions all followed Jefferson's charge to bring order out of chaos and firmly established the primacy of the federal government in the region.

What these early federal explorers all shared was a way of looking at the natural environment for its market potential, and some of the first white Americans to venture into these newest territories in search of profits were the fur traders and mountain men, whose epic treks often swung them out ahead of the nation's advancing borders. In 1811, John Jacob Astor established the first American settlement on the Pacific Coast at Fort Astoria near the mouth of the Columbia River. As the far western headquarters for his Pacific Fur Company, Astor's trading post set precedent for American presence in the region and his "Overland Astorians" were the first whites to discover Wyoming's South Pass, which later became the main trade route over the continental divide to Oregon. Befitting their democratic heritage, many enterprising American mountain men sought to avoid costly allegiances with fur trading companies and became "free trappers," signing short-term contracts instead and hiring themselves out basically as fur free-agents. To fully realize pelt profits, these American "free traders" needed access to the market, and the annual rendezvous along the Green River (about 100 miles south of today's Jackson Hole, Wyoming) provided it. Begun in 1825, the rendezvous was a yearly frontier trade fair that attracted mountain men, Indians, international traders, and women, who all exchanged goods and many services (other rendezvous occurred less frequently in Utah's Cache Valley and in Taos, New Mexico). John Colter, for example, who had first ventured west as part of the Corps of Discovery, trapped from the Rockies to the Pacific and was the first to describe the weird and wonderful sights of Yellowstone, which also became known derisively as "Colter's Hell." Some of these mountain men/trapper/explorers became part of the western mythology – Jedediah Smith, Jim Bridger, Kit Carson, and Jim Beckwourth – as they blazed new trails and gained renown as America's first western wilderness romantic heroes. If the mantra was "go West, young man," Smith, Carson, and others led the way, both for migration and profitability.

In the first half of the nineteenth century, "the fur trade was a reciprocal system which had to be bicultural and symbiotic in order to succeed," historian William Swagerty has argued. Native laborers provided the foundation upon which the American Rocky Mountain Fur Company and its older, larger British-Canadian competitor the Hudson's Bay Company (HBC) built the fur trade. As white diseases ravaged newly exposed Native populations, Indians actively turned toward the market as a more efficient means of securing subsistence. White free traders were usually single men who married or cohabited with Native women for companionship, to facilitate positive cultural relations, and to increase their trapping and processing efficiency. Their mixed-race descendants, called the Métis in the case of French-Indian offspring and mestizo for Spanish-Indian ones, created a cultural middle ground of interaction and inter-marriage between trappers and Native people, and anticipated the truly multi-cultural nature of the modern American West. In the Southern Rockies, too, where the fur trade emanated out of Taos, New Mexico, white trappers like Kit Carson married or allied with New Mexican women of Indian, Mexican, or mestizo descent for the same reasons. These usually mutually satisfying and reciprocal relationships allowed white mountain men to trap and hunt while Indian/Hispanic women, whose language skills and knowledge of the local natural environment was essential to their husbands' success, tended to domestic duties, gathered and prepared food, and dressed pelts for travel and trade. Beaver pelts were not so much valued for their thick outer fur as for the fine underhairs that women pounded into felt that was then rendered into hats. The fur companies also utilized and exploited Indian transportation and communication networks and employed Native men as hunting guides. The transforming influence of the fur trade thus rippled out in all directions, affecting even the human landscape by modifying and shifting gender roles and facilitating cultural blending. Indian peoples made their own choices in participating in the fur trade, and often profited from it early on; at the same time, the fur trade served as a powerful accelerant to the demographic shift from Native to white dominance in the Pacific Northwest and northern Rockies.

In a sense, the fur companies were agents of the American empire that ushered the region into the global economic network. The British had pioneered the beaver fur trade in the Pacific Northwest to feed Europe's insatiable hat fetish, but by the 1820s, thanks in part to the Lewis and Clark Expedition and Fort Astoria, the United States entered the fray. Although the two countries had agreed to "joint occupation" of Oregon Country in 1818, Britain's HBC knew that competition was bad for business and so it sent trappers like Peter Skene Ogden to "trap out" areas ahead of the Americans. Hoping to affect a geopolitical checkmate, one HBC Governor explained, "we have convincing proof that the country is a rich preserve of Beaver and which for political reasons we should endeavor to destroy as fast as possible."

This strategy brought short-term profits, to be sure, but it also produced serious long-term environmental consequences. Ogden's tactics were stunningly effective and his men quickly wiped out the entire Snake River Basin beaver population. The "war" on these dam-building animals continued throughout the Northern Rockies: in just six years, for example, between 1824 and 1830, Ogden's trappers "harvested" about 18 000 beavers south of the Columbia River, and as early as 1824, Ogden proclaimed of the Bitterroot River in today's Montana, "this part of the Country tho' once abounding in Beaver is entirely ruined." By 1840, for all intents and purposes, the HBC had fully realized its goal of creating a "fur desert."

The insatiable demands of the market paid little heed to ecological balance. Without the influence of beavers and their dams, this largely arid region failed to retain water beyond seasonal run-offs, which in turn negatively affected native flora, fauna, and soils, and increased erosion. As the first big extractive corporations to work in the West, the fur companies set in motion a powerful precedent. In many ways the resource depletion wrought by the fur trade was analogous to the environmental costs of the bison/horse trade on the Plains. Both the fur trade and the bison hide trade systematically commodified nature, treating it solely as something to sell, which in turn bound participants into the larger emerging system of global capitalism. Ironically, the success of the fur traders had led to their own demise much as the success of bison hunters would do the same. Similarly, the sustainability of Native American communities became increasingly impossible when demand for "merchantable commodities" dictated the "value" of nature. Indian reliance on white trade goods ultimately led to dependency, even though it created new opportunities in the short to medium run. By 1840, the year of the last rendezvous, the fickle whims of fashion had turned to silk hats, Indian reliance on the market intensified, and the beaver population hovered near extinction in the West. This was certainly no pristine "Eden."

In 1846, though, the consequences of American involvement in the fur trade seemed entirely positive for white traders, and also many of their Indian counterparts, as the United States and Great Britain peacefully negotiated their long-standing dispute over control of the Pacific Northwest. Because of her presence in the area now, the United States claimed the 183 million-acre Oregon Territory south of the 49th parallel, while the British retained control over Canada to the north. For an ambitious nation like the United States, the acquisition of this region's giant old-growth timbers, teeming rivers of salmon, rich agricultural lands, and soon-to-be-discovered ore deposits was like hitting a natural resource jackpot. White farmers, missionaries, and settlers streamed into Oregon Country along the Oregon Trail and, by 1859, the territory had a large enough population to enter the union as the nation's 33rd state. During this explosive growth period, the western border of the United States surged toward the Pacific from the 49th parallel all the way south to Mexico, and by mid-century, the "West" lying between the Great Plains and the Pacific, had become solidly American. But not all territorial acquisition was peaceful.

The Southwest first belonged to Spain and then Mexico before the United States finally wrested control. Spanish sovereignty dated back to their original arrival in the New World at the turn of the sixteenth century, but by the early nineteenth century Spain's glory days as a world power were waning, and in 1821, a powerful Mexican nationalism successfully asserted its independence. For the United States, this changing of the guard proved significant, as a flourishing trade with Santa Fe strengthened American interest in acquiring the region. Mexico knew it. In addition to mineral, cattle, timber, and agricultural wealth, the arid Southwest held few, and thus extremely valuable, waterways. Tensions between these two uncomfortable neighbors grew as land lust and trade routes piqued US desire to acquire more West, particularly Texas, and legal Americans settlers and illegal squatters slid across international borders. Mexico, however, had no intention of relinquishing her new territories.

The Mexican government understood that the key to sovereignty – power and authority – was control of the land itself: essentially, settlement equals sovereignty. So in order to strengthen her hold on the far north, Mexico encouraged loyal colonists to claim cheap land in Texas. The requirements were simple: recognition of Mexican sovereignty and, ideally, conversion to

Roman Catholicism. Mexico's goal was to develop stable, patriotic settlements in the far north that would bind these distant holdings more tightly to Mexico City, much like the Spanish missions had bound these lands to New Spain in the 1600s. But the scheme backfired. Most of the settlers who claimed Texas farms and ranches were not Mexicans but slave-holding Americans from the Deep South seeking affordable and fertile cotton lands. Loyalty to Mexico and religious conversion were annoying but relatively simple obstacles to overcome, and soon Mexico's Texas filled with Americans – "Texians" in the parlance of the time. Despite numerous attempts to oust floods of illegal squatters, who quickly outnumbered legal settlers, the Mexican government failed to halt the white southern tide, and by 1835 skirmishes between the two jostling neighbors finally erupted into war. Although the Texians won their independence from Mexico the following year, slavery thwarted their hopes of immediately joining the United States. In 1836, Texas was populous enough to become a new state, but 1836 was an election year, and the "Texas question" would most certainly thrust the polarizing North–South slavery debate back into the center of American politics. So President Andrew Jackson declined to annex Texas territory and the Lone Star Republic forged ahead as an independent country (at least in its own mind, as Mexico did not recognize this) until 1845, when calmer domestic politics made its admission into the United States less controversial. At least at home.

Mexico, however, had never formally recognized Texas independence, so US annexation amounted to an act of war. And by 1846, the same year as the peaceful settlement of the Oregon Territory dispute with Great Britain, the United States was prepared to go to war to gain the invaluable natural resources of the Mexican Southwest. This near feverish desire to expand the nation westward became known as Manifest Destiny, a term coined by newspaperman John O'Sullivan in 1845. It perfectly encapsulated the unique sense of mission and predestination that Euro-Americans had cherished since the Puritans had proclaimed, "we shall be as a city upon a hill." O'Sullivan's argument that expansionism was "the fulfillment of our manifest destiny to overspread the continent alloted by Providence for the free development of our yearly multiplying millions" was, in essence, a politicized nineteenth-century restatement of the seventeenth-century utopian vision of Puritan John Winthrop. It quickly became a national mantra and served as the perfect justification for imperialism.

By 1846, the United States was interested in a far bigger prize than just Texas. Farther west lay California, whose riches included livestock, verdant farmland, vineyards, and a seemingly enslavable Indian workforce. That year, President James Polk upped the ante by arraying American troops provocatively along the Rio Grande River, facing Mexico. The Mexican government countered. The predictable result was the Mexican–American War, which began in May of that year and lasted until early 1848, when the Treaty of Guadalupe-Hidalgo provided for American acquisition of the Mexican Cession – the entire 338 million-acre Southwest from California to Texas – in a $15 million steal. Five years later, in 1853, the United States paid Mexico an additional $10 million for the Gadsden Purchase, nearly 19 million acres in what is today southern Arizona and New Mexico, to complete the continental outline of the nation.

White settlers followed federal explorers, traders, and the US military into the West, and their epic treks soon transformed the natural landscape and the lives of those already living there. The possibilities inherent in the wide-open West tantalized easterners, who saw endless possibilities for renewal and revenue. The first whites to head west in significant numbers were pioneer farmers, who followed on the heels of the fur trappers and mountain men along the California and Oregon trails in their covered wagons seeking to claim and tame the West as their own manifest destiny. Although Indian and Hispanic agriculturalists had preceded them, Euro-American farmers trailed townspeople behind them – the merchants, missionaries, and medical personnel who in turn created markets for finished goods, food, and real estate. They also brought with them familiar plants and animals that would affect their own version of the earlier Columbian Exchange on the flora and fauna of the coastal West. In 1847, for example, one intrepid Overland Trail migrant hauled hundreds of apple, pear, cherry, and peach tree saplings, along with grapes, currants, and gooseberry bushes from Iowa to Oregon. He immediately planted them into the orchards, berry patches, and vineyards near present-day Portland that would in time evolve into the multimillion dollar fruit industry all along the temperate zones of Oregon and California.

This was "progress" and "civilization," but not from the perspective of region's native flora and fauna. During the 1840s and 1850s alone, nearly a quarter of a million settlers made their way west along the overland trails, and they took their toll on valuable timber stands along the way for wagon repairs, firewood, home construction, and fencing. White displacement of Native peoples also caused thick fir forests to replace the park-like oak savannahs that the Indians' seasonal burning had maintained. Native prairie grasses retreated against the onslaught of exotic wheat and Kentucky bluegrass lawns, and salmon runs began their precipitous decline toward endangered species protection in the twentieth century. These changes represented the price of "progress."

One of the most remarkable of these overland pioneer migrations belonged to the Mormons of Utah. In 1847, this uniquely American faith group sought protection and salvation in The Great American Desert – testimony, indeed, to the powerful forces pushing the Saints westward. The Church of Jesus Christ of Latter-day Saints (Mormons/LDS) arose in 1830 as the divine vision of a charismatic prophet named Joseph Smith during the foment of religious revivals in upstate New York that historians call the Second Great Awakening. But non-Mormons grew to resent the church's isolationist tendencies and unorthodox theology (from the viewpoint of most Americans), its growing political and commercial influence, and the newly-sanctioned practice of polygamy and in June of 1844, a vicious Nauvoo, Illinois, mob took matters into its own hands and murdered Smith and his brother. During this nadir, Brigham Young emerged to lead the fractured faithful, and he quickly determined that the safest refuge for the Mormons lay to the west, outside the boundaries of the United States near the Great Salt Lake. John Fremont's 1844 California expedition had described "a region of great pastoral promise abounding with fine streams ... [and] soil that would produce wheat" along the Wasatch Front. For Young and the Mormons, this would be the place.

The Saints' migration, led by Young, was a feat of organizational skill and coordination; there would be no wandering in the desert for this Mormon Moses and his people. Their trek/flight from Nauvoo to the Great Salt Lake would be church-organized, church-financed, and church-led, establishing both Young and the LDS apostles as *the* authorities in the region. In the beginning, in their new Promised Land, the church was omnipresent and it placed a strong emphasis on cooperation and community. This theocracy laid out and assigned new communities, and distributed land based on family size and ability to cultivate. Even more importantly, it presided over a collective communal irrigation system that was a notable departure from the "first-in-time, first-in-right" allocation practices in other parts of the West. Young declared that the Saints would take the "fallen" deserts of Northern Mexico (because the desert still belonged to Mexico at that time), and turn them into the "Garden of Eden." Water was the key. The LDS prophet preached a message of communalism that suffused Mormon settlement of the American West and set it apart from the many individualistic and capitalistic pursuits that had dominated other Euro-American colonization efforts. Thus, even in the driest years, community welfare prevailed and everyone received at least some water to irrigate their fields and farms.

"The Lord's Beavers," as environmental historian Donald Worster has labeled the hardworking Saints, utilized strategies similar to earlier Indian practices of communal control and usufruct rights in their remarkable conquest of the desert they chose to make bloom. Native peoples had lived in the region for thousands of years, of course, and had altered the natural environment to suit their own needs. Paleolithic hunters had stalked mammoths perhaps into extinction, and ancestors of the Anasazi had extracted life from the harsh and arid environs through hunting and gathering until the rise of agriculture and irrigation allowed the Anasazi and Fremont cultures to thrive, while the Utes and Paiutes encountered by the Mormons used fire for hunting and to promote open grasslands enticing to game. But it was the *scale* of the Mormon transformation that was so striking. Although they brought zero experience in water management with them, by 1850, the Mormons were irrigating more than 16 000 acres in what Worster has called "one of the most river-deprived areas in the United States." By 1890, these thrifty and persevering pioneers, who called their provisional state "Deseret," which means "honeybee" in the *Book of Mormon*, had adopted the beehive as the symbol of their work ethic and were watering more than 260 000 acres to support a population in excess of 200 000. The church planned, financed, and managed the web of canals and dams that produced bountiful harvests, which, in turn, filled the pantries of enterprising Saints, albeit with non-native plants and animals. Young and his followers fulfilled their promise to "make the desert bloom as a rose," but the environmental price for success here and in the rest of the American West would be high.

More than 70 000 Mormons trekked to Utah over the two decades following Young's arrival, heeding the call to come to "Zion" and "be gathered unto one place" and bringing about significant changes in this arid land lying at the foot of the Wasatch Range. Although their religious zeal distinguished the Saints from other overland emigrants, their basic outlook on the natural environment mirrored that of pioneers generally. They, too, sought fertile soil for their non-native crops, sufficient grasslands and meadows for their non-native livestock, and suitable timber stands for building materials. The Mormons also exposed local Indians to deadly waves of smallpox and measles, and often refused to respect Indians' title to their ancestral homelands.

The long-term success of Mormon settlement belies some initial ecological difficulties. For example, the nearly 2000 original migrants who struggled through their first winter in this Deseret "Eden" faced a plague of crop-destroying crickets the following spring. Although flocks of seagulls soon descended to feast on the insects, the chirping hordes continued to menace these newest agriculturalists for years to come (and still billow up in vexing clouds today). Starvation and food shortages plagued early settlers and various predators took their toll on the farm animals kept by the Saints. Hungry pioneers soon depleted the region's big game populations at the same time as they introduced thousands of sheep, cattle, and other easy "prey" – nearly 70 000 domesticated animals by 1870. The predictable livestock mortalities led to a pioneer "war" on predatory "wasters and destroyers." As one Salt Lake Valley resident explained, "There is a general raid by the settlers on bears, wolves, foxes, crows, hawks, eagles, magpies and all ravenous birds and beasts." One two-month toll was impressive: 2 bears, 2 wolverines, 2 bobcats, 9 eagles, 31 mink, 530 magpies, hawks, and owls, 1026 ravens, and 1192 foxes, coyotes, and wolves were killed. Within a decade of their arrival, Salt Lake settlers had also ravaged local timber stands and their livestock had over-grazed the grasslands, which in turn led to damaging flash floods and debris flows. Woody sagebrush and exotic Russian thistles (tumbleweeds) capital-ized on the disturbed soils and soon drove out native bluestem and gramma grasses. Although the church endeavored to manage Deseret's natural resources for the good of the people, all of the people, the mirage of paradise soon faded; Mormon economic stability would ultimately rest to a large extent on a growing trade with westward-bound migrants along the overland trails.

Mormon prosperity derived from their successful communal conquest and transformation of nature as well as their fortuitous settlement at an important waypoint along the Oregon and California trails. Thus when a California Mormon named Samuel Brannan bellowed "gold" through the streets of San Francisco in 1848, spilling Marshall's secret, the Saints stood poised to make a handsome profit by supplying the rush of Forty-niners destined to flow through their territory. For the United States, the timing of the California gold rush was perfect. Just as the Mexican–American War concluded and California passed into American hands, the nation hit the jackpot about 50 miles east of present-day Sacramento. On the eve of the discovery, California was sparsely populated by about 14 000 non-Indians and the remnants of disease-ravaged Native peoples; in less than two years, there were more than 100 000 settlers, and by 1852 the two-year-old state's population stood at 250 000. As the world rushed in, however, the rising human tide brought with it techniques to wrest gold from the land that paid little heed to the environmental costs such a bonanza incurred.

Initial discoveries like those of James Marshall's focused on the gold nug-gets that settled out along the stream-bed edges of California's rivers, so miners adopted various "placer" techniques to swirl and scratch the precious metal from the earth. Placer mining relies on the relative density of gold versus other alluvial deposits – the loose rocks, sand, and soils left behind by flowing water. Miners swish the sediments around in some water and the dense gold pieces settle to the bottom while the other lighter materials get washed away. The simplest technique is "panning" for gold and it literally involves scooping up some sand, gravel, and water in a shallow pan, swirling it around, and picking out the shiny pieces. Simple but also very small-scale. Usually, once a miner located a gold deposit, he (rarely she) switched to rocker boxes and sluice boxes. As its name suggests, the rocker box was like a big cradle that the miner could agitate, like a much larger version of the pan, to sift through significantly greater amounts of silt, sand, and gravel alluvium.

If "rocking the golden baby," as rocker boxing was known, still seemed too small-scale, miners could employ a sluice box. This technique utilized a long chute or walled run (usually 3–10 feet long) with a corrugated or stepped bottom. Miners shoveled debris into the top of the box and then rushing water sluiced the material over the rungs, grabbing the heavier gold and flushing away the lighter "waste rock." For the most part, none of these early placer techniques extracted a significant environmental toll because they were all still relatively small-scale.

But as obvious surface deposits quickly played out, miners resorted to more elaborate schemes of river mining. Between about 1853 and the early 1880s, increasingly aggressive techniques diverted entire streams through chutes to expose the gold lying in now-dry beds and then quickly shifted to hydraulic mining, which eroded away entire mountains and washed countless tons of silt and debris downstream (see Figure 3.3). The rationale was simple: the

Figure 3.3   Malakoff Diggings, 1905, by Carleton E. Watkins. In an effort to maximize mining efficiency, entrepreneuring extractors shifted from small-scale panning and sluicing to large-scale hydraulic mining, which strafed entire hillsides with high-pressure water jets to expose valuable ores and caused serious environmental damage. Source: Reproduced with permission of The Bancroft Library.

more gravel miners could process, the more gold they could discover. The hydraulic process that California gold seekers perfected involved trapping water in holding ponds and diverting it through increasingly narrow channels until the concentrated stream finally blasted out of a canvas hose like a mighty water cannon and erosionary force. One observer remarked that "the stream when it leaves the pipe has such force that it would cut a man in two if it should hit him. Two or three and sometimes even six such streams play against the bottom of a hill, and earth and stones, often of great size, are washed away until at last an immense slice of the hill itself gives way and tumbles down." The scale of these hydraulic operations was epic. Armed with these water cannons, miners strafed entire hillsides and sent roaring debris rivers through enormous sluices in their quest to strike it rich. It was monstrously successful. In just over 30 years, hydraulic extraction yielded 11 million ounces of gold worth more than $700 million – the equivalent of approximately $14.5 *billion* in 2014 dollars!

The California Gold Rush may have perfected hydraulic mining, but the environmental costs were staggering and enduring. Moreover, miners transported this stunningly efficient and massively destructive technique throughout the Rocky Mountain West, providing the model for subsequent fortune seekers to wreak havoc on other mountain ecologies. Historian Raymond Dasmann has estimated that this mere three-decade onslaught caused more environmental damage along the Sierra Nevadas than any other event in the past 600 million years. Hydraulic mining in the "land of milk and honey" flushed torrents of rubble down on farmlands, fouled the region's streams and rivers, and destroyed salmon runs. Debris streaming down into the Central Valley of California, for example, raised the overall level of the area by 7 feet, threatening the agricultural endeavors of farmers with sterile soils and raging spring floods, and pitting these two extractive resource users against one another. One contemporary hydraulic critic lamented, "Hills melt away and disappear under its influence... The desolation which remains ... is remediless and appalling."

"The diggings," as California's vast extractive operation was called, also required huge amounts of timber for fuel and construction, and both mines and communities dramatically accelerated the deforestation of the territory. This in turn exposed big game animals to hungry hunters, who decimated California's elk herds to feed the insatiable demands of the burgeoning mining camps – from an estimated high of 500 000 animals, for example, the entire population of tule elk, native only to California, flirted with extinction as their population plummeted to just 28 individuals by the 1890s. Pronghorns faced similar near-elimination.

River diversions and dams also altered historic stream flows and in some cases relocated waterways wholesale into new channels and beds. Aquatic flora and fauna simply could not follow or adapt rapidly enough. Flushed sediments clogged flow regimes, muddied waters, and silted up lakes and harbors. Returning salmon, which rely on clean gravel beds for their redds (spawning nests) and are extremely sensitive to changes in water temperature, turbidity, and flows, found a muddy mess. The twin pressures of miner over-fishing and polluted habitat sent salmon numbers into a free-fall – a collapse that rippled throughout the California ecosystem. Salmon comprise an invaluable component of any riparian nutrient cycle; having spent much of their lives fattening up in the oceans, salmon return to their freshwater origins to spawn and die, and their decaying carcasses nourish everything from aquatic invertebrates to eagles, bears, and humans. California may still proudly fly a state flag emblazoned with a grizzly from its (brief) days of independence as the Bear Flag Republic (in 1846), but without salmon to sustain them, the big bears disappeared in just a couple of generations. Although the courts finally banned hydraulic mining in 1884 as "a public and private nuisance," the salmon runs would never recover.

The environmental impact of gold lust reached far beyond California; the Gold Rush, it turned out, was bad for bison. The Forty-niners and other western fortune seekers had to get to California first, and to do so, some of them crossed the Great Plains. There, they helped precipitate a momentous ecological collapse that would have deep and abiding historical repercussions. For white emigrants, the Great Plains presented a great obstacle – a formi-dable, seemingly endless stretch of grass and wind that lay between them and the promised lands of California and Oregon. For Native people like the Comanches, though, the wide-open prairie offered opportunity. Indian adop-tion of horse culture in the eighteenth century and participation in a wider market economy had enabled them to effectively exploit the bison wealth that teemed all around them. Or so it seemed. Buffalo were central to Plains Indians' lives, providing the foundation of their diet, their material culture (attire, teepees, etc.), their religious identity, and their primary means of trade. But by 1840, the herds were in serious decline. Yet the "usual suspects" in this story – white overland travelers, hide hunters, or the Army – were not the main culprits. In fact, several historians have demonstrated that white emi-grants could not possibly have precipitated such a disastrous bison decline all on their own. For one thing, the early pioneers were notoriously lousy hunters who had neither the time nor the energy to devote to the hunt – they were pressing hard to beat the November snows in the Sierra Nevadas to reach their California (or Oregon) destinations. Plus, bison numbers had already begun to drop precipitously by 1840 before the incursion of whites; indeed, many emigrant journals describe the skeletal remains of these shaggy beasts along the trails, indicating that the die-off was already well underway. Hide hunters and the Army arrived only in the final years of bison decline.

The near extinction of bison, then, was not the result of some single, catastrophic event or agent, but rather the consequence of a complex web of colliding changes that beset the Great Plains at a particular and critical moment in history. In other words, any one of the challenges, in and of itself, would not have been enough to deliver the knock-out blow. It was instead the collective barrage – the perfect storm – that doomed bison, and in turn, the people whose lives depended on them. The Comanches, Arapahos, and Cheyennes certainly shouldered some responsibility, since they used buffaloes for both subsistence and trade. Buffalo robes had become the medium of exchange on the Plains – the "money" – and Native Americans needed this "cash" for commodities such as agricultural foods, guns and ammunition essential to warfare, alcohol, and other items, and so they hunted well beyond their need for meat/subsistence. Unfortunately, to get more guns to defend and take hunting grounds, the Indians had to kill more bison, for which they needed more guns – it was an insatiable and ultimately unsustainable cycle. The robe trade also focused on female bison, thus constricting the reproductive abilities of the herds.

But other factors were also at work. Just as white emigrants crossing the Plains infected Indians with deadly diseases such as smallpox and cholera, their livestock transmitted deadly diseases to bison such as brucellosis and anthrax. Both people and animals suffered predictable population declines as a result. These same emigrants and their livestock also competed with Indians and their horses and the bison for grass. But by winter, the emigrants had moved on to greener grounds in the far West; the Indians, horses, and bison had to fend for themselves in the increasingly depleted micro-environments of the Plains, such as river bottoms. When spring finally arrived, all three emerged weakened, only to repeat the cycle in a downward spiral of starvation, desperation, and increased market dependency. Already vulnerable due to these multiple stresses, both human and animal Plains populations teetered on the edge of survival at precisely the moment that drought seared the region. From the mid-1840s to the 1860s, there was too little grass and too many mouths. It was too much. White market hunters streamed onto the Plains in the 1870s to finish the job that nature, the Indians, and white emigrants had begun, slaughtering bison by the thousands, taking only their valuable hides to sell, and leaving behind their carcasses to rot. By 1882, the deed was done. As one bison hunter remembered, "there settled over them [the Plains] a vast quiet ... the buffalo was gone." Buffalo-centric Indians met a similar fate of drastically reduced numbers and confinement to reservations.

The bison story is an illustration of both Liebig's Law and the "Tragedy of the Commons" concept. As discussed in the introduction, ecologist Garrett Hardin introduced the "Tragedy of the Commons" dilemma in a 1968 article in which he argued that individuals acting in their own self-interest will ignore the best interests of larger society and deplete "common" resources.

In this instance, the common resource was the unregulated, shared prairies of the Great Plains. As more lives came to depend on this ultimately finite resource, the limited supply of grass became too depleted and could no longer sustain the Plains' bison ecology. Liebig's Law then led to declining populations that at least for bison, flirted with extinction.

In the end, then, change, both economic and environmental, killed the bison. To be sure, "change" had wrought wondrous progress for the nation, too, which celebrated the realization of its Manifest Destiny to "overspread the continent." But at what cost? Exploration had opened up vast new territories to Euro-American settlers from the United States and immigrants from abroad, revealed previously unknown peoples as well as plant and animal species, and ensured that the nation would have a natural resource base capable of catapulting it to the forefront of world power and influence. Exploitation of the West's bounty was the most obvious way to supply the demands of the burgeoning country; in 1783, the nation's population had been just 3.25 million people, but by 1850, there were 30 million Americans, and immigrants continued to pour in every year.

Yet while the West's natural resources constituted the region's greatest asset, they would also ensure its colony-like status for more than a century. Quite simply, eastern factories would render western raw materials into finished products for decades. The same market-driven perspective that had "opened" the West, bringing "civilization" and "progress," had also driven beavers and bison to the brink of extinction, decimated pristine waterways in the fevered search for gold, introduced exotic agricultural species into an arid West that, in turn, demanded irrigation works on a scale previously unimagined, and systematically destroyed Indian lives and culture at a level approaching genocide. This was never Eden. The West may have been "the right place" for many, but they took a heavy toll on the region's land and water and the Native peoples already living there. Abundance often bred abuse or, as environmental historian William Cronon has suggested, "the people of plenty were a people of waste."

Suggested Reading

Diana L. Ahmad, "'I Fear the Consequences to Our Animals': Emigrants and Their Livestock on the Overland Trails," *Great Plains Quarterly*, Vol. 32 (Summer 2012), 165–182.

Kent Curtis, "Producing a Gold Rush: National Ambitions and the Northern Rocky Mountains, 1853–1863," *Western Historical Quarterly*, Autumn 2009, 275–297.

Sara E. Dant, "Brigham Young's 'All the People' Quote Quandary," *Western Historical Quarterly*, Vol. 46, No. 2 (Summer 2015), 219–223.

Raymond F. Dasmann, "Environmental Changes Before and After the Gold Rush," *California History*, Vol. 77, No. 4 (Winter 1998/1999), 105–122.

Dan L. Flores, "Bison Ecology and Bison Diplomacy: The Southern Plains from 1800 to 1850," *The Journal of American History*, September 1991, 465–485.

Dan L. Flores, "Zion in Eden: Phases of the Environmental History of Utah," *Environmental Review*, Winter 1983, 325–344.

William H. Goetzmann, *Exploration and Empire: The Explorer and the Scientist in the Winning of the American West* (New York: History Book Club, 1993).

Garrett Hardin, "The Tragedy of the Commons," *Science*, Vol. 162, No. 3859 (December 1968), 1243–1248.

Andrew Isenberg, "Toward a Policy of Destruction: Buffaloes, Law and the Market, 1803–83," *Great Plains Quarterly*, Fall 1992, 227–241.

William Lang, "Describing a New Environment: Lewis and Clark and Enlightenment Science in the Columbia River Basin," *Oregon Historical Quarterly*, Fall 2004, 353, 360–389.

Jennifer Ott, "'Ruining' the Rivers in the Snake Country: The Hudson's Bay Company's Fur Desert Policy," *Oregon Historical Quarterly*, Summer 2003, 166–195.

William R. Swagerty, "Marriage and Settlement Patterns of Rocky Mountain Trappers and Traders," *Western Historical Quarterly*, April 1980, 159–180.

Elliott West, "Becoming Mormon," in *The Essential West: Collected Essays* (Norman: University of Oklahoma Press, 2012), 176–193.

Elliott West, "Lewis and Park: Or, Why It Matters That the West's Most Famous Explorers Didn't Get Sick (or at Least Not *Really* Sick)," in *The Essential West: Collected Essays* (Norman: University of Oklahoma Press, 2012), 15–43.

Elliott West, *The Way to the West: Essays on the Central Plains* (Albuquerque: University of New Mexico Press, 1995).

David M. Wrobel, "The Politics of Western Memory," in Jeff Roche, ed., *The Political Culture of the New West* (Lawrence: University Press of Kansas, 2008), 332–363.

4

The Great Barbecue

In 1878, one-armed Civil War veteran John Wesley Powell laid before Congress a document writer T.H. Watkins has characterized as "quite possibly the most revolutionary document ever to tumble off the presses of the Government Printing Office": *Report on the Lands of the Arid Region of the United States*. Despite its rather dry title, Powell's account of the American West outlined a radical new proposal for the logical and rational utilization and settlement of this largely waterless region, so different from the East. Beginning in 1867, this intrepid explorer and scientist had roamed far and wide across the Great American Desert – ascending its peaks, traversing its basin-and-range topography, and pioneering its rivers. By 1878, perhaps no single man in the nation knew the West's geography more intimately than Powell. Armed with his careful observations, particularly of the Mormon model of collective and cooperative resource use, Powell felt confident endorsing a novel approach to settlement in the region. He divided the arid West into three categories: irrigable lands, timber lands, and pasturage lands. Each of these, he argued, demanded a unique approach – an environmentally responsible land-use solution. With these demands in mind, he called for a halt to all settlement of the West until federal surveyors could complete a thorough classification of the entire region. Needless to say, Powell's caution clashed with western boosterism, and Congress essentially ignored his careful report in favor of "booming" the region's natural resources and transferring public lands into private hands as quickly as possible. In the end, western

Losing Eden: An Environmental History of the American West, First Edition. Sara Dant.
© 2017 John Wiley & Sons, Inc. Published 2017 by John Wiley & Sons, Inc.

development would bear little resemblance to Powell's proposals, for better and for worse, yet his prescient observations masterfully identify the environmental challenges still confronting the West even in the twenty-first century.

While much of mid-nineteenth-century American history often focuses on slavery and the Civil War, these traditional markers of time were not central to the issues confronting westerners. To be sure, as the nation became increasingly agitated by the slavery question during the 1850s, the fate of that "peculiar institution," as it was sometimes called, became intimately intertwined with the West's lands – would slavery expand all the way to the Pacific or remain confined to the Deep South? But even as these debates widened the fissure between the North and the South until civil war convulsed the nation, the West's relationship to the rest of the country remained largely unequal, dependent, and colonial. For the West, the real consequence of the Civil War was that it significantly ramped up the Industrial Revolution in the eastern portion of the country, which in turn created heavier demands for the natural resources of the western portion of the country. Thus while Union forces battled their Confederate foes over questions of slavery and states' rights east of the Mississippi River, the federal government began binding the West to the nation by subsidized the building of the nation's first transcontinental railroad and fighting wars to force the region's Indian nations onto reservations.

As discussed in the previous chapter, rapid US territorial acquisition meant that by the 1850s, the entire West was open to American settlement – a process the federal government sought to promote as the surest means of extending national sovereignty over the region. But, as always, successful settlement was beholden to the realities of the natural environment. Lack of trees and water on the Great Plains had pushed earlier overland trail pioneers on to California and Oregon, but new federal laws would encourage migrants to reconsider these assumptions and revise their homestead plans. The rise of corporate capitalism and big business, particularly after the Civil War, would also fuel an extractive frenzy in the West. This, too, the federal government encouraged by eagerly adopting legislation designed to funnel the resultant ores, timber, and produce to a hungry and economically expanding East. Historian Vernon Parrington called this give-away The Great Barbecue: "Congress had rich gifts to bestow -- in lands, tariffs, subsidies, favors of all sorts; and when influential citizens made their wishes known to the reigning statesmen, the sympathetic politicians were quick to turn the government into the fairy godmother the voters wanted it to be. A huge barbecue was spread to which all presumably were invited."

This exploitative environmental attitude would help establish a long-term unsustainable pattern of resource consumption destined to haunt the United

States until the present day. Powell's vision of tempering extractive western settlement with solid science might well have moderated future scarcities and environmental problems, but his ideas largely fell on deaf ears as eager settlers, spurred on by bullish capitalists and gung ho politicians, overran the West and tried to claim their place in the sun.

Discussions of western settlement and development, and thus the region's environment, often fail to account for the significant influence of science. But in the nineteenth century, the scientific method began to reshape the ways in which people not only interacted with nature but also the very ways in which they understood the world and how it worked. As discussed in the previous chapter, the invention of the steam shovel, nitroglycerine, and hydraulic mining radically altered the scope and scale of mining in the West, but scientific innovation was also beginning to explain species' diversity and change over time in rational, logical ways. No one was more influential in this area than Englishman Charles Darwin, who published his seminal work *On the Origin of Species* in 1859. Darwin's simple and profound conclusion was that the diversity of all life on earth was the product of generations of evolution, branching from a common origin through a process of natural selection. Darwin's discovery of the signal importance of the environment to all life forms certainly influenced the thinking of Powell and others. For example, following the publication of Darwin's masterpiece, what had previously been vaguely lumped together as "natural history," separated out into the separate fields of botany, zoology, and ethnology. In 1879, Powell became the first director of the nation's new Bureau of Ethnology, dedicated to the linguistic, archeological, and ethnographic study of North American Indians – the nascent field of anthropology.

In western environmental history, Darwin's influence is most apparent in the writings of George Perkins Marsh, who some consider America's first environmentalist. In 1864, Marsh published *Man and Nature*, a pioneering work that introduced the concept of ecology – the study of the relationship among and between organisms and their environment (although the term "ecology" first appeared in an 1866 German publication). A brilliant linguist, scholar, and scientist, Marsh served in a variety of public capacities – foreign ambassador to Turkey and later Italy, Representative from Vermont, member of the state railroad commission, etc. – that gave him a rich foundation upon which to base his argument. His keen observations and experiences in Europe, in particular, convinced him that the primary culprit in the collapse of ancient Mediterranean civilizations (e.g. Rome) had been environmental degradation, deforestation in particular. And quite remarkably for the time, Marsh did not hesitate to name the primary perpetrator: "man is everywhere a disturbing agent. Wherever he plants his foot, the harmonies of nature are turned to discords." Technology and myopic economic development had enabled humans to conquer and "civilize" in the name of progress, he conceded, but at what cost? *Man and Nature*, every bit as influential in its time as Darwin's *Origin*, painstakingly detailed the destruction and degradation to plants, animals, forests, water, and land: "the ravages committed by man subvert the relations and destroy the balance which nature [has] established." Surprisingly, this unflinching nineteenth-century polemic remains strikingly modern. Marsh understood the symbiotic relationship between man *and* nature – how each shapes and is in turn shaped by the other. "We can never know how wide a circle of disturbance we produce in the harmonies of nature when we throw the smallest pebble into the ocean of organic life," he wrote.

For the West, Marsh's ideas translated directly into policy. His observations of destruction in the Alps, backed by impeccable science, led him to conclude that in the arid West, where lands were fragile and water was scarce, public stewardship of mountain streams and watersheds was essential, lest private interests wreak havoc on communities in their blind pursuit of profit. "When the forest is gone," he argued, "the great reservoir of moisture ... returns only in deluges of rain ... the well-wooded and humid hills are turned to ridges of dry rock ... [and] the whole earth, unless rescued by human art from the physical degradation to which it tends, becomes an assemblage of bald mountains, of barren, turfless hills, and of swampy and malarious plains." This early expression of the later Progressive conservation ideal of the greatest good for the greatest number, illustrates the forward nature of Marsh's thinking and set in motion the movement that would become in time the preservation of public lands (as national parks, forests, wilderness, etc.). Interestingly, Powell disagreed with this idea, recommending instead that the "timber lands must be controlled by lumbermen and woodmen," while fire protection "will be largely accomplished by removing the Indians." But Marsh's insights signaled the emergence of scientific conservation.

For the American West, Marsh's focus on wood and the protection of watershed-source forests was prescient. By the mid-nineteenth century, the nation's voracious appetite for timber was beginning to produce the very degradation that Marsh warned of. Until the Civil War, 95% of Americans heated their homes with wood. Steamboats, mines, and the nascent (and soon-to-boom) railroads all demanded wood. Americans constructed their homes out of wood, fenced their property with wood, built their saloons and wharfs and city halls and sidewalks out of wood. They sat on it, slept on it, ate on it, and occasionally got paddled at school with it, too. Wood was *the* building block of American society. In the decade from 1850 to 1860, alone, this timber appetite consumed 30 million acres of forest, and the acquisition of new territory in the West unleashed the heavy harvest on the region's vast timberlands. The ability to easily transport raw lumber via the railroads to eager eastern consumers and nascent western boom towns would only exacerbate the destruction.

As the United States added more territory, the previous and current residents of the West found themselves bound by East Coast interests intent on funneling western natural resources to eastern markets. With the Civil War erupting around them, northern members of Congress schemed to harness this economic engine by connecting the West to the East via railroad. The vision of a great connective steel ribbon had emerged as transportation to and through the West evolved during the first half of the nineteenth century. By this time horse or mule wagon trains had begun to replace steamship travel, as entrepreneurs sought more efficient – both in terms of time and money – means of connecting the resources of the West to the markets of the East. The federal government provided both political and economic support for these efforts. By the 1860s, the short-lived but infamous Pony Express (1860–1861) had given way to more predictable Wells Fargo stagecoaches, whose freight monopoly expanded to include passenger service. Traveling at roughly 10 miles per hour, people and parcels crossed the vast West in about three weeks, rather than the four months endured by earlier overland pioneers. Still, stagecoaches and wagons could not haul raw materials in any large quantities. The railroad was the obvious solution. But the road's route would be critical – the economic boom it would bring (or the bust its absence would ensure) led to intense sectional rivalries between the North and the South. The Civil War resolved the debate. Southern secession, which began in December of 1860, not only ultimately removed 11 states from the Union but also eliminated the South's ability to influence the route for the first transcontinental railroad.

Thus in 1862, Congress passed the Pacific Railroad Act authorizing a cooperative federal–private construction enterprise linking the Midwest to the West. The Central Pacific Railroad built east from California while the Union Pacific Railroad built west from roughly the 100th meridian. Their fevered construction competition would lay track across California, Nevada, Wyoming, and Nebraska – a decidedly northern route – before the two rival companies finally met on May 10, 1869, at Promontory Summit about 50 miles west of Ogden, Utah. This East–West link would prove economically vital to the nation and in many ways began to re-configure American sectionalism away from its historic North–South orientation and toward an East–West alignment.

The railroad became the primary means of connecting the West's natural resource supply – timber, gold, silver, coal, copper, iron, wheat, cattle, and more – to the East's nearly insatiable demand, and began to transform the nation into an eventual world powerhouse (see Figure 4.1). Between 1850 and 1900, the total US population ballooned from 23 million to 76 million people, which meant that in addition to the growing raw materials demands of eastern factories, and the need for gold to fund the war effort, eastern population growth had

Figure 4.1 After the United States completed construction of the first transcontinental railroad in 1869, the nation's network of rails expanded dramatically; by 1900, five transcontinental roads linked the East to the West and more than 200 000 miles of track criss-crossed the country.

outpaced the production capabilities of local farmers, necessitating importation of foodstuffs. Environmental historian Richard White has documented the extensive nature of West-to-East railroad commerce, which included such diverse commodities as livestock, sugar, wine, fruit, freight, and cash. Science and the Industrial Revolution prompted western farm families to move away from subsistence agriculture, where they planted a variety of crops on each farm and sold whatever modest surplus they had locally. Instead, their production became commercial, focusing on single, more specialized crops intended for the market: corn in the Midwest, wheat on the Great Plains, dairy farming in New England, cotton in the South, and fruits and vegetables in the West. Complementing this shift were improvements in mechanization that enabled fewer farmers to cultivate increasingly larger acreages. Reapers (grain cutters), iron plows, threshers (grain separators), and tractors were all manufactured in eastern factories and shipped west on the railroads to supply the region's demand for finished consumer goods.

An additional spur to railroad development had been the 1849 California gold rush, which boomed that state's population to 380 000 by 1860, and subsequent ore bonanzas in Nevada, Colorado, Idaho, and Montana. These strikes acted as powerful magnets drawing easterners to the West, especially as the Panic of 1857 created economic hardship throughout the country. The possibility of "striking it rich" was a tantalizing temptation. The railroads would provide not only the conduit for transporting settlers out West, but would also provide the means to ship the products of their labor back East. As Powell declared, "the railway has brought to our doors the harvest of our fields; handed to our mints the vast resources of our mines, and opened to us direct communication with the older worlds."

Faced with wide-open western spaces, growing eastern consumer demands, and population pressure, Congress responded with a series of settlement acts, beginning with the 1862 Homestead Act, passed on May 20 in the same year as the Railroad Act. It was no coincidence; these two pieces of legislation formed two parts of a larger whole. The Homestead Act represented a concerted effort on the part of the federal government to lure settlers onto the Great Plains. It was also what some historians have called a cruel hoax. Under the Homestead Act, anyone over the age of 21 who had never raised arms against the United States and intended to become a citizen could file application for 160 acres, a quarter-section, of federal land. After five years, if the settler had made "improvements," a very loosely defined and oft-fudged term, he or she could file for a deed of title and the land passed from federal lands into private hands. While the act was designed to promote the yeoman farmer of Jeffersonian agrarianism, in reality, it was fraught with problems.

To begin with, the Jeffersonian 160-acre parcel size, an obvious legacy of the Land Ordinance grid system discussed in Chapter 3, was an *eastern* ideal wholly unsuited to the aridity and soils of the West. This was Powell's concern. In a region where dry farming – cultivation without irrigation – was not feasible, 160 acres was far too large for an individual farmer to afford to irrigate. It was also too small for ranching; aridity made vegetation sparse and it simply took far more acres to sustain cattle or sheep in the thinly leafed West than in the lush, green East. Powell himself said, "I think it would be almost a criminal act to go on as we are doing now, and allow thousands and hundreds of thousands of people to establish homes where they cannot maintain themselves."

The federal government complemented the Homestead Act with the Desert Land Act of 1877 and the Timber and Stone Act of 1878 in a naïve effort to "solve" the problem of settlement in the arid West. The first of these offered an adult married couple the "opportunity" to purchase 640 acres, a full section, at the bargain price of $1.25 per acre if they irrigated the land within three years. The government's complete misunderstanding of the issue was obvious: if 160 acres was difficult to irrigate, 640 acres would be better? The Timber and Stone Act of the following year offered the enshrined 160-acre parcel at $2.50 per acre to those who wished to log or collect building stone (for homesteaders) on the West's public lands. All three of these acts ably fulfilled the federal government's purpose of settling the West, but they also played into the hands of land speculators, who used "dummy" claims to gain control of tens of thousands of acres of public lands. Cattlemen could assemble vast spreads by setting up each of their ranch hands as "dummy" claimants, while others "proved" they had irrigated their lands by pouring out a bucket of water in front of their "witness" friends.

Yet arguably one of the most influential, exploitative, and certainly long-lasting federal acts designed to encourage western migration and settlement was the 1872 Mining Law, which is still largely in effect today. Like the aforementioned acts, the Mining Law was borne out of economic necessity and exigency. The California gold rush had poured thousands of eager miners into the newly acquired territory without adequate laws to govern either the miner's rights to their claims or the federal government's sovereignty over the land. The result had been a hodgepodge of local ordinances of questionable legal standing that had inspired violence and claim jumping (often at gunpoint). Subsequent western ore strikes and the gold and silver rushes that followed had only exacerbated the problem of justice by lynch-mob, forcing Congress finally to act. In its original configuration, the Mining Law allowed a miner to stake a claim on public lands, and thus keep competitors at bay, for the usual gold, silver, and copper, but it also permitted "other valuable minerals" to fall under the law's purview. Once a miner had actually discovered a mineral, he or she could then transfer the public domain into private property for the bargain price of between $2.50 and $5 per acre, no matter how rich the lode might prove to be (remarkably, these prices/acre are still in effect in the twenty-first century). Subsequent twentieth-century legislation would withdraw petroleum, coal, oil shale, and sand and gravel from these sales, but the Mining Law furthered the capitalist resource plunder of the West significantly. None of these acts and laws, however, would effectively promote the thoughtful and rational settlement of the West, and perhaps no one understood that fact better than John Wesley Powell.

In 1878, the man who knew the West was Powell. Born in New York in 1834, he and his family gradually drifted westward, through Ohio, Wisconsin, and Illinois. Although he had limited formal education, Powell possessed a voracious appetite for natural history and pursued knowledge of the peoples, plants, and animals around him with a passion. His life's trajectory and abolitionist convictions landed him in the middle of the Civil War, where he fought for the Union, met and forged a close bond with then General, later President, Ulysses S. Grant, and lost his right arm in the pyrrhic April 1862 Union victory at Shiloh. The horrors of war led many men, including Powell, to look to the West as the source of national renewal. It was their and the nation's manifest destiny, after all. In 1867, Powell headed west to Colorado on what would become the first in a long series of exploratory expeditions on which he collected geological samples, made extensive ethnographic notes and observations of flora and fauna, and meticulously mapped the terrain. Perhaps the most famous of these adventures was his epic 900-mile journey down the previously uncharted wild Colorado River through the Grand Canyon in 1869. "What falls there are, we know not; what rocks beset the channel, we know not; what walls rise over the river, we know not," he wrote in his journal, "Ah, well!" These experiences provided the foundation for his visionary 1878 analysis *Report on the Lands of the Arid Region*.

Although the term "bioregionalism" is a twentieth-century creation, Powell was one of the first to see the West in this way. The term refers to "a geographic area defined by natural characteristics, including watersheds, landforms, soils, geological qualities, native plants and animals, climate, and weather ... [which] includes human beings as a species in the interplay of these natural characteristics." Geographers have broadened the concept, defining a bioregion as "a kind of unifying principle, a way of thinking about land and life within a regional framework ... an action-oriented cultural geography." More recently, environmental historians have utilized the approach in an effort to draw "the boundaries of the places we study in ways that make real sense ecologically and topographically." The ultimate goal of bioregional analysis is to supersede arbitrary political boundaries and gain insight into the dynamics of the natural world.

Powell fits the bioregionalist definition as someone who keenly understood that western state, county, and property boundaries derived from a Land Ordinance grid system that paid no attention to the natural geography of the land. In the green East, these arbitrary demarcations were of less consequence, but in the brown West, where access to water could mean the difference between life and death, Powell recognized that the settlement of the West could fail on a scale unimaginable – economically, socially, and environmentally – without thoughtful and careful planning. His *Report* thus proposed partitioning the whole of the American West into what he called watershed commonwealths (see Figure 4.2), defined not by political boundaries but by the waterways

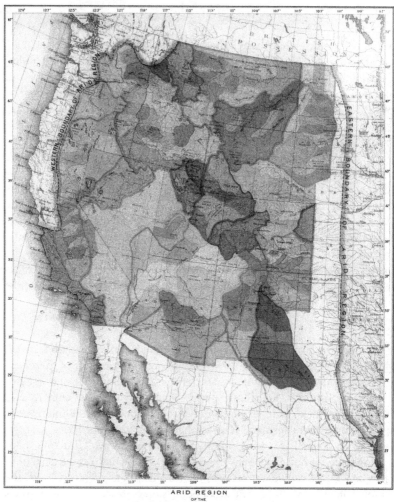

ARID REGION
OF THE
UNITED STATES
Showing Drainage Districts.

Figure 4.2 In his provocative 1878 *Report on the Lands of the Arid Region of the United States*, John Wesley Powell offered a radical alternative to traditional township and range grid settlement patterns. In order to combat western aridity, Powell proposed partitioning the whole of the American West into what he called watershed commonwealths (shown here), defined not by political boundaries but by the waterways themselves, and outlined sustainable settlement and development patterns. Source: US Geological Survey, "Arid Region of the United States, Showing Drainage Districts," in J.W. Powell, *Eleventh Annual Report of the United States Geographical Survey to the Secretary of the Interior, 1889–'90, Part II – Irrigation*, Plate LXIX (Washington: GPO, 1891), p. X. Courtesy Jack Loeffler.

themselves, and outlined sustainable settlement and development patterns. He understood that westerners had to live *within* the limits of nature, aridity, and the environment; they had to homestead where there was water. Powell's vision for the West included a comprehensive federal survey of the regions' geology and topography, although the federal government would not occupy a supervisory role (assuaging some western concerns). The day-to-day land-use decisions would be local and communal, creating a novel federal–private hybrid model to conform to the unique challenges the West presented. His theme was simple: westerners must adapt to the land and not vice versa. Aridity could be overcome, but only through cooperative efforts, much like those of Utah Mormons and Southwestern Hispanics in New Mexico. The desert could "bloom," he argued, but only in oasis settlements.

"There are values too critical and resources too perishable to be entrusted entirely to private exploitation," Powell's biographer Wallace Stegner argued. Politics and the federal government were to play a pivotal role in the West, Powell believed, overseeing the development of irrigation and the regulation of forest and pasture lands to promote democracy and ensure "the growth and prosperity of the Arid Region." Even if the government did not get land management right all of the time, the alternative was worse. Later, in testimony before Congress, Powell proposed that "the General Government organize the arid region … into irrigation districts by hydrographic basins." Although "some of these districts lie in two States," Powell nevertheless argued that the states should ignore these artificial political boundaries and "provide statutes for the organization of the districts and for the regulation of water rights, the protection and use of forests, and the protection and use of pasturage." Bioregionalism before its time.

Powell's "integrated understanding of the requirements of western lands was profound, if not prophetic," historian William deBuys has observed. Powell's ideas were also enormously unpopular at the time. Powell's assertion that the West's aridity *limited* settlement possibilities seemed to fly in the face of America's can-do spirit, not to mention the greedy desire to exploit resources and get rich quickly. While his proposals were logical and sound, they were a bitter pill politically. Congress had designed federal land policies to encourage the rapid settlement of the West – to transfer public lands into private hands as quickly as possible. Orderly surveys and watershed analyses were not only unglamorous but time-consuming. And Powell's emphasis on communalism failed to square with American virtues of rugged individualism, democracy, free enterprise, and independence. In the end, the massive effort to survey the irrigable lands of the West took too long, obstructed eager migrants, and ran afoul of the nation's rampant Manifest Destiny. Watershed governance may have looked good on paper, but it could never surmount the politics, and Congress took out its frustration on Powell by slashing the budget of his US Geological Survey, created in 1879, ultimately forcing him to resign.

The federal government may not have been interested in pursuing Powell's surveys, but it had been keen on building transcontinental railroads. To facilitate western exploration, exploitation, and settlement, Congress struck a deal with the Union Pacific and Central railroads and later track-builders. The government offered financial incentives for each mile of track laid, including cash payments that varied based on terrain ($16 000/mile for level ground, $32 000 in foothills, and $48 000 in mountains), and land grants of alternating sections of land alongside the iron roads amounting to 6400 acres/track mile. To maximize their profits, the railroad companies had to sell these lands, even on the Great Plains. It was a win–win for the United States: empty-space settlement expanded national sovereignty and railroad corporations raked in even larger earnings. The result was often fantastic advertising claims designed to lure unsuspecting immigrants and naïve easterners to try their farming luck on the prairies. "This is the sole remaining section of paradise in the western world," claimed one promotion. "All the wild romances of the gorgeous Orient dwindle into nothing when compared to the everyday reality of Dakota's progress." And it worked. Thousands of sod-busters poured onto the plains, claiming homesteads and buying railroad lands in the hopes of plowing their way into middle-class stability.

It also worked because western boosters and eager easterners were far more willing to believe railroad advertisements that promised "rain follows the plow" than a dour geologist like Powell who predicted drought. There was even "science" to back up the railroads' dubious claim. According to a railroad-hired biologist, farmers' plows tilling packed prairie soils would churn dust into the atmosphere thereby attracting tiny water particles like a giant sponge and, voila!, increased rainfall. The "proof" for such a theory? Ever since the passage of the Homestead Act, annual rainfall totals had increased across much of the Great Plains – "dry farming" (not irrigated) west of the 100th meridian had been possible for much of the 1870s and early 1880s. "Rain follows the plow," this amateur scientist promised. What the arid West needed, then, was not "watershed commonwealths" but more farmers.

This faulty science ignored the reality that for millennia, the climate of the Great Plains had cycled between wet and dry years often with wild unpredictability. The late 1870s and early 1880s *were* unusually wet, but the key word here is *unusually*; no amount of plowing could stave off the withering drought that bore down on these financially strung-out farmers (and ranchers). The epic year of 1886, in particular, followed up a searing, fire-scorched summer with an early, harsh, snow-lashed winter that was, by many accounts, the worst in memory. Eager homesteaders had thwarted the treeless prairies by building sod houses, fencing with barbed wire, and burning cow and buffalo dung for heat. But they had also torn up deep-rooted prairie bunch grasses to plant seasonal wheat and corn crops, exposing the region's precious topsoil to erosion by nearly ceaseless winds that laid the foundation for the future Dust Bowl of the 1930s. By the mid-1880s, short growing seasons, declining rainfall, accelerated erosion, and poor soils further frustrated naïve Great Plains farmers, leaving them with anemic crop harvests, mounting debts, and collapsing grain prices. Confronted by the very aridity Powell had predicted, many homesteaders packed up and moved back east, signaling a major bust at the end of the frantic boom that had lured too many west of the line of aridity. On the side of his loaded wagon, one thoroughly defeated sod-buster painted a fitting epitaph for this prairie experience: "In God We Trusted, In Kansas We Busted." The boosters were wrong. Powell was right. And farm families paid the price. Giant corporate agribusinesses quietly acquired these failed family farms one by one and began to transform the Plains into endless amber waves of grain.

As historian Richard White has compellingly shown, for all the hype of "progress" and "civilization" heaped upon the transcontinental railroads (by 1900 there were five), they categorically failed to improve the lives of westerners. The region was simply "too arid, too infertile, [and] too distant from markets to sustain the density of settlement and agricultural development" promoted by the railroads, proving Powell's points perfectly. In the end, despite western demand for it, the railroad's environmental impact was twofold: it created an efficient extractive pipeline for sending western raw materials east, while its construction and boosterism left behind long-term scars on western lands and peoples.

Furthermore, the railroads, and the mines and towns they sustained, ramped up the regional appetite for raw materials to rapacious rates. As Marsh had so wisely predicted, the timber toll on the West was staggering. On average, a mile of rail consumed more than 2500 ties, most of which were treated with a toxic mercury bichloride that could leach into surrounding soils. But the iron road also demanded wood for telegraph poles, support beams, bridges, fences, and even cars and stations. By the late 1880s, the railroads alone consumed nearly one-quarter of the nation's timber production. The Homestead Act had encouraged timber exploitation by railroad companies and timber barons, who used the same "dummy claim" tactics as their farming and ranching compatriots. Although the entire West bore the cutting burden, western law scholar Charles Wilkinson has argued that "the fraud was most pervasive in the Pacific Northwest, where the spruce, cedar, redwood, and Douglas fir stands amounted to green gold." Once again, speculators had successfully redefined the ecological wealth of the West in capitalist terms.

To supply this nearly insatiable demand, independent western timber contractors cut on both railroad-owned and federal lands and sold directly to the railroads. One of the major concerns early on in the building of the railroad, however, was the excessively high cost of ties, primarily due to transportation costs. The solution that readily emerged was to eliminate the most costly aspect of tie-supply, overland transport, and replace it with the free labor of the region's rivers. During the winter months, then, tie contractors deployed cutting crews into the steep canyons of the mountainous West to cut and roughly shape logs into ties, which they left piled on the banks of frozen rivers to be flushed downstream to the waiting railroads during spring floods. These tie and log drives were common all along the Rocky Mountain front – New Mexico, Utah, Colorado, Wyoming, Idaho, Montana – and once the major railroads had moved through, the timber demand switched to supplying booming mines (like Park City, Utah) with support timbers and cordwood and providing replacement ties. Not surprisingly, these massive tie and log drives could wreak incredible destruction when they finally cut loose, destroying riparian zones (ecosystems along water bodies), causing massive back-up floods, and clogging the rivers for aquatic flora and fauna.

Not everyone ignored Powell, however. In 1902, the federal Bureau of Forestry made a rather remarkable and extremely thorough survey of Utah's forests that provides excellent insight into the condition of that state's (and by extension much of the interior West's) forests at the turn of the twentieth century. The account describes the impact of mining, sawmills, and stockyards on the forests. In almost every canyon of the Weber and Provo rivers in northern Utah, the report documents the remnants of the previous years' tie and timber harvests – old sawmills, camps, and areas "cut out." Top grade timber was a rare commodity in many mountain valleys by the turn of the century and sheep ranching had fully invaded the now timber-less high country. Indeed, the evidence for the overuse of the mountain areas was extensive, corroborating Marsh's own observations. Mountain watersheds were routinely sloughing landslide debris down bare slopes into the irrigation works and settlements of the intrepid Mormon communities nestled up against the Wasatch Front. As environmental historian Dan Flores has concluded, by the 1920s, "a widespread land collapse had begun," paving the way for Marsh's proposed federal protections, if not Powell's watershed commonwealths.

The Plains were also suffering by the turn of the twentieth century. The decimation of the tall-grass prairies by farmers wielding McCormick Reapers, twine binders, harrows, and plows rippled out across the ecosystem. Historian Geoff Cunfer notes that "between about 1870 and 1930 Americans plowed more than 100 million acres of biologically diverse grassland ecosystems and replaced them with single-species cropland." Since land sales, whether federal homestead or railroad-owned, conformed to the artificial township and range grid established by the Land Ordinance of 1785 and ignored environmental obstacles and problems, settlers were motivated to clear forests and drain wetlands that occupied their potential farmlands. Settlement, agriculture, and competing cattle nearly drove prairie species like black-tailed prairie dogs and bison into extinction. Industrial hunting, complemented by the efficiency of transcontinental railroad transportation, drove bison to the brink. And as contemporary naturalist Joe Truett explained, "the foot of the buffalo was necessary for their [prairie dogs'] existence. As soon as the ground ceased to be tramped hard and the grass and weeds grew they perished." Without the prairie dogs, black-footed ferrets and burrowing owl numbers collapsed as well. Run-off from exposed fields clogged and silted streams and rivers and, in combination with intensified harvests, crippled native fish populations. Everywhere, the loss of species diversity – including charismatic predators like wolves, bears, and mountain lions – accompanied the movement of the masses into the West. As Cunfer concludes, there was never a condition of "sustainable agriculture" on the Great Plains.

For Native Americans, the consequences of this commercialization and commodification of the Great Plains were even more dire. After the Civil War between the North and South ended in 1865, another kind of war between East and West – between whites and Native Americans – began in earnest. Although the federal government had been engaged formally in the forcible removal and relocation of Indians since the Jacksonian Era, the shocking 1864 massacre of peaceful Cheyennes and Arapahos at Sand Creek, Colorado, and the subsequent Plains Indian Wars mowed down Native people, communities, and cultures with stunning efficiency. Applying tactics and strategies perfected by the Union, military commanders began systematically to remove Indians as "obstacles to progress." General Philip Sheridan, for example, who had utilized a scorched earth tactic the Shenandoah Valley locals simply called "The Burning" to successfully defeat Confederate soldiers and destroy the southern ability and will to fight during the Civil War, employed a similar technique on Plains tribes the army assigned him to subdue. Called "winter campaigning," Sheridan's strategy was to attack Native American encampments during the lean winter months, when food and resources were scarce and populations were smaller (during the summer months, by contrast, some Indian camps could exceed 3000 individuals). By this time, extensive horse herds, white expansion, and habitat erosion had fundamentally weakened Plains ecology and economy. With their bison teetering on the brink of extinction, their horses slaughtered or starving, and their lands over-run by eager homesteaders, ranchers, and railroads, fleeing Indian bands could neither rest nor hunt and soon succumbed to the relentless pursuit of a well-supplied (by the railroads) army. The December 1890 massacre of desperate Lakotas/Sioux in Wounded Knee, South Dakota, signaled the final and complete collapse of Plains Indian resistance as the last remaining bands reported to reservations. This triumph of "progress" meant that white settlers were now free to fill the West.

In the years following the Civil War, the federal government eagerly promoted western settlement and resource extraction with little oversight or regulation. This "laissez-faire" mining of resources without consequence found broad support within the Republican Party, the party of Lincoln, which abandoned the plight of former slaves by the 1870s and embraced instead the more exciting and lucrative lures of big business. The Great Barbecue also coincided with an age of invention and innovation that not only produced new and more efficient means of wresting western wealth (dynamite, for mining; reapers, binders, and threshers, for farming; steam engines and steam-powered sawmills, for logging), but also for transporting it to the East via the railroads. It was a classic "tragedy of the commons." In the end, John Wesley Powell's rational West failed to jibe with national expansionist goals leaving the region to its arbitrary political borders, more than a century of wrestling with aridity, and a largely subordinate role as larder to the East. The question was whether the voices of scientists like Powell and Marsh, and the few politicians who listened to them, would be able sustain the region's natural wealth and ecological health for the future of man *and* nature.

Suggested Reading

Thomas Andrews for "'Made by Toile': Tourism, Labor, and the Construction of the Colorado Landscape, 1858–1917," *The Journal of American History*, Vol. 92, No. 3 (December 2005), 837–863.

Peter Berg, "Bioregionalism Comes to Japan: An Interview with Peter Berg," interview by Richard Evanoff, *Japan Environment Monitor*, E-mail Edition, Issue 97 (June 1998). www.sustainable-city.org/intervws/berg.htm (accessed February 3, 2016).

Geoff Cunfer, *On the Great Plains: Agriculture and Environment* (College Station: Texas A&M University Press, 2005).

Sara Dant Ewert, "Bioregional Politics: The Case for Place," *Oregon Historical Quarterly*, Winter 2002, 439–451.

Dan L. Flores, "Zion in Eden: Phases of the Environmental History of Utah," *Environmental Review*, Winter 1983, 325–344.

David Lowenthal, "Nature and Morality from George Perkins Marsh to the Millennium," *Journal of Historical Geography*, Vol. 26, No. 1 (2000), 3–27.

John Wesley Powell, *Seeing Things Whole: The Essential John Wesley Powell*, William deBuys, ed. (Washington DC: Island Press, 2001).

Martin Ridge, "Disorder, Crime, and Punishment in the California Gold Rush," in Kenneth N. Owens, ed. *Riches for All: The California Gold Rush and the World* (Lincoln: University of Nebraska Press, 2002), 176–201.

James E. Sherow, "Workings of the Geodialectic: High Plains Indians and Their Horses in the Region of the Arkansas River Valley, 1800-1870," *Environmental History Review*, Vol. 16, No. 2 (Summer 1992), 61–84.

James Tejani, "Dredging the Future: The Destruction of Coastal Estuaries and the Creation of Metropolitan Los Angeles, 1858–1913," *Southern California Quarterly*, Spring 2014, 5–39.

Joe C. Truett, "Migrations of Grassland Communities and Grazing Philosophies in the Great Plains: A Review and Implications for Management." *Great Plains Research: A Journal of Natural and Social Sciences*, Vol. 13 (Spring 2003), 3–26.

Richard White, "Introduction," "Creative Destruction," and "Appendix," in *Railroaded: The Transcontinentals and the Making of Modern America* (New York: W.W. Norton & Company, 2011), xxi–xxxix, 455–493, 519–534.

5

The Pivotal Decade

On January 1, 1889, during a rare solar eclipse, a northern Paiute man named Wovoka had a prophetic vision of environmental renewal. Since his birth approximately 33 years earlier, this mystic, also known as Jack Wilson, had witnessed the rapid and often destructive transformation that the shift from Native to white dominance had visited on the American West: typhoid fever and other European diseases had killed one out of every 10 of his people, while drought and diminished populations seriously impeded Paiute subsistence hunting and foraging efforts. In fact, by 1900, white agricultural practices, encouraged by the Homestead Act, had almost completely eradicated traditional Paiute food sources such as piñon nuts. Faced with severe economic hardship, starvation, and crisis, Wovoka sought salvation and healing through faith. Synthesizing various Indian ceremonial traditions with Christian tenets, this modern messiah envisioned a restorative ritual called the Ghost Dance that would bring about earthly renewal, material abundance, and the disappearance of whites. The five-day ceremonial circle-dance Wovoka prescribed was hope made manifest (see Figure 5.1). Ultimately, 30 western tribes adopted, adapted, and participated in the Ghost Dance in an almost desperate attempt not only to retain Indian authority and identity, but also to address the real failure of white promises of "progress" and "civilization."

Historians are often reluctant to write about watershed years, and mostly with good reason, as currents of history rarely begin or end at a particular moment in time. Yet the 1890s come as close to being just such a pivotal

Losing Eden: An Environmental History of the American West, First Edition. Sara Dant.
© 2017 John Wiley & Sons, Inc. Published 2017 by John Wiley & Sons, Inc.

Figure 5.1 Famed western artist Frederic Remington drew this scene of the Oglala Lakota Ghost Dance at the Pine Ridge Agency, South Dakota, in 1890 from sketches he took down during the ceremony. Source: Reproduced with permission of the Library of Congress.

moment as any. These years not only inspired a new and influential historical interpretation of the genesis of American "character," but also captured a moment in time when Americans attempted to grapple with the environmental costs of their rapid westward expansion even as they celebrated the romantic and nostalgic icons they had nearly destroyed. By 1900, the transition from subsistence to market so effectively implemented by Euro-American pioneers and settlers meant that the environment of the American West looked profoundly different than it had just a century earlier. In many cases, scarcity or absence replaced natural abundance. Westerners – all of them, Indian, Anglo, Hispanic, and others – would have to live with and adjust to this new reality.

At the close of the nineteenth century, Native Americans were not the only westerners anxious about their future. Four years after Wovoka's vision, in the summer of 1893, the World's Columbian Exposition created a utopian "White City" amid the entrepreneurial vitality, urban upheaval, and industrial squalor of daily life in Chicago that exemplified a nation struggling to reconcile its rural, frontier past and an urban, industrial future. For six months, between May and October, nearly 27 million people visited this celebration of the 400th anniversary of Columbus' voyage of "discovery." In addition to offering midway attractions such as the first Ferris wheel, the fair celebrated and demonstrated technological innovations such as electrical generators, transformers, and motors. It featured historic steam engine and log cabin displays, and provided scholarly lectures and public performances by prominent musicians. Perhaps one of the most enduring elements of this fair was a talk delivered on a sweltering July evening at the meeting of the American Historical Association by a 31-year-old history professor named Frederick Jackson Turner. Turner's "The Significance of the Frontier in American History" did not garner much attention that July, but over the next decade, he presented versions of it to countless civic organizations and historical societies. Consequently, by the beginning of the twentieth century, his "frontier thesis" had become the dominant explanation for American exceptionalism – the nation's professed historical uniqueness and qualitative superiority – and it would influence writing and thinking about the American West well into the twenty-first century.

The essence of Turner's oft-quoted thesis is that "the existence of an area of free land [the frontier], its continuous recession, and the advance of American settlement westward, explain American development." Turner defined the frontier as "the meeting point between savagery and civilization" and his thesis about its formative influence contains strong Darwinian undercurrents. In the story he tells, Europeans both shaped and were shaped by their interaction with the American natural environment and ultimately had to evolve into a new and better adapted species: the American. As they struggled against the land and its Native peoples, Turner argued, these evolving Americans developed a "composite nationality" (called the melting-pot effect by a later generation) and independent individualism. Americans embraced economic independence and physical mobility, and their confrontation with the frontier promoted the "growth of democracy." The unique contribution of Turner's thesis then and ever since was that it identified the frontier – the wild *environment* really – as the source of American uniqueness and a mighty engine of change.

The inspiration for Turner's thesis had been a relatively simple statement by the United States Census Bureau. As of 1890, the agency announced, the American frontier was officially closed. Statistically, this meant that population densities had now reached at least two people per square mile everywhere in the contiguous United States. In short, the nation had effectively occupied its open spaces. But the seeming finality of such a pronouncement exerted a significant cultural influence and forced a national reckoning with the nation's future, that of the West in particular. In essence, where do we go from here? What's next? For Turner, the Census Bureau's findings were sobering: "the frontier has gone, and with its going has closed the first period of American history." Many other Americans were worried too. Without a frontier to assimilate immigrants, in a nation more urban than rural, what would provide moral order and vital physical health for the nation? What would maintain American exceptionalism?

Although other historians have since attacked Turner's frontier thesis, his basic argument about the formative influence of nature in the West has endured. For many, it simply made sense that "civilization" arrived when people conquered nature. Turner believed, as did a majority of the population at the time, that whites were the civilizing force in the West and that Indians served as a "common danger" and unifying force against which evolving Americans struggled for success and identity. Turner's focus was fundamentally exploitational and agrarian. His hero was the yeoman farmer, whose ingenuity, integrity, and resourcefulness allowed him to triumph over the adversity of the wilderness and bring agrarian order out of environmental chaos, much as Jefferson had advocated nearly a century earlier. Historians have pointed out that Turner's thesis essay ignored Native peoples, other non-whites, and women for that matter. Indeed, historian Patricia Limerick has even labeled his core idea, "the frontier," as the "f-word" in western history for its racist, sexist, and over-simplified explanations of the American past. For all of its shortcomings, Turner's nationalistic, patriotic thesis that American cultural identity was indeed a product of the frontier experience has endured in part because he told a story Americans wanted to hear about themselves and in part because he was correct in asserting that a way of life in the West was passing from the land. No one understood this more clearly than Native Americans.

By 1890, indigenous societies had collapsed to their nadir; their collective populations would never be lower. The natural environments of the West in which they had lived for tens of thousands of years also reflected their removal and relocation onto reservations. Although variations on that story could be told for Indians in the deserts of the Southwest, the Rocky Mountains, and the Pacific Northwest, the Plains in particular no longer sustained an Indian–horse–bison ecology. As discussed in Chapter 3, bison were already in decline by 1850, but by the 1890s they teetered on the brink of extinction. Plains Indians had long traded horses and many Indian peoples had traded furs and hides, including buffalo, but after the Civil War, bison hide robes became a valuable commodity on a global scale. Industrial America prized bison leather for machine belts, furniture, shoes, etc., and aggressive hide hunters and increasingly market-oriented Indians fanned out across the Plains in pursuit of these lucrative animals. At a time when many day laborers struggled to earn a dollar a day, a single bison hide robe could bring anywhere from $3–50, although by the 1870s, the robe trade had disappeared as the harvest became centered around greater efficiency in leather processing and prices dropped. If hunters could provoke a herd to mill around the lead cow of the herd, it was possible to shoot hundreds of bison at one time. Skinning crews then moved in to strip the hides and ship them to eastern tanneries. They left the rest of the carcasses to rot. As environmental historian Richard White writes, "what was left looked less like a corpse than a stillbirth," and the revolting stench of "tens of thousands of rotting corpses" spread like a pall over the Plains. Passengers crossing the country on the newly constructed transcontinental railroads also wantonly shot buffalo from trains purely for sport and with no pretense of harvesting any part of the animal. This decimation of buffalo culture, so central to Plains Indian food, clothing, shelter, and ceremony, likely telescoped white control over the Great Plains by a decade or more. And the federal government tacitly approved. In 1874, President Ulysses S. Grant pocket-vetoed a bill granting federal protection for bison; while his inaction ultimately allowed the market hunt for animals to continue to flourish and hastened Indian removal from potential homesteads to reservations by helping to eliminate their subsistence sources, there is no indication that Grant himself intended such consequences. As White concludes, "the whole episode was pathetic."

By the time of the Ghost Dance, which promised to restore bison as part of an overall environmental renewal, there were only about 350 wild bison left in the United States, 200 of which lived in Yellowstone National Park. A few hundred more lingered in Canada. By 1892, even the Yellowstone herd had dwindled to fewer than 25, the ghostly remnants of a vast shaggy ocean that had once undulated across the prairies in numbers estimated at 30 million or more. The deadly convergence of market hunters and a global market for bison hide leather, white settlement, disease, drought, competition for grass from cattle and horses, and the removal of Indian stewards had finally eroded the ecological niche that this buffalo super-organism had not only occupied but thrived in for thousands of years. The costs were ruinous. As bison historian Martin Garretson has written, "it was a decimation of race as well as species." In 1884, more than a quarter of the Blackfeet nation starved due to the loss of their bison sustenance. By the turn of the century, captive breeding efforts by Native peoples and white ranchers had rescued bison from complete eradication, but they never restored the wild buffalo commons that had so dominated the western landscape. Unlike deer, elk, or antelope, bison remained a commodity, a new form of domesticated livestock animal whose ecological relationship to the Plains conformed to the supply and demand dictates of a capitalist market system. Bison lost their wildness.

Unfortunately, the destruction of the West's great wild bison herds was not the only natural catastrophe marked by the symbolic closing of the frontier, but instead it was one of several examples of species and natural resource depletions that began to alarm some Americans. Historian Joseph Cone has suggested that the most appealing definition of the Pacific Northwest is "anyplace the salmon can go." Or at least where they *used* to go. By the 1890s, once-mighty salmon runs showed obvious decline and this precious subsistence resource that had seemed limitless to early settlers was now in peril. For thousands of years prior to the arrival of the first peoples in the Americas, six species of salmon and steelhead had teemed in almost every Pacific Coast river. Some of these fish were monsters, too; Columbia River "June hogs" or "Royal Chinook" bound upriver for Canada could weigh as much as 125 pounds! Each year, currents swept millions of salmon "smolts" from their natal freshwater gravel redds to the sea, where they fattened up for as many as five years, before returning home to their exact birthplace to spawn and die in a round-trip journey that could exceed 10 000 miles.

On their journey downstream, salmon smolt fed countless birds and other fish; on their upstream return, adult salmon not only filled the bellies of eagles and bears but their spent bodies provided a nutrient-rich fertilizer for adjacent lands. Writer Bruce Brown remarked that salmon "are an engine of general enrichment, and an important element in the long-range stability of the Pacific Coast ecosystem." In the early nineteenth century, their sheer numbers were astounding and their rich flesh ably sustained sizeable human and animal communities. In 1805, when Meriwether Lewis and William Clark had journeyed west for President Thomas Jefferson, Clark had recorded in his journal (in his typically poor spelling) that the Columbia River was "crouded with salmon."

Remarkably, Pacific Coast peoples depended on salmon even more than Plains peoples depended on bison. Historians have estimated that prior to the arrival of Euro-Americans, the annual catch in the Columbia River system alone approached 42 million pounds! It is roughly 5–8 million pounds annually today. Traditional fishing grounds demarcated community boundaries, while the harvest itself defined family and gender roles: men fished, women cleaned and smoked the salmon, children gathered wood. To ensure the safe and plentiful return of their essential animal totem or symbol, Native peoples developed elaborate rites and religious customs such as the First Salmon Ceremony. This widely practiced observance – which usually involved the ritualistic capture of the first salmon in the run, its preparation and distribution among the tribe, and the return of its bones to the river – honored and reinforced the relationship between the people and their food source. Because salmon provided the foundation for Native trade economies, communities also protected this important resource (as a kind of "commons") by implementing various conservation measures such as seasonal closures, exclusive fishing rights, and laws prohibiting waste. Each year thousands of Indians converged at The Dalles in present-day Oregon to barter for items such as shells, obsidian (for making arrowheads), bison robes, pipestone, and feathers. As the Supreme Court ruled in 1905, salmon were "not much less necessary to the existence of the Indians than the atmosphere they breathed."

In 1846, when the United States extended its sovereignty over the Pacific Northwest, Native peoples theoretically retained control over their lands and fishing rights, but successive treaties deprived them of both title and access, making way for large-scale commercial interests to move in. In 1854–1855, for example, Washington's territorial governor Isaac Stevens negotiated a series of treaties (10) that granted the federal government clear title to most of the present-day states of Washington, Oregon, Idaho, and Montana, and diminished tribal land holdings by 80–95%. Although all of Stevens' treaties promised that tribes would retain the "right of taking fish, at all the usual and accustomed grounds and stations," those rights quickly fell victim to the supply and demand whims of an emerging capitalist system and hostile state governments. Like bison, salmon soon became a valuable commodity for the global market and once sustainable harvests careened toward a crash. Legal scholar Charles Wilkinson later ominously observed, "there would be a great toll on the river, and also on Indian people and societies, and on the fish themselves." He was right.

Like bison, salmon suffered from the devastating combination of excessive harvest and habitat loss. By the 1890s, the depredation of the seemingly invincible salmon runs by industrial fishing and canning industries produced a collapse. Although the fish canning process had originated in the early 1800s, the scale was at first too small to exert an environmental influence, But by the 1860s, the commercial potential of Columbia River canned salmon had inspired fishers to innovate. Fish already evaded hooks, gill nets, traps, weirs, harpoons, and occasionally even dynamite, but soon super-efficient fish wheels were scooping salmon from the rivers in staggering numbers (see Figure 5.2). Fish wheels harvested day and night, operating much like an indefatigable water-powered mill wheel. A single wheel could potentially catch more than 400 000 pounds of fish in a season. In 1883 alone, 40 Columbia River canneries neatly packed nearly 37 million pounds of the highest quality Chinook salmon (and threw away lower quality varieties) into 1-pound cans that they shipped across the country and the planet. The total Chinook harvest for non-Indians that year was 43 million pounds, a pinnacle Columbia fishers would never again attain.

As early as the 1870s, catch, gear, and season restrictions began to emerge in Oregon and Washington territories, in dim recognition that salmon runs were in fact not limitless. But they accomplished little. It simply made no sense for fishers to conserve salmon for their competitors. Consequently, with no break in the harvest, salmon fisheries could never fully recover. By the 1880s, spring and summer Chinook salmon runs were in notable decline, which led to intensified harvests of other species. The dominance of market fishing by the late 1880s also meant that, as with bison, Indian tribes such as the Nez Perces and Yakamas became active and aggressive participants in the harvest that was undermining the foundation of their way of life. By 1894,

Figure 5.2 Fish wheel on the Columbia River, Oregon. Operating much like a water-powered mill wheel, fish wheels first appeared on the Columbia River in the 1870s, where they facilitated the dramatic expansion of the canning industry and ultimately helped decimate the river's salmon runs. Source: Reproduced with permission of the Gerald W. Williams Collection, Oregon State University Libraries.

after just 26 years of commercial fishing in the Pacific Northwest, an official with the United States Bureau of Fisheries declared "not only is every contrivance employed that human ingenuity can devise to destroy the salmon of our west coast rivers, but surely more destructive, more fatal than all is the slow but inexorable march of these destroying agencies of human progress, before which the salmon must surely disappear as did the buffalo of the plains."

In addition to the human predation of industrial-scale fishing, the opening of the "frontier" ushered in other changes to the natural environment that salmon depended upon for their survival. Timber clearcuts, livestock grazing, and hydraulic mining all fouled pristine gravel spawning redds with silt and chemicals, and irrigation works and dams increasingly blocked rivers and streams. Like the bison, salmon teetered in the balance. The "tragedy of the commons," in this case free access to salmon runs, played out once again as the frontier closed.

While the destruction of bison and salmon represented the profound, if not entirely intended consequences of an unrestricted harvest of seemingly infinite wildlife for national and global markets, elsewhere in the West, species faced the threat of eradication as the result of very concerted efforts. For the earliest settlers who arrived in North America from Europe, the "wilderness" constituted a threat; it was filled with the dangerous, predatory animals that provided the scare in every children's fable. As white settlers moved onto the western frontier during the nineteenth century, they brought these attitudes with them and encouraged both private and governmental agencies to eliminate the danger these "killers" seemed to represent. The result was yet another war on nature, this time on any animals that white settlers deemed a nuisance. That list was long.

At the top were wolves. In the seventeenth and early eighteenth centuries the West teemed with wolves. Deer, elk, antelope fawns, and bison provided a wealth of prey for the canny *Canis lupis* and even the initial arrival of whites failed to blunt their numbers as wolves quickly understood that wasteful hunters often left discarded carcasses behind. As discussed in Chapter 3, it was the fur trade, primarily beavers, which lured white trappers westward "indirectly bringing wolves into the maw of a colonial economy" according to historian Michael Robinson. By the mid-1850s, wolf pelts were worth about 75 cents each, and some entrepreneurs managed to sustain themselves through the winter months by baiting the above-mentioned abandoned carcasses with the poison strychnine. Like bison robes and canned salmon, wolf pelts became a lucrative commodity in national and trans-Atlantic trade systems.

But it was ultimately not for their fur that wolves died. By the 1840s, as western ranchers began to graze livestock on the prairies, they also began systematically eliminating species that competed with their cattle and sheep for grass (bison, deer, elk, antelope) and threatened their investment (wolves, mountain lions, bears, etc.). Refrigerated boxcars, which appeared after the Civil War along with the transcontinental railroads, made beef an important national commodity. Millions of hungry customers in American cities provided increased motivation for ranchers to protect their herds. This market reality proved deadly for wolves. By the end of the nineteenth century, bighorn sheep had disappeared from the Plains and pronghorn antelope teetered on the brink of extinction, ranchers successfully exterminated several subspecies of elk in New Mexico and Arizona, and bison, of course, had all but vanished. With their primary prey sources so fully depleted, wolves naturally turned to the readily available substitute: open-range cattle and sheep, which proved too tempting for hungry packs searching for their next meal. It was a fatal choice; stockmen were not about to sit idly by and allow wolves to ravage their herds.

The first efforts at systematic wolf eradication were private and commercially motivated. Stockgrowers' associations began offering bounties – cash payments for dead wolves – as early as the 1860s. These influential cattlemen soon convinced their territorial and state legislatures to follow suit (see Figure 5.3). By the time of Turner's frontier thesis, most western states and territories offered up rewards for dead wolves, bears (especially grizzlies), mountain lions, coyotes,

Figure 5.3   According to the US Fish and Wildlife Service, "To protect livestock, ranchers and government agencies began an eradication campaign. Bounty programs initiated in the 19th century continued as late as 1965, offering $20 to $50 per wolf. Wolves were trapped, shot, dug from their dens, and hunted with dogs. Poisoned animal carcasses were left out for wolves, a practice that also killed eagles, ravens, foxes, bears, and other animals that fed on the tainted carrion." Source: Reproduced with permission of the Arizona Historical Society.

and bobcats. Most were in addition to private bounties. In 1889, for example, Colorado paid $1.50 for each wolf or coyote killed and a whopping $10 for mountain lions and bears, as much as most factory workers earned in a week. The commodification of dead wolves worked to accelerate their decline; by the 1890s, they were "very scarce" in the Rocky Mountains of Colorado and Wyoming. But unlike bison, whose near extinction brought, finally, a public outcry to save the species, the big, bad wolf was almost universally detested. As Robinson writes, "wolves remained at the bottom of a moral hierarchy so obvious that it needed no articulation." Yet despite these concerted efforts, wolves persisted into the twentieth century, albeit in greatly reduced numbers, in part because their litter sizes increase when faced with adversity and also because wolves became far more wary and reclusive.

As with wolves, the role of the economy in the health of the West's natural environment was central and ominous. By 1900, the United States was the most productive industrial economy in the world thanks to three key ingredients: capital, labor, and the natural resources of the West, especially minerals and timber. The market system still bound the West to the East like a colony, but commodification of bison, whales, redwoods, and salmon had dramatically depleted the western store. As homesteaders poured into the West to take advantage of free land, their numbers swelled the region's population and accelerated their agricultural and ranching toll on the natural environment. By 1890, there were 3.5 million irrigated acres in the West. Salinization (excessive salt accumulation) began to affect some of the region's soils, run-off poured chemicals and sediments into formerly pristine salmon runs, and the dams and irrigation works necessary to water the arid West irreparably altered and blocked riparian zones. Exotic flora and fauna introduced by these "frontier" agrarian entrepreneurs pushed native species to the margins and sometimes into extinction; by the end of the nineteenth century, for example, California had lost between 50 and 90% of its native grasses to invasive weeds.

The story on the cattle frontier was much the same. For decades, profit-hungry ranchers had severely overgrazed the western range. Cattle die-offs in the early 1880s had been a harbinger of the devastation that finally materialized in 1886–1887; a hot dry summer with little moisture for grass, a winter of memorable blizzards, and an overstocked range proved a recipe for disaster (represented so poignantly in Charles Russell's painting *Waiting for a Chinook*, see Figure 5.4). Known as the "Big Die-Up" (as opposed to Round-up), mortality rates surpassed 75% on the northern Plains and up to 90% in other locations. Future President Theodore Roosevelt lost at least 60% of his North Dakota ranch's cattle, lamenting "Well, we have had a perfect smashup all through the cattle country of the northwest. The losses are crippling." When the spring thaw finally came, it came in a flooding fury. As Roosevelt's ranching neighbor recounted, "countless carcasses of cattle [were] going down with the ice, rolling over and over as they went, so that at times all four of the stiffened

Figure 5.4 "Waiting for a Chinook" by Charles M. Russell conveyed the desperation of western cattle herds ravaged by drought and blizzards during the brutal summer and winter of 1886–1887 far more poignantly than any written descriptions. Source: Reproduced with permission of the Buffalo Bill Center of the West.

legs of a carcass would point skyward, as it turned under the impulsion of the swiftly moving current and the grinding ice cakes." By the 1890s, ranchers could no longer simply turn their livestock out onto the open range to fatten up on public lands; now they had to fence in their herds, feed them over the winter, experiment with better breeds that carried more beef on the hoof, and generally operate like a business rather than a romantic cowboy novel.

The rest of the West suffered, too. By the turn of the century, California's Native population was a fraction of what it had been 50 years earlier, before the gold rushes had pulverized the state's mountains, contaminated her soils with mercury, and fouled her rivers and streams. In his 1890 book *Life Amongst the Modocs*, Joaquin Miller lamented that Indians were "moving noiselessly from the face of the earth" and that "the whole face of the earth was perforated with holes; shafts sunk and being sunk by these men in search of gold, down to the bed-rock." Hydraulic mining in California had caused such severe flooding and devastation that the state's Supreme Court finally outlawed the practice. Undaunted miners replaced it with arguably even more destructive practices like stream dredging, open-pit extraction, and the beginnings of cyanide heap-leach mining. The 1890s also saw the beginnings of the oil boom in California, Texas, and Oklahoma, and within two decades, the West would supply 75% of the nation's petroleum products and begin to suffer the pollution and contamination consequences.

By the 1890s, both the West's Native peoples and its iconic fish and mammal species faced fundamental threats to their very existence, but timber exploitation also undermined regional environmental stability. A national recognition that a unique era in American history was passing, as Turner articulated in his frontier thesis, inspired some to conservation efforts, but exploitation still ruled the day. Ironically, it was the 1878 Timber and Stone Act that facilitated rapacious western timber harvests. Congress designed the act to extend national sovereignty by transferring public lands "unfit for farming" into the private hands of individuals, but it was timber barons like A.B. Hammond who used the act to snap up the "green gold" of the Pacific Northwest's (PNW) Douglas fir, giant redwood, spruce, and cedar stands through "dummy" claims and other schemes, as discussed in the previous chapter. Transportation difficulties confined most PNW harvesting to the coasts until the 1880s, however. But the 1883 completion of the Northern Pacific Railway, linking the Pacific to the Great Lakes, made it possible to connect the rich forests of the PNW to eager eastern markets. Ever the entrepreneur, Hammond built his own railroads, like the Astoria and Columbia River Railroad, to make this West-to-East conduit even more profitable. While some of the harvest stayed in the West, rebuilding San Francisco after the one-two punch of earthquake and fire in 1906, Hammond and others reinforced western resource colonialism by extracting and shipping wood wealth across the nation and around the world and often relying on eastern financing to pay the bills.

Like iconic salmon, towering old-growth forests served as ancient totems of the region. And by the close of the nineteenth century, the PNW came to the fore of the nation's timber harvest after corporations had reduced the forests of the Great Lakes region to endless stumplands. However, despite the extensive control the timber barons exerted over the PNW, it was the federal government that was destined to play a major role in managing the West's forests. As discussed in the previous chapter, early concerns about clearcutting forests were less about the visual abomination they presented and more about protecting the headwaters of the West's rare rivers to ensure that summer irrigation waters ran predictably. George Perkins Marsh had sounded the alarm in 1864 by arguing that deforestation could lead to desertification. By the 1870s, the idea of conservation to condone the wise use of natural resources began to appear more widely in scientific circles. New organizations such as the American Forestry Association pushed for forest reform and regulation, and their concerns about erosion and flooding found a receptive audience in Congress.

In 1891, Congress passed the Forest Reserve Act, which allowed the president to withdraw public forest lands from further settlement and appropriation, although it did little else initially. There were no provisions for protection and management, for example. Despite these omissions, by 1893, Presidents Benjamin Harrison (1889–1893) and Grover Cleveland (1885–1889, 1893–1897) had added 18 million acres to the system. Then in 1897, Cleveland more than doubled that by adding another 21 million acres in honor of George Washington's birthday. Some westerners were furious. In their minds, the distant (eastern) federal government was directly interfering with their right to exploit and plunder the public "commons" for commercial gain. But without federal oversight, it was clear the PNW was threatening to follow the cut-over deforestation precedent set in Michigan. So, who would control the public forests? In 1897, the pendulum of power swung decisively toward the federal government when Congress enacted the Organic Act, which created and provided funding for the national forest system and outlined new managing criteria for the nation's forest reserves. According to the act, the reserves were intended "to improve and protect the forest within the reservation, ... securing favorable conditions of water flows, and to furnish a continuous supply of timber for the use and necessities of citizens of the United States." This supervision represented a significant shift. Prior to the 1890s, the primary effort of the federal government in the West had been to give lands away. Now it began to regulate and manage them for the good of all the people, in a nascent effort to thwart the "tragedy of the commons."

Despite the potential of a federally managed forest reserve "commons," in the 1890s, timber harvests in the Pacific Northwest often mimicked the extractive ruin pioneered in California's gold fields. Wood was a major fuel that stoked the industrial engines of the United States in the late nineteenth century, not just coal – steam engines, steamboats, boilers, and stoves devoured 36 billion board feet of timber by 1900. And much of this wood wealth came from the West. In the 1890s, the timber giant Weyerhaeuser began permanently relocating its operations from the stumped-over Great Lakes region to the largely untapped timber reserves of the far Northwest, and the swath of devastation it had left behind earlier would soon reappear along the Pacific coastline. By the end of the nineteenth century, California and Oregon each supplied the market with more than 700 000 board feet of timber annually, while Washington out-produced both of them combined.

Despite the destruction, or perhaps because of it, the effort to conserve at least some elements of the natural West spawned a powerful frontier nostalgia that artists like Frederick Remington and Charles Russell sought to capture before it faded away forever. Both men journeyed to the West for the first time in the 1880s, and the "closing" of the frontier had a profound impact on their art. In his paintings, bronzes, and magazine illustrations, Remington sought to capture all of the wild romance, danger, and action-adventure of the "Old West," and his work, along with Russell's became instrumental in the development of "cowboy art" as a genre. Remington's simplified, glamorized West meshed almost perfectly with Turner's frontier, where good (white) guys in white hats triumphed over bad (non-white) guys in black hats (or head-dresses). The natural environment merely served as background. Art critics and collectors celebrated his nostalgic frontier art as "modern" and quintessentially American and his first one-man show appeared, fittingly, in 1890. "The School of Remington," as his work and that of scores of imitators was sometimes called, focused on the people and animals of the late nineteenth-century West and often featured the galloping horse as a central image. President Theodore Roosevelt would later proclaim that "the soldier, the cowboy, the rancher, the Indian, the horses and cattle of the plains, will live in his pictures and bronzes for all time."

Like Remington, Charles Russell also strove to recreate an authentic vision of the fast-disappearing West on canvas and in bronze, but his work was more sympathetic to Indians, particularly tribes of the Northern Rockies such as the Blackfeet, and even the animals paying the price for white "progress" such as bison, wolves, and bighorn sheep. Russell's formative experiences had come as a cattle hand in Montana, where he began to record his first-hand impressions of the evolving ranching business, the demise of bison, and the defeat of Plains peoples. He, too, saw that the West was no "Eden." His 1890 oil on canvas called "Cowboy Sport – Roping a Wolf," for example, offers a perfect snapshot of this fleeting moment, both for cowboys and for wolves. Russell himself lamented that he was glad he knew the West "before natures enimy [sic] the white man invaded and marred its beauty." As historian-artists, Remington and Russell helped establish a simplified western iconography that endures into the twenty-first century – cowboys and Indians, cattle and horses, saddles and guns. But as historian Dan Flores has argued, "what Russell's art offers ... is not so much the celebration of the cowboy world that everyone assumes, but actually the basis for a very valid critique of the history of the West." Russell's title for his 1911 one-man show seemed to sum up this exact sentiment: "The West That Has Passed."

Remington and Russell were internationally recognized and respected artists to be sure, but for mass appeal, perhaps no cultural expression captured the era's romantic fascination with the mythic "frontier" better than Buffalo Bill's Wild West and Congress of Rough Riders of the World. In 1893, Cody's show played twice a day, every day, right next door to Turner at the Chicago World's Columbian Exposition. Cody even invited members of the American Historical Association to see the show, as "fellow historians" of the West. William Cody, known as "Buffalo Bill," the show's founder and star, had lived an iconic western life. Before creating the Wild West (he never called it a "show"), Cody served in the Civil War, rode for the Pony Express, fought in the Indian wars, and hunted buffalo, among other endeavors. For many, he was the epitome of the rugged, individual, masculine American Turner believed the frontier forged. Cody's Wild West, which debuted in 1883 and played for three decades, was middle-class mass entertainment – part-circus, part-theater, part-variety show, all action. Looking backward, it celebrated the white taming of the Plains by manly, virile (white) men protecting their women and children from marauding Indians and Mexicans, and the West's inevitable Turnerian "progress" from savagery to civilization. Crowds thrilled to reenactments of stagecoach attacks, the Pony Express, and even the Battle of Little Bighorn, shooting demonstrations (including the famous Annie Oakley), various rodeo-type events and races, parades of Indians (including Sitting Bull, who joined the show in 1885), Mexican vaqueros and bandits, and of course Cody, whose skilled horsemanship was accompanied by frequent costume changes that allowed him to be a scout, Indian fighter, frontiersman, and hunter. The Wild West was multi-ethnic and wildly entertaining, but it was also designed to be educational, and it generated and reinforced a powerful western mythology and iconography. The show also conveyed a certain ambivalence about the frontier, at once a celebration of the nation's triumphant conquering of the "wilderness" and a reckoning with the costs of such a victory. Yes, the cowboys *had* vanquished the Indians, but audiences also recognized that the Indians and bison and even the cowboys they cheered were only the faintest remaining echoes of what had once been, in their minds, the Wild West.

Yet for all of their entertainment value, Cody's Wild West performances were remarkably place-less. True enough, they contained all the familiar western icons accurately rendered and outfitted, but the Indians and bison and cowboys and horses existed completely out of context with the natural environment that had sustained them. *The West itself was missing.* In its place was a generic stage. The show's spectacle and theater played equally well in Chicago, New York, London, and Paris precisely because it ignored the historical setting that had generated the "frontier" in the first place. Cody simply appropriated short-hand symbols of the region to spin a nostalgic American mythology – the Western – with little consideration for the root cause of change: the West's environment could no longer sustain traditional subsistence economies and complex ecosystems against the onslaught of market capitalism.

For Buffalo Bill and Frederick Jackson Turner, access to free land in the West had been the defining characteristic of American life; the process of winning the West, whether by vanquishing Indians in Cody's Wild West or plowing the prairies and establishing log cabins in Turner's thesis, had made Americans unique. And now, at the end of the century, the West was "won." But at what cost? By the 1890s, the environmental degradation that accompanied the triumph of "civilization over savagery" was sobering: numerous species in peril, overgrazing and land erosion, and obvious limits to once abundant resources. Local self-regulated "commons" (bison, salmon, timber stands) had often utilized effective resource management customs and practices, only becoming unstable when outside capitalists (including other westerners) attempted to satisfy extra-local market demand with limited resources, leading to Hardin's "tragedy." Both Cody and Turner worried about what the end of the frontier meant for America and the West, but neither offered a viable answer to the inevitable follow-up question: now what?

Wovoka's Ghost Dance echoed these lamentations of loss *and* offered a vision for the future. This peaceful pan-Indian religious response to the closing of the frontier proclaimed that earth itself would be renewed, essential in an arid landscape devastated by three decades of invasive mining and failed agriculture. In many ways, it constitutes an early environmental protest. Wovoka's prediction that Indian salvation would come through the redemptive power of nature not only expressed a Native requiem for the "West that has passed," but also sought to restore a reverence for the natural environment that offered an alternative to exploitation by emphasizing the deep connections between people and the land. Various tribes synthesized the Ghost Dance ritual with their own beliefs, but all ceremonies interacted intimately with the environment – some circled around a sacred tree, others incorporated animals into ceremonial garments, most "shook the earth" with pounding feet and chanted "the buffalo are coming."

Like Turner's thesis and Buffalo Bill's Wild West, Wovoka's Ghost Dance ritual recognized that the "frontier" had closed, but unlike the first two, the latter also understood that life in the West would have to be lived differently and that a healthy, sustainable environment was central to future success. Indians who danced the Ghost Dance, worked hard, and lived clean, honest lives would not only be saved from the coming natural disaster that would purge the land of whites and reunite them with their dead ancestors, they would be restored to a new world teeming with the animals and plants that had always sustained them. Wovoka's millennial vision prophesied that "elk and deer and antelope and even the vanished buffalo will return in vast numbers as they were before the white man came. And all Indians will be young again and free of the white man's sicknesses." Not surprisingly, the Ghost Dance spread quickly.

Among the groups who welcomed Wovoka's message of salvation during these grim times were western Lakotas (aka Sioux) in South Dakota. In 1890, the federal government had violated its treaty agreements with the tribe and carved up their reservation into five smaller units to force assimilation (incorporation into white society) and the practice of individualized agriculture. When the lands proved too thin to support agrarianism – Plains drought withered Native crops as effectively as it did busted-out homesteader crops – the government punished "lazy Indians" by cutting federal rations in half, making the specter of starvation very real. Faced with the near extinction of vital bison, economic decline, and desperation, abject Lakotas sought spiritual assistance by embracing the Ghost Dance. But white Indian agents on many reservations feared that the Ghost Dance was some kind of war dance, particularly because in the Lakotas' version of the ritual, the Ghost Dance rendered Native shirts "bulletproof" – the warriors couldn't be killed. Alarmed that the Dance was simply another stage in the prolonged Plains Indian Wars, panicked white Indian agents called in federal troops.

On December 15, 1890, events came to a head: as soldiers arrested the Lakota leader Sitting Bull for failing to halt the spread of the Ghost Dance, a tribal police officer accidentally shot and killed him. His murder provoked a small band that included women and children to flee the reservation with the US Army in hot pursuit. It was late December in South Dakota; the Indians didn't get far. On December 29, at Wounded Knee Creek, officers forced the desperate, cold, starving group to surrender their weapons. When a scuffle ensued, the soldiers opened fire. By the time the shooting stopped, 153 Lakotas (again mostly women and children) lay dead. Although public outrage erupted over the shameful massacre and resulted in the restoration of full treaty rights and rations for Lakotas, the massacre effectively ended Plains Indian resistance and eliminated their central role in the complicated ecosystems of the region. Not surprisingly, the millennial fervor of the Ghost Dance waned considerably in the wake of Wounded Knee, although other elements of the faith endured well into the twentieth century. But the closing of the frontier had meant something entirely different to Native peoples than it had to Turner and Buffalo Bill. As Black Elk, the famous Lakota medicine man proclaimed, "the nation's hoop is broken and scattered. There is no center any longer, and the sacred tree is dead."

Turner and Cody may not have had a clear vision of the post-frontier West, but a Scottish immigrant named John Muir did. Muir's veneration of the natural West was not economic but aesthetic and echoed the sentiments of Wovoka: "Brought into right relationships with the wilderness, man would see that his appropriation of Earth's resources beyond his personal needs would only bring imbalance and begat ultimate loss and poverty by all." In 1892, the year prior to Turner's frontier thesis, Muir co-founded an alpine hiking group called the Sierra Club that would become a leading advocate for environmental protection in the twentieth century – one that sought to promote sustainability not Edenic mythology. It seemed the fulfillment of statesman George Perkins Marsh's prescient prediction nearly four decades earlier that "the destructive agency of man becomes more and more energetic and unsparing as he advances civilization, until the impoverishment, with which his exhaustion of the natural resources of the soil is threatening him, at last awakens him to the necessity of preserving what is left, if not of restoring what has been wantonly wasted." Muir would make preservation his passion.

Suggested Reading

Thomas G. Andrews, *Killing for Coal: America's Deadliest Labor War* (Cambridge, MA: Harvard University Press, 2010).

Robert Block, "Frederick Jackson Turner And American Geography," *Annals of the Association of American Geographers*, Vol. 70, No.1 (March 1980), 32. www.jstor/org/stable/2562823 (accessed February 3, 2016).

William Cronon, "Revisiting the Vanishing Frontier: The Legacy of Frederick Jackson Turner," *Western Historical Quarterly*, Vol. 18, No. 2 (April 1987), 157–176.

Mark Fiege, "Iron Horses: Nature and the Building of the First U.S. Transcontinental Railroad," in *Republic of Nature: An Environmental History of the United States* (Seattle: University of Washington Press, 2013), 228–270.

Dan Flores, "Frederic Remington's Kiss of Death" and "In the End, What was Charlie Russell Trying to Tell Us?" in *Visions of the Big Sky: Painting and Photographing the Northern Rocky Mountain West* (Norman: University of Oklahoma Press, 2010), 151–157, 204–211.

Greg Gordon, *When Money Grew on Trees: A.B. Hammond and the Age of the Timber Baron* (Norman: University of Oklahoma Press, 2014).

David Igler, "The Industrial Far West: Region and Nation in the Late Nineteenth Century," *Pacific Historical Review*, Vol. 69, No. 2 (May 2000), 159–192.

Randy McFerrin and Douglas Wills, "Searching for the Big Die-Off: An Event Study of 19th Century Cattle Markets," in *Essays in Economic and Business History*, Vol. XXXI (Mount Pleasant: Central Michigan University, 2013), 33–52.

Joaquin Miller, *Life Amongst the Modocs: Unwritten History* (Berkeley: Heyday, 1996).

Edmund Morris, "The Winter of Blue Snow, 1886–1887," in *The Rise of Theodore Roosevelt* (New York: Modern Library, 2001), 361–367.

James Muhn, "Early Administration of the Forest Reserve Act: Interior Department and General Land Office Policies, 1891-1897," in Harold K. Steen, ed. *The Origins of the National Forests: A Centennial Symposium* (Durham: Forest History Society, 1992). www.foresthistory.org/Publications/Books/Origins_National_Forests (accessed February 3, 2016).

Brian Richard Ott, "Indian Fishing Rights in the Pacific Northwest: The Need for Federal Intervention," *Boston College Environmental Affairs Law Review*, Vol. 14, No. 2 (December 1987), 313–343. http://lawdigitalcommons.bc.edu/cgi/viewcontent.cgi?article=1596&context=ealr (accessed February 3, 2016).

Michael J. Robinson, *Predatory Bureaucracy: The Extermination of Wolves and the Transformation of the West* (Boulder: University Press of Colorado, 2005).

Louis S. Warren, "Wage Work in the Sacred Circle: The Ghost Dance as Modern Religion," *Western Historical Quarterly*, Vol. 46, No. 2 (Summer 2015), 141–168.

Richard White, "Creative Destruction," in *Railroaded: The Transcontinentals and the Making of Modern America* (New York: W.W. Norton & Company, 2011), 455–493.

Charles F. Wilkinson, "The River was Crouded with Salmon," in *Crossing the Next Meridian: Land, Water, and the Future of the West* (Washington DC: Island Press, 1992), 175–218.

John Willis, "The End of the (Old) World," in *US Environmental History: Inviting Doomsday* (Edinburgh University Press, 2012), 28–49.

6

Conservation and Preservation

"I want to drop politics absolutely for four days and just be out in the open with you." In 1903, this charming and unusual request came to John Muir from none other than President Theodore Roosevelt. Muir could not resist. That summer, the two men set out on an intimate three-night camping trip through the spectacular scenery of Yosemite Park in California to "talk conservation" (see Figure 6.1). Although Yosemite Valley and the Mariposa Grove belonged to the state at the time, Muir hoped to convince the commander-in-chief that both deserved protection within the national park. While the specifics of their talks and rambles remained private, the outcome of their adventure was not only the federal preservation of Yosemite Valley and Mariposa Grove and a preliminary outline for what would become the Antiquities Act, but also effusive declarations of respect and affection from both men. "I shall always be glad that I was in the Yosemite with John Muir," Roosevelt wrote, while Muir simply gushed: "I fairly fell in love with him." As this rapprochement illustrates, these two men, who often appear as over-simplified adversaries – Roosevelt the Conservationist versus Muir the Preservationist – in fact aligned closely on many key environmental issues. Both men dedicated their lives to protecting the scenic wonders of nature and both viewed wilderness as a necessary respite from civilization. By the time he left office, Roosevelt had created 5 national parks (many influenced by Muir), 18 national monuments, 55 national bird sanctuaries and wildlife refuges, and 150 national forests. "We are not building this country of ours for

Losing Eden: An Environmental History of the American West, First Edition. Sara Dant.
© 2017 John Wiley & Sons, Inc. Published 2017 by John Wiley & Sons, Inc.

Figure 6.1 President Theodore Roosevelt and John Muir atop Glacier Point in Yosemite during their formative May 1903 camping trip. Source: Reproduced with permission of the National Park Service.

a day," Roosevelt avowed, "It is to last through the ages." Muir's writings and advocacy ultimately established his legacy as the "Father of the National Parks," and his biographer Donald Worster has argued that Muir's mission was nothing less than "saving the American soul from total surrender to materialism." But for all their points of agreement, the two men also had their differences. Ironically, Yosemite would provide the setting for both their happy 1903 camping expedition and their apocryphal showdown over damming the park's Hetch Hetchy Valley.

As the twentieth century dawned, exploitative market demands and the West's resource-based colonial-like status continued – acerbic writer Bernard DeVoto labeled the early West "the plundered province," but the region began to assert its own unique identity as a result of its extensive public lands. This federal variation on "commons" comprised of forest reserves, parks, monuments, and wildlife refuges quickly became the distinguishing hallmark of the American West and began to establish a new way to "value" nature beyond commodification. In 1889, a former Secretary of Interior, Carl Schurz, had railed that Americans were "a spendthrift people recklessly wasting [their] heritage" and saddled with "a government careless of the future"; four years later, Frederick Jackson Turner ominously warned that "the frontier has gone and with it has closed the first period in American history." So, what was next? Roosevelt and Muir. Together these two men personified the foundational ideas, conservation and preservation that would shape both thought and policy about the natural environment of the West well into the twenty-first century.

Public commitment to protecting natural resources grew through the first two decades of the twentieth century as one of the central issues championed by Progressives. As a political ideology, Progressivism sought to improve the human condition through governmental reforms designed to redress the social inequalities that emerged as the nation rapidly urbanized and industrialized. Although it began at the local and state levels as a kind of municipal housekeeping, Progressive reform had become a full-fledged national phenomenon by the turn of the century. Avid modernizers, Progressives typically held white, middle-class values, used science and statistics to support their causes, promoted efficiency and education, and viewed government, especially at the federal level, as a positive instrument for social change. Progressivism also had a strong religious undercurrent that attempted to reconcile Protestant morality with capitalism and democracy to promote a kind of Christian stewardship of the nation and its resources. Never a really unified "movement" per se, Progressivism championed reforms as diverse as temperance, birth control, urban sanitation, anti-child labor laws, settlement houses, anti-prostitution campaigns, women's rights, and environmental protection.

In this final area, Progressive's concerns about the limits of the nation's natural resources prompted two different, if related, responses: conservation and preservation. While by the late twentieth century these two terms had become interchangeable in popular parlance (along with "environmentalism"), at the beginning of the century each had a very unique meaning and associated values. Essentially, conservation advocated the wise *use* of nature, while preservation advocated the protection of nature from exploitation.

The first of these, conservation, was utilitarian and emphasized the role of science and rational planning in the efficient development and use of natural resources, especially in the West. Conservationists advocated protecting resources for the good of the nation to ensure that they would always be available for future consumers. Theodore Roosevelt and his chief forester Gifford

Pinchot would become the most high-profile advocates for this idea, which arose out of concerns about the nation's declining timber supplies. The myth of inexhaustibility in the nation's forests had begun to reveal its perfidy as early as the 1870s with the stark deforestation of the Great Lakes region. Interior Secretary Schurz had lamented that "the destruction of our forests is so fearfully rapid that if we go on at the same rate, men whose hair is already gray will see the day when … there will be no forest left worthy of the name." He was right. By the 1890s, the avaricious take had also stripped many West Coast forests of their prize trees to feed housing booms in San Francisco and Los Angeles, and provide milled timber to east coast markets. Congress had responded with the 1891 Forest Reserve Act, discussed in the previous chapter, which empowered the president to set aside/conserve "forest reserves" for the future. The subsequent 1897 Organic Act reinforced this conservation agenda by stipulating that the reserves were designed to "furnish a continuous supply of timber for the use and necessities of citizens of the United States." In 1898, President William McKinley appointed the 33-year-old Pinchot to preside over these holdings, and by the turn of the twentieth century, the system comprised more than 47 million acres.

In 1901, McKinley's assassination suddenly thrust Vice President Theodore Roosevelt into the Oval Office. At the news, one conservative senator purportedly lamented, "Now look! That damned cowboy is president," but for the West, the elevation of the "cowboy" proved a fortuitous promotion. Progressives now had a powerful new ally in the White House, and so did Pinchot. An early and avid advocate for protecting the wild places of the American West, the once-frail president had used ranching and hunting in the region to reinvent his sickly eastern self as a virile and manly "cowboy" and so shed early effeminate nicknames such as "Jane-Dandy" and "Punkin-Lily." In the early 1880s, Roosevelt made several trips to the Dakotas, even buying a couple of ranches, and working on them, which allowed him to "harden" himself, bulk up, shed childhood ailments like asthma, and even swap out his squeak for a voice "hearty and strong enough to drive oxen." "Cowboy" was apt. In 1887, as part of his effort to protect the very West that Turner and Buffalo Bill would soon warn was vanishing, Roosevelt co-founded the Boone and Crockett Club, named after frontiersmen Daniel Boone and Davy Crockett, to "promote the conservation and management of wildlife, especially big game, and its habitat." A kind of grown-man's Boy Scouts, the Club's socially elite membership advocated ethical hunting and sportsmanship and began lobbying for the protection/conservation of wild animals – at least the ones these sportsmen liked to hook and shoot – and American masculinity. As good Progressives, they believed that the federal government served as the best steward of the public's natural resources and guardian against rampant capitalist exploitation.

As President, Roosevelt was in a unique position to implement change. By the end of his administration, the nation could boast 51 wildlife refuges and 4 game preserves in 17 states and 3 territories that protected birds from the hat plume trade as well as the few remaining bison and elk herds. Roosevelt had a number of prominent allies in his quest to protect the West's charismatic megafauna, including William Temple Hornaday, prolific author, taxidermist, and director of the New York Zoological Park. Like Roosevelt, Hornaday had grown alarmed by the near extermination of bison and other western game species and became a convert to conservation. "Here is an inexorable law of Nature," Hornaday wrote, "to which there are no exceptions: No wild species of bird, mammal, reptile or fish can withstand exploitation for commercial purposes." Hornaday's pithy "law" certainly applied to almost all of the natural resources of the West. Roosevelt concurred.

In 1905, Roosevelt set aside the nation's first large game wildlife reserve, the Wichita National Forest and Game Preserve in Oklahoma, as a cooperative bison restoration effort between the federal government and Hornaday, who donated 15 of the zoo's captive bison to reestablish the species. Indeed, if any one person deserves credit for rescuing bison from the brink of extinction, it's Hornaday. His book *Our Vanishing Wildlife*, published in 1913, passionately called for wildlife reform; the "birds and mammals now are literally dying for your help," he warned. By 1919, thanks in large part to Hornaday's activism, the great American bison had begun its slow rebound to ecological health, from a frighteningly low point of a few hundred wild individuals, to nine growing herds. In 1905, Roosevelt had also consolidated several federal agencies into the Bureau of Biological Survey (which in 1940 became the Fish and Wildlife Service) to manage the growing reserve system. The agency's focus, however, remained the protection of fish and game, not predators, which they continued to exterminate in astonishing numbers. It would take the ecological imagination of later men like Aldo Leopold, a forester who embraced both conservation *and* preservation, to begin seeing things whole, rather than as a piecemeal attempt to protect trophy species and eliminate their predators. But the wildlife refuges constituted a start and an important foundation upon which the coming environmental movement could build.

In 1905, the same year that he organized the Bureau of Biological Survey, Roosevelt transferred the country's "forest reserves" into a newly minted United States Forest Service, renamed them "national forests," and designated Pinchot Chief of the Forest Service. Significantly, the Department of Agriculture housed the Forest Service, an assignment befitting the utilitarian/conservation mission of the new agency. Trees were a crop, and the Service would manage them accordingly. Pinchot himself argued that "the object of our forest policy is not to preserve the forests because they are beautiful ... or because they are refuges for the wild creatures of the wilderness. The forests are to be used by man. Every other consideration comes secondary."

A classic Progressive, Pinchot combined a formal education in forest management with practical experience gleaned from his family's private estate. Pinchot adhered to "the gospel of efficiency" – an almost religious dedication to the scientific management of the forests (as a crop) to ensure "that the water, wood, and forage of the reserves are conserved and wisely used for the benefit of the home builder first of all." This "multiple-use" philosophy sought to avoid the "tragedy of the commons" by regulating cutting, mining, grazing, and recreation to ensure that the forests could be both used *and* saved, the hallmark of efficient conservation. The national forest system flourished under Roosevelt and by the end of his tenure in the White House, he had set aside 150 national forests. In the West, Pinchot endeavored to counter the heavy hand of this new, often resented federal landlord by creating a hierarchical US Forest Service that placed much of the administrative responsibilities and decisions in the hands of local rangers and regional supervisors. But ultimately, the agency bowed to efficiency of scale, and Pinchot frequently gave preferential treatment to large cattle and timber operations over small resource users because it made good conservation, if not democratic, sense. In the end, he argued, conservation meant "the greatest good" to "the greatest number in the long run." Like many of the West's natural resources, timber acted as a commodity and the market determined its ultimate value; scientific management of the forests made them profitable.

Not all Progressives followed Pinchot's utilitarian lead, however, and an important, and often competing, ideology emerged at the turn of the century called preservation. Preservationists advocated the protection of nature for its own sake and for the physical and spiritual health of people rather than purely for economic utility. This was the argument of John Muir, who believed that "the hills and groves were God's first temples." In many ways, Muir serves as an illustrative transitional figure between the Romanticism of the nineteenth century and the environmentalism of the twentieth. Both Romantics and Transcendentalists like Henry David Thoreau and Ralph Waldo Emerson had emphasized the primacy of the imagination and emotions, celebrated the individual, and waxed rhapsodic about the wonders of nature. Muir's writings certainly bore the imprint of these influences. Born in Scotland in 1838, Muir and his family immigrated to America when he was 11. A curious, if eclectic, student, Muir took college courses in the sciences and read Thoreau, Emerson, and George Perkins Marsh, absorbing natural history and developing an abiding appreciation for "the infinite lavishness and fertility of Nature." For several years, he traipsed across much of the West, including Alaska, studying at what he called "The University of the Wilderness." By the 1870s, he made his living as "John of the Mountains," writing about wilderness and the West's wild places he had come to love. Like many Progressives, Muir believed that the federal government could most effectively and efficiently protect these natural wonders.

As historian Thomas Wellock has argued, "Muir blended the idealism of Henry David Thoreau with the political activism befitting a modern lobbyist." In classic Progressive fashion, Muir co-founded the Sierra Club in 1892 as an organization "to explore, enjoy, and render accessible the mountain regions of the Pacific Coast; to publish authentic information concerning them; to enlist the support and cooperation of the people and the government in preserving the forest and other natural features of the Sierra Nevada Mountains." He also cultivated friendships with businessmen/powerbrokers like Edward Harriman, head of the Southern Pacific Railroad, President Roosevelt, and even Pinchot, because they had the political and financial clout to translate his advocacy into action, as the opening Yosemite anecdote illustrates. These pragmatic alliances also reveal that the divide between conservation and preservation could often be more imagined than real.

During the Roosevelt years, however, conservation won the day. The American West was still developing economically and serving as a national resource warehouse, so that Muir's preservationist ideals seemed a luxury, even a "waste," to many people in the region and the nation. The Sierra Club and Muir continued to lobby for the protection of "sublime" nature, but these more romantic notions about the environment would not attain primacy in the West or the United States as a whole, until after World War II, when tourism became a mass phenomenon, and middle class and even blue collar Americans began taking vacations to enjoy the "wilderness." Nowhere was this triumph of conservation more evident in the West than in the push for reclamation, the effort to use irrigation to "reclaim" arid lands. Despite the federal government's best efforts and intentions to distribute western lands cheaply and quickly via the Homestead Act and others like it, settlers inevitably ran up against the vexing aridity of much of the West: too dry to dry-farm and too vast to irrigate. Progressives once again turned to the federal government for assistance and, in 1902, Congress passed one of the most influential laws for the West: the Newlands Reclamation Act.

The Reclamation Act alluded to the vision of John Wesley Powell, who had vigorously advocated for a West settled and developed around watershed basins managed by the federal government (see Chapter 4). Powell's proposals may have been too restrictive for gung ho settlers, but in the Progressive Era, the idea that the federal government should fund large-scale water projects – dams, canals, irrigation – found many adherents. In contrast to Powell's plan, though, reclamation endeavored to bring water to the people instead of settling people where there was water. Essentially "multiple use" for rivers, reclamation promoted the rational, efficient development of water resources to manage power and provide irrigation, flood control, navigation, and recreation. Indeed, the reclamation movement tugged hard at long-held, core American values: it promised to make the desert bloom, promote Jeffersonian democracy by providing for the yeoman farmer, and prevent corporate monopolies. As one of reclamation's biggest boosters Elwood Mead proclaimed, "the result will determine whether Western agriculture will be corporate or cooperative; whether rivers shall become an instrument for creating a great monopoly, as the dominant element of Western society, or be a free gift to those who make a public return for their use."

With the Progressive Roosevelt in the White House, the reclamation movement gained momentum. Roosevelt explained how reclamation fit within the conservation movement in a December 1901 speech written by Pinchot: "The forests alone cannot ... fully regulate and conserve the waters of the arid region. Great storage works are necessary to equalize the flow of streams and to save the flood waters." Conserving water for future *use*. Congress agreed and six months later it passed the historic Newlands Reclamation Act, named after Senator Francis Newlands of Nevada, the act's sponsor. The act created the federal Reclamation Service, soon renamed the Bureau of Reclamation, within the Department of Interior, provided for all states on or west of the 100th meridian (Texas was added in 1906) to receive federal funds for reclamation projects, and proclaimed its intention to serve the small family farmer by limiting access to reclaimed water exclusively to local residents irrigating between 40 and 160 acres of land. The optimistic act also stipulated that the projects would pay for themselves within 10 years through land sales and farmer payments. Not surprisingly, western states chafed at federal control over western resources, and so to mollify them, the Reclamation Act also provided for a strange hybrid of federal funding for reclamation projects and state control over the water they conserved. Social critic DeVoto summed up the West's arrangement: "Get out and give us more money." Reclamation represented a utopian, democratic vision of the West not wholly incompatible with Powell's. And like most utopian visions, it was doomed to failure, as corporate agribusiness and booming cities soon monopolized the water intended for small family farms.

Reclamation projects did spur western settlement, however; settlers filed by far the largest number of homestead patents ever in the first 20 years of the twentieth century, and reclamation water accounted for nearly 30% of the irrigated acreage in the 11 western-most states. In its first five years, the Bureau began about 30 projects in western states. But the fiscal and environmental costs proved excessive. Farmers' meager profits left them unable to repay the high costs of dams and irrigation projects. To address this problem, Congress began to stray from the actual language of the act, first by extending repayment periods out to four decades, then by making the building loans interest-free, and finally by allowing the debts to linger, in some cases, until the present day. According to one estimate, "86 percent of the total reimbursable construction costs have not been and will not be repaid." It was an awesome tax-payer subsidy. But not to the intended small farming families. Like the Homestead Act before it, reclamation quickly came to benefit entrepreneurs, who identified water as *the* lucrative western commodity.

Cheap land plus cheap water proved a powerful lure to agribusiness speculators, who snapped up 160-acre parcels and took advantage of a reclamation loophole that allowed families to collectively manage each member's individual (maximum) holding and then lease the entire landmass to corporate farmers. In other words, a family of six could claim six separate 160-acre land parcels and the federally subsidized reclamation water to irrigate it, and then lease all 960 acres and the cheap water to an agribusiness entrepreneur. The bigger the "family," the bigger the leased land/water parcel. Like earlier Homestead Act "dummy" claims, these reclamation sleight-of-hand maneuvers undermined the act's original Jeffersonian intent to support small farmers. California speculators elevated the subterfuge to a near art form. Lobbyists for the state's development managed to convince Congress to exempt the entire Imperial Valley from the acreage limitations stipulated in the act, while agribusiness farmers in the Central Valley circumvented the same restrictions when the Army Corps of Engineers built their hydraulic system. Throughout the West, the Army Corps often competed with the Bureau of Reclamation for federal funding to build, among other things, dams, canals, and flood control projects. The Army Corps' water, it turned out, was not bound by reclamation laws. Ultimately, neither were federal bureaucrats, who found it increasingly inconvenient, if not impossible, to enforce the act's limitations.

In his influential book, *Rivers of Empire*, environmental historian Donald Worster argues that the legacy of the 1902 Newlands Act was the development of a "hydraulic society," where ownership and control of the West's massive reclamation infrastructure became consolidated into the hands of an oligarchic elite comprised of large western land owners and federal technocrats from the East. Instead of the utopian, democratic ideals the act seemed to embody, Worster argues, the massive scale of arid lands reclamation created a "coercive, monolithic, and hierarchical system, ruled by a power elite based on the ownership of capital and expertise." In the West, capitalism had captured the water. Los Angeles and San Francisco certainly fit this description. Growing and thirsty, their grasping for water added another layer of complexity to the West's environmental history, and they provide two provocative non-federal illustrations of Worster's thesis.

William Mulholland personified Worster's "power elite" and he had a vision for Los Angeles. For the City of Angels to become a thriving metropolis, it would need water … lots of it. And as the head of that burgeoning city's Department of Water and Power, Mulholland was painfully aware that the go-go growth of Los Angeles was quickly outstripping the thirst-quenching ability of the Los Angeles River. He also understood the basic premise of western water law: first in time, first in right. The answer to LA's aridity riddle, Mulholland realized, lay 200 miles north of Los Angeles on the eastern side of the Sierra Nevadas in the Owens River Valley. There, small farmers eagerly awaited the kind of federal reclamation promised by the Newlands Act that would make their desert bloom. Mulholland had a different idea … one that would make LA bloom instead.

In 1905, after securing a vaguely worded municipal bond issue for the "purchase of lands and water and the inauguration of work on the aqueduct," the City of Los Angeles began quietly buying up Owens Valley farmland and the riparian/water rights-of-way along the Owens River. By the time local residents figured out the hijacking scheme, it was too late. Mulholland supervised construction of the 233-mile-long, gravity-powered Los Angeles Aqueduct that took the river south and *over* the mountains into Los Angeles (see Figure 6.2). Along the way, it also provided irrigation to the San Fernando Valley, just north of the city. Developers and investors in on Mulholland's confidential plan snapped up dirt-cheap soon-to-be-irrigated property in the San Fernando Valley before its real value became apparent. On November 5, 1913, when the water began to flow, Mulholland, like a good oligarch, empirically declared: "There it is; take it."

So what about the "small family farmer" whom reclamation was supposed to support? Ever the pragmatic and efficient Progressive conservationist, Roosevelt embraced the "greatest good of the greatest number" reasoning and threw his support behind the Owens River water transfer as "a hundred or thousandfold more important and more valuable to the people as a whole." Federal reclamation abandoned the Owens Valley and doomed its farmland to aridity. The loss of the river also devastated the local Owens Valley environment. The Owens Lake ecosystem, which once served as an important rest stop for millions of migrating waterfowl, shriveled into a parched alkali flat that still generates debilitating dust storms. A second LA Aqueduct, built in the 1970s, further exacerbated the situation by siphoning off the valley's springs and seeps and withering groundwater-dependent vegetation and the valley's lush meadows. Although two environmental lawsuits and court-levied fines finally forced the city to restore water to a 62-mile stretch of the Owens River in 2007, desertification had already taken a heavy toll. In an area that receives less rainfall than Phoenix, saltbrush and tumbleweeds now flourish where native grasses and wildflowers once thrived. Today, the Owens River supplies between 30 and 50% of distant Los Angeles' water needs and the dried-out local lakebed constitutes one of the largest sources of dust pollution in the United States.

Figure 6.2 A portion of pipeline in the Jawbone Siphon of the Los Angeles Aqueduct, San Fernando Valley, California, engineered by William Mulholland to transfer water from the Owens Valley more than 200 miles south to thirsty Los Angeles. Source: Reproduced with permission of the Los Angeles Department of Water and Power.

As recently as 2014, one resident complained that "the city of Los Angeles regards Inyo County as a resource colony to be exploited to whatever means they see fit. They are taking all the water they possibly can. Water tables are dropping precipitously." Los Angeles built the aqueduct in spite of farmers and ranchers who bombed and vandalized it in the so-called California Water Wars of the 1920s. And in the end, the Owens River flowed out of its valley into a concrete ditch and made a distant metropolis, not the desert, bloom. In 1890, 50 000 people had called Los Angeles "home"; by 1900 that number had doubled to 100 000; and by 1910, the population had exploded to 320 000. As Worster concludes, "the smaller, weaker party lost out to the more powerful one while the federal government looked on and abetted."

For John Muir and Theodore Roosevelt, the sometimes conflicting objectives of conservation and preservation, evident in the Owens Valley, came into even sharper focus in the Hetch Hetchy Valley of Yosemite. Once again, the catalyst was water. Like Los Angeles, the city of San Francisco sought a reliable source that could slake its thirst for decades into the future. In 1903, city officials proposed damming the Tuolumne River in the Hetch Hetchy Valley in Yosemite National Park to create a public water supply. It was classic conservationism. Outraged, Muir and the Sierra Club protested vigorously, arguing that such a proposal violated the *preservation* mandate of the park. Following the devastating earthquake and ensuing calamitous fires of 1906, however, San Francisco's quest took on a new urgency; the city needed a bigger, better, more reliable source of water. The Roosevelt administration, largely at the prodding of utilitarian-minded Pinchot, agreed, and shifted its support to the proposal.

The Hetch Hetchy clash pitted two different visions of the valley against one another: Muir and other preservation activists, who hoped to promote nature tourism and scenic protection through the development of hotels and campgrounds, versus conservationists, who wanted to dam the valley to create a public water supply and thwart avaricious private utility companies that could ransom power to the highest bidder. Both sides slung epithets. Muir blasted his opponents as "Satan and Co." and "temple destroyers" who were beholden to the "Almighty Dollar." Dam supporters ridiculed preservationists as "short-haired women and long-haired men" and argued that the economic utility of damming Hetch Hetchy outweighed the sentiments of tourists, who could always go marvel at Yosemite Valley. Conservation won this round. In 1913, Congress passed the Raker Act authorizing the city's construction of O'Shaughnessy Dam, completed a decade later, and the creation of the Hetch Hetchy Reservoir. Muir was devastated; he died the next year. Yosemite and the Range of Light may have brought Roosevelt and Muir together to hike and camp in 1903, but Hetch Hetchy demonstrated that sometimes conservation and preservation were irreconcilable. In the early twentieth-century West, the development/exploitation mindset still prevailed, although sometimes by the hands of westerners themselves, and a full-blown commitment to preservation was only a faint glimmer in the distant future.

The Hetch Hetchy fight may have broken Muir's spirit, and perhaps even his heart, but preservationists emerged from it more powerful and influential than ever before, and ironically their loss in Yosemite helped ensure that other parks, like the Grand Canyon, would not suffer such a fate. Unlike federal and municipal reclamation, the parks movement allowed conservation/use and preservation to overlap extensively. Conservationists championed national park "use" for the enjoyment and moral and physical health of visiting tourists, while preservationists celebrated federal protection of scenic wonders. By the time Roosevelt took the presidential oath of office, the United States had already committed itself to the idea of parks for the people, particularly in the

West where the federal government still held and controlled much of the land. In 1872, Congress had set aside Yellowstone as the first national park and assigned its administrative duties to the Department of Interior. In 1886, when the agency proved unable to keep poachers and squatters out of the park, the US Army took over and expanded its jurisdiction over the next two decades to include each newly added western jewel such as Yosemite, Sequoia, General Grant (which later became Kings' Canyon), Mount Rainier, Crater Lake, and Glacier.

Progressives enthusiastically embraced the park concept and so did Roosevelt, especially after 1906 when Congress passed the Antiquities Act. The Antiquities Act gave the president extraordinary and unchecked executive authority to by-pass the cumbersome congressional park designation process and unilaterally set aside "historic landmarks, historic and prehistoric structures, and other objects of historic or scientific interest" as national monuments. Roosevelt, and his successor William Howard Taft, wasted little time putting the new law into action; Devil's Tower, El Morro, Montezuma's Castle, Petrified Forest, Chaco Canyon, Lassen Peak, Grand Canyon, Jewel Cave, Natural Bridges, and Mount Olympus all came into the system as western national monuments. Significantly, these first parks and monuments were visually stunning *and* economically marginal, so setting them aside didn't jeopardize western development. During Roosevelt's tenure alone, from 1901–1909, the conservation president set aside 18 national monuments and 5 national parks, which in addition to national forests, wildlife preserves, and refuges, protected approximately 230 000 000 acres of public land. By 1911 the number of national parks and monuments administered by various governmental agencies had swollen to nearly 40. The time had clearly come to create a new agency to manage this public resource "commons" collectively rather than individually.

The national parks have been called "America's best idea," and it makes sense that their organizational genesis lies in the Progressive Era. The Hetch Hetchy fight had demonstrated the vulnerability of the parks, and the effort to establish an agency to manage them had gained serious momentum by the time Woodrow Wilson came into the White House in 1913. Support for such a federal agency ran the gamut from governmental administrators to tourist organizations. But the complaint of borax millionaire Stephen Mather finally tipped the scales. In the summer of 1914, Mather visited Sequoia and Yosemite national parks and became incensed at their poor management. He wrote of his concerns to his friend, Secretary of Interior Franklin Lane, who responded quite simply: "If you don't like the way the parks are being run, come on down to Washington and run them yourself." Mather took the bait. As someone who had been on the losing side of the Hetch Hetchy fight, Mather understood that both he and the parks needed to finesse a delicate balance between conservation and preservation, and so Mather began a national campaign of articles and photographs to drum up support for a federal parks agency.

In 1916, Mather's crusade triumphed when Congress passed and President Wilson signed the National Park Service (NPS) Organic Act and named Mather as its first Director. The NPS's stated mission was "to conserve the scenery and the natural and historic objects and the wild life therein and to provide for the enjoyment of the same in such manner and by such means as will leave them unimpaired for the enjoyment of future generations." This hybrid and often contradictory assignment would prove difficult to carry out in the long run. With "tourism" as its prime directive, the newly minted Park Service struggled to reconcile protecting the sublime and providing pit toilets.

Furthermore, the aesthetic appreciation for nature borne out of leisure experiences such as hiking, camping, hunting, and fishing sometimes gave conservationists and preservationists an elitist perspective. Although the creation of the park system seemed to reinforce core democratic values of community and openness, the parks themselves were really only accessible to

Figure 6.3 Cliff Palace, Mesa Verde. Once home to ancestral Pueblo peoples, Mesa Verde became a national park in 1906 when President Theodore Roosevelt set it aside to "preserve the works of man." Source: Reproduced with permission of the National Park Service.

those with the financial resources to travel and explore. Not until the post-war boom in the 1950s and 1960s would travel to the national parks become a mass phenomenon. Moreover, conserving nature for recreation and tourism at times meant *preventing* subsistence users from hunting, gathering, fishing, and utilizing timber resources. In other words, parks tended to benefit the middle and upper classes at the expense of non-whites and the rural poor. Policies of Indian removal at Yellowstone, Glacier, and Yosemite, for example, attempted to create a "pristine" and "safe" wilderness experience for park visitors as part of a larger attempt to "protect" nature. Buffalo Bill's Wild West had already primed audiences with a nostalgic western Indian mythology, but these romantic portrayals only resonated once Native peoples no longer constituted any real threat or danger. Interestingly, all three parks were willing to pay Native peoples to "play Indian" as "tourist bait" for visitors, so long as this controlled contact constituted the extent of their presence in the park. To be sure, several of the new national parks and monuments protected Indian sites such as Mesa Verde, Chaco Canyon, and Gran Quivira, but they were all *ruins*, the silent, ghostly, abandoned reminders of an ancient America that had long since vanished (see Figure 6.3). Tourists expected that *their* parks would be uninhabited, and that required dispossession. Yet for all its shortcomings and seeming frivolity to many who labored in the West, public lands tourism nevertheless served as a cultural common denominator and the region's iconic landscapes, flora, and fauna proved especially captivating.

Both the conservation and preservation movements represented an important shift in the relationship between the federal government and the nation's public lands. Prior to the Progressive Era, the government's primary objective had been putting public lands into private hands through massive incentive programs such as the Homestead Act and the 1872 Mining Law. Now, however, the federal government aggressively set aside lands in the public domain with the specific goal of *preventing* their conversion into private property. By doing so, the government, through its various land-management agencies, ensured that it would continue to be a dominant presence in the West. In the end, the twin Progressive Era reform impulses of conservation and preservation sought to remedy open-access exploitation through federal oversight and regulation and avoid the "tragedy of the commons" dilemma. National forests, wildlife preserves, reclamation, and parks – a kind of federal "commons" – would ensure that no matter how zealously individual Americans pursued their own economic and self-interest, there would always be sufficient natural resources to fuel the nation's growth and development, and sublime landscapes where one could discover, as Muir evangelized, "that wildness is a necessity; and that mountain parks and reservations are useful not only as fountains of timber and irrigating rivers, but as fountains of life."

Suggested Reading

Marshall E. Bowen, "Crops, Critters, and Calamity: The Failure of Dry Farming in Utah's Escalante Desert, 1913–1918," *Agricultural History*, Vol. 73, No. 1 (Winter 1999), 1–26.

Lincoln Bramwell, "When the Mountains Roared: The 1910 Northern Rockies Fires," *Montana: The Magazine of Western History*, Autumn 2010, 54–69, 96.

Douglas Brinkley, "TR's Wild Side," *American Heritage*, Vol. 59, No. 3 (Fall 2009), 26–35.

Bernard DeVoto, "The West Against Itself," in Douglas Brinkley and Patricia Nelson Limerick, eds, *The Western Paradox: A Conservation Reader* (New Haven: Yale University Press, 2001), 45–73.

Benjamin Heber Johnson, "Conservation, Subsistence, and Class at the Birth of Superior National Forest," *Environmental History*, Vol. 4, No. 1 (January 1999), 80–99.

Robert B. Keiter, *To Conserve Unimpaired: The Evolution of the National Park Idea* (Washington DC: Island Press, 2013).

Robert H. Keller, Jr and Michael F. Turek, *American Indians and National Parks* (Tucson: University of Arizona Press, 1999).

Tom Knudson, "Outrage in Owens Valley a Century after L.A. Began Taking its Water," *The Sacramento Bee*, January 5, 2014. www.sacbee.com/2014/01/05/6046630/outrage-in-owens-valley.html (accessed February 4, 2016).

Curt Meine, "Roosevelt, Conservation, and the Revival of Democracy," *Conservation Biology*, Vol. 14, No. 4 (August 2001), 829–831.

John Muir, "The Wild Parks and Forest Reservations of the West," in Fred D. White, ed., *Essential Muir: A California Legacy Book* (Berkeley: Heyday Books, 2006).

David A. Nesheim, "Profit, Preservation, and Shifting Definitions of Bison in America," *Environmental History*, Vol. 17, No. 3 (July 2012), 547–577.

Mark Reisner, *Cadillac Desert: The American West and its Disappearing Water* (New York: Penguin Books, 1993). See also the June of 2000 PBS four-part documentary by the same name.

Robert W. Righter, *The Battle over Hetch Hetchy: America's Most Controversial Dam and the Birth of Modern Environmentalism* (New York: Oxford University Press, 2005).

Mark David Spence, *Dispossessing the Wilderness: Indian Removal and the Making of the National Parks* (New York: Oxford University Press, 1999).

Ian Tyrrell, *Crisis of the Wasteful Nation: Empire and Conservation in Theodore Roosevelt's America* (Chicago: University of Chicago Press, 2015).

James Wilson to The Forester [historians believe Gifford Pinchot authored the letter for Wilson's signature], 1 February 1905, Forest History Society. www.foresthistory.org/ASPNET/Policy/Agency_Organization/Wilson_Letter.aspx (accessed February 4, 2016).

Donald Worster, *Rivers of Empire: Water, Aridity, and the Growth of the American West* (New York: Oxford University Press, 1985).

Donald Worster, "The Troubled Nature of Wealth," in *A Passion for Nature: The Life of John Muir* (New York: Oxford University Press, 2011).

Michael J. Yochim, "Beauty and the Beet: The Dam Battles of Yellowstone National Park," *Montana: The Magazine of Western History*, Vol. 53, No. 1 (Spring 2003), 14–27.

7

Roll On

More than 10 000 people braved the scorching 102 °F heat of the Arizona/
Nevada border desert on September 30, 1935, to hear President Franklin
Roosevelt (FDR) dedicate "the greatest dam in the world," Boulder Dam (see
Figure 7.1). Begun in 1931 and completed in 1935, Boulder Dam was a world-
class construction feat accomplished during the darkest days of the Great
Depression (Congress renamed it Hoover Dam in 1947 in honor of former
president Herbert Hoover and after the death of his rival FDR). Built by the
Bureau of Reclamation and 21 000 laborers, it was the highest dam on earth
at the time, and even today its graceful, almost delicate arching form gleams
in the Black Canyon as it holds back twice the annual flow of the once-
raging lower Colorado River. The dam was a triumph of human ingenuity
and innovation.

In many ways, Boulder Dam stands as a monument to the federal government's rising power over the West's economy and environment during the
period between the end of World War I and 1940. The region's relationship
to the rest of the nation remained largely unchanged during this interval between the wars as the West continued its frenzied exploitation of raw materials such as food, timber, ores, and petroleum to fuel eastern factories,
support western development, and expand foreign trade. But unlike the rest
of the country, much of the West did not enjoy the Roaring Twenties economic
boom before the Great Depression bust. Instead, the region's heavy reliance
on natural resource extraction sent it on a rollercoaster of economic boom

Losing Eden: An Environmental History of the American West, First Edition. Sara Dant.
© 2017 John Wiley & Sons, Inc. Published 2017 by John Wiley & Sons, Inc.

Figure 7.1 Boulder Dam and Power House, November 23, 1935. Source: Reproduced with permission of Weber State University, Stewart Library, Special Collections.

and bust – California mostly boomed while the inter-mountain West mostly busted – nearly a full decade before the 1929 stock market crash jolted the rest of the country, revealing the environmental toll that market-based decisions wrought. Conservation ideals remained viable in the West during the lull between the wars, as reclamation and new federal agencies like the Soil Conservation Service promoted the wise *use* of nature. But as extraction continued to link inextricably the region's environment and economy, there was little consideration for long-term sustainability. Too few really asked, "At what cost?"

In the summer of 1914, Europe collapsed into war. The United States attempted to remain "neutral in thought as well as in action" under President Woodrow Wilson, but the truth was that the US cared a great deal about who won "the Great War." (It didn't become World War I until there was a second "great war" and we began numbering them.) The nation's ties were far stronger with the Allies, with Great Britain in particular, though German immigrants had swelled the ranks of the American population in recent decades. Long our primary trading partner, Great Britain and the United States had also enjoyed increasingly strong diplomatic relations since Theodore Roosevelt's tenure in the White House. By 1917, the United States could no longer ignore the carnage across the Atlantic, and it reluctantly joined the war, as Wilson declared, "to make the world safe for democracy." Despite the nation's April entry into the fray, however, it took nearly a year before the full strength of American troops found its way to the front. In the meantime, the United States became the Allies' primary materials supplier. To facilitate the most efficient production and distribution of critical war goods, the federal government created the War Industries Board (WIB) and tapped into the natural resource wealth of the West.

The WIB's influence on the western economy, and indirectly on the western environment, was significant. During its two-year administration (1917–1919), the agency set industrial production quotas and prices, implemented wage hikes to keep down labor unrest, and allocated raw materials to key manufacturers. The result was a spectacular 20% increase in industrial production. While production and labor incentives primarily affected the East, the WIB's influence over raw materials had long-term consequences for the West. The agency became directly involved in shaping the region's extractive economy with slogans such as "Food will win the war," "Save Gasoline, It's a War Necessity," and "Uncle Sam says – garden to cut food costs." On January 1, 1919, however, the federal government brought this massive agency's broad powers over the national economy to a screaming halt. The guns of the Great War had fallen mercifully silent the preceding November, and with the cease-fire came the end to the nation's federally managed economy. In the East, factories attempted to re-tool from war to peace-time production – from tanks to washing machines – even as labor unrest erupted into deadly strikes. In the West, however, the cancellation of WIB price supports and federal largesse contributed to the region's steady slide into economic recession and depression, ahead of much of the rest of the nation.

Initially, as the WIB set prices and encouraged production in the name of patriotism, western farmers, miners, loggers, and oil drillers answered the call. The result was an unprecedented expansion of extraction. During the 1910s, above-average rainfall across the Great Plains washed away earlier concerns (and experiences) that the region might not be the best place to raise wheat and corn. Federal WIB incentives and the still-active Homestead Act, which granted land to individuals, encouraged farmers to till previously unplowed prairies and "send wheat to the Allies!" This demand only grew after late 1917, when Europe's primary wheat producer Russia, pulled out of the war to contend with her own communist revolution. The United States, especially the West, stepped into the void.

WIB price supports also helped keep mines and timber companies operating at full capacity. At the WIB's behest, mining companies ramped up production to meet wartime demands and shifted their priorities from precious metals such as gold and silver to industrial metals such as copper, zinc, and molybdenum (a metal alloy). Ore extraction had always exacted a steep environmental toll on the lands of the West, but the twentieth century ushered in a devastating new practice: open-pit mining. Open-pit mining involved epic-scale excavation; mining corporations literally moved mountains as they leveled hills and dug deep holes in the earth, crushed and processed tons of rock, and deposited the toxic tailings (leftover rubble) into huge terraced piles. Mines sprang up (or dug down) throughout the interior West, but Utah and Arizona soon surged ahead, especially once "the richest hole in the earth," Bingham Canyon, began operating. In 1906, steam shovels made their first cuts into Bingham Canyon, located 28 miles southwest of Salt Lake City, and the site soon proved that open-pit mining of low grade ores could be profitable. The demand for copper wiring skyrocketed as the Great War gathered momentum and the nation embraced electricity as the power source to drive the second Industrial Revolution. Bingham Canyon became not only one of the first but eventually the largest open-pit copper mine in the world. The scale of excavation predictably led to numerous environmental problems, including soil and groundwater contamination and the poisoning of the complex marsh and wetland ecosystems surrounding the Great Salt Lake.

Wartime priorities often overrode preservation and conservation concerns, as Bingham Canyon and the environmental consequences of open-pit mining suggest. In 1909, for example, President Theodore Roosevelt had set aside Mount Olympus National Monument on Washington's Olympic Peninsula, in part to protect its scenic beauty but also to conserve its herds of rare Roosevelt Elk. The United States Forest Service (USFS) managed the monument and adjacent national forest in the classic Gifford Pinchot model of the greatest good for the greatest number, making little distinction between the two federal classifications. The Great War took precedence, however. The monument's prime Sitka spruce forests became a prized Allied resource for airplane frame fabrication. In 1915, eager western timber barons convinced Congress to slash the size of the monument in half to facilitate both logging and mining.

Much of the newly available spruce forest was located in rugged terrain, so the USFS excavated hillsides, dynamited tunnels, and financed 36 miles of railroad track to expedite the harvest. In a bit of ironic timing, the Spruce Division Railroad laid its final tie just as the combatants declared armistice in 1918, but the scar remained. Logging of the former monument's lands continued into the 1920s as hundreds of millions of board feet of timber found its way into regional sawmills. The primary extractive challenge here was inaccessibility, a problem the USFS hoped to overcome "as other more accessible supplies are exhausted." The solution: by 1931, roads completely encircled the Olympic Mountains making formerly elusive timber more accessible.

Miners also benefitted from the downsized Olympic Monument, and their claims pockmarked the original acreage. Prospectors dug and excavated in search of gold, silver, copper, and manganese, and shipped tons of ore to regional smelters throughout the 1910s and 1920s. Only the presidency of Franklin Roosevelt brought a merciful end to the worst of the extraction. In 1933, FDR transferred management of Mount Olympus National Monument, like all national monuments, into the hands of the National Park Service (NPS). Five years later, he signed legislation that re-designated the monument as Olympic National Park and doubled its size. Depression-era work programs such as the Civilian Conservation Corps helped to develop roads within the park, but NPS management shielded Olympic from further extractive endeavors.

By the end of the 1920s, thanks in part to the war and the WIB, a new extractive industry had become king in the American West: petroleum. In 1901, the Spindletop gusher on the east Texas Gulf Coast (slightly east of the 100th meridian) had anointed the state as the oil capital of the West. Bolstered by the nearly insatiable petroleum demands of war, the region quickly became the nation's leading oil producer, pumping out more than 70% of the country's total production. The entire Lone Star State had produced a mere 1000 barrels per year in 1896; Spindletop and others like it pushed oil production to an astounding 21 million barrels per year just six years later. By 1910, oil fever had infected North Central Texas and, by the 1920s, the Texas Panhandle had joined the rush. "Wildcat" drilling dotted the landscapes of Texas and Oklahoma with oil fields, but California also joined the prospecting frenzy. It often out-produced the two traditional oil powerhouses in the first four decades of the twentieth century. During the 1920s, for example, oil remained the Golden State's largest business enterprise. But Texas surged to the zenith of petroleum production in 1930 when a wildcat driller once again struck black gold in East Texas and tapped into the biggest oil field in US history. The flows peaked in 1933, when the seemingly ubiquitous wells pumped out an astonishing 200 million barrels per year and replaced cattle and cotton as the state's leading industry. Spurred on by this liquid wealth, the rest of the state eagerly pursued black gold extraction, sinking wells in places like Odessa and Midland and along the Canadian River.

The environmental consequences of the nation's long love affair with petro-leum began almost immediately. In addition to the audio and visual blight of clanking, nodding derricks on the landscape, the extraction process posed significant health and safety risks. Crowded wells erupted into gigantic fire-balls (Spindletop itself raged as an inferno for a week in 1902) and high-pressure drilling often spewed thousands of gallons of crude oil into the air and saturated the surrounding soils with toxic sludge. Drilling and refining by-products fouled surrounding ecosystems. Sulfurous strike fumes settled like a pall over surrounding communities, for example, and the saltwater by-product the wells dredged up contaminated drinking water and got dumped in local rivers and streams, creating riparian death zones that stretched for miles. Oil also ended up in the water systems, polluting rivers and harbors, coating unsuspecting swimmers, and wreaking havoc on birds, fish, and other wildlife. Gas flares from the wells roared into the skies to burn off their (then) worthless natural gas by-product. One resident even recalled driving through east Texas at night without headlights, the roadway perfectly illuminated by the massive flames.

The booming petroleum industry weathered the transition from war to peace better than most western resource endeavors in part because the 1920s ushered in America's full-blown love affair with the automobile. The Model T was first available in 1908. It cost $850 (equivalent to about $22 600 in 2014) and was available in any color, "so long as it is black," Henry Ford said. Although Ford invented neither the automobile nor the assembly-line technique for producing it, he had perfected both by the time the United States emerged from the Great War. By the 1920s, Ford dropped the Model T price to $260 (roughly $3500 in 2014 dollars) and his company manufactured two million cars each year. Its affordable price, reliable performance, and quality workmanship put the Tin Lizzie, as the Model T was affectionately known, within the purchasing reach of ordinary Americans. Nearly half of all families owned a car by the end of the decade, but no one owned more automobiles per capita than southern Californians, who roared around with the top down through sun-drenched, beachy air. Historian Tom McCarthy has called Los Angeles "a driver's paradise … ideal for those twin pleasures of early automobiling, speeding and touring." This "Eden at the end of the road of making it in America" soon boasted "the world's greatest metropolitan freeway system, an engineering marvel that would triumphantly reconcile speed and safety." The long-term environmental repercussions of the nation's love affair with the automobile, however, would include smog, urban sprawl, abandoned automobiles, and lead pollution (lead was first sold as a fuel additive in 1923 to help engines run more smoothly). Hardly Edenic. But Americans clung tenaciously to their cars, even through the Great Depression. Despite numerous studies and growing complaints about the resultant noxious air pollution that the federal government would eventually have to address, consumers continued to prioritize automobile ownership as a conspicuous measure of success.

The federal government's growing influence in the western economy and environment was nowhere more evident than in reclamation. The legacy of Progressive-era conservationism, the Bureau of Reclamation and Army Corps of Engineers built dams and reservoirs for flood control and to harvest and hold the rare waters of the arid West's rivers. Aqueducts then delivered water to the region's growing cities, industries, and massive corporate farms, all of which demanded ever more in the name of economic growth and progress. Westerners had long since abandoned John Wesley Powell's rational proposals to settle people near water sources, expecting instead that the federal government would bring the water to the people.

"Water. It's about water," writer and historian Wallace Stegner replied succinctly when asked what a newcomer should know about California. The same could also be said of the West as a whole. In addition to wartime production incentives, federal reclamation had boomed the region's agricultural production rates and transformed the natural environment. The 1902 Newlands Reclamation Act re-purposed the American West by bringing federally subsidized water to its parched lands. The Bureau of Reclamation built 22 projects in the West during its first three decades. Those dams and water projects brought 14 million new acres under cultivation and catapulted the region to the forefront of national agricultural production. Farm output surged during the Great War to meet Allied demands for food, but as Europe slumped into recession during the 1920s and could no longer afford American foodstuffs, prices collapsed. This early-onset Depression in some parts of the West sent farmers into an economic death spiral and allowed the Bureau of Reclamation to emerge as the region's economic hero. Corporate agribusiness was the primary beneficiary as it bought out bankrupt farm families and used its wealth to monopolize scarce water resources. The federal government aided and abetted the coup.

Its first major multipurpose dam was Boulder/Hoover Dam on the lower Colorado. Begun in 1931 and completed ahead of schedule and under budget in 1935, Hoover Dam was an engineering marvel and aesthetic wonder designed to supply water and electricity primarily to southern California and provide jobs during the worst period of unemployment in the nation's history. Its spectacular success spawned 19 more major Depression-era dam projects throughout the West. These water works boomed cities like Phoenix, Los Angeles, and Las Vegas, provided cheap electricity for nascent industry in the Pacific Northwest, irrigated California mega-farms in the Central Valley, and made the Bureau one of the most powerful agencies in the federal government.

At the Boulder Dam dedication, FDR clarified the economics of reclamation. "As an unregulated river, the Colorado added little of value to the region this dam serves," he observed. Before the dam, the mighty Colorado River had been a tempestuous torrent that wound more than 1450 miles from its headwaters in the Colorado Rockies to its mouth in Mexico's Gulf of California. The only significant source of water in the vast, arid region, this fickle "Lifeline of the Southwest" also often wiped out farms, irrigation projects, and communities with massive sediment loads that roiled in its spring fury of floods. Taming such a wild beast was too daunting for private interests and so the federal government had stepped in. Congress authorized the Boulder Dam project in 1928 with little thought to the environmental costs such a monumental project would incur. As the nation sunk into the Great Depression and unemployment rates soared, however, dam construction became a rare bright spot in an otherwise grim economic landscape. Federal projects like Boulder Dam, Roosevelt argued, gave "relief to several million men and women whose earning capacity had been destroyed by the complexities and lack of thought of the economic system of the past generation."

As if uttering a mantra for the extractive West, Roosevelt continued, "Labor makes wealth. The use of materials makes wealth." And when Boulder/ Hoover Dam was finished in 1935, the world stood in awe as the waters of Lake Mead began to rise behind the 726-foot high, 1244-foot-long marvel. The dam was just the beginning, Roosevelt believed. "Across the desert and mountains to the west and south run great electric transmission lines by which factory motors, street and household lights and irrigation pumps will be operated in Southern Arizona and California." Continuing the conservation agenda of his distant cousin Theodore Roosevelt, FDR sought to use the wealth and might of the federal government to lift the West out of its economic malaise and make the desert bloom.

The Boulder/Hoover Dam not only exemplifies the dominance of and the region's dependence on the federal government during the protracted economic depression of the 1920s and 1930s, but it also illustrates the considerable environmental costs incurred by the West's continued reliance on extractive industries to fuel the region's economic engines. For environmental historian Donald Worster, "the death of the Colorado River began with Hoover Dam." For FDR, though, the commodification of such a valuable resource was an occasion for celebration: "The mighty waters of the Colorado were running unused to the sea. Today we translate them into a great national possession."

The environmental costs of such a use-it-or-lose-it wholesale redistribution of West's waters were significant. In 1935, the gates closing on Boulder/Hoover Dam near present-day Las Vegas set in motion a series of long-term consequences. First of all, the impounded Lake Mead would spread out over one of the most arid reaches of the American West, creating a gigantic evaporation pond, which in turn reduced the overall flow in the Colorado River. The dam also blocked the heavy sediment load that annually scoured down the river and replenished riparian zones and distributed fertile soil along the Colorado's banks and flood plains. Without this yearly flush, lands adjacent to the river became nutrient-deprived and salinized, and invasive plants began to take root and drive out native species. The water now flowing in the river below the dam further exacerbated the destruction of native species. For eons, the temperature of the Colorado had fluctuated with the seasons, but Boulder/Hoover Dam's turbines drew water from deep below Lake Mead's surface and then released it in a clear, cold rush downstream. Aquatic life, both floral and faunal, that had evolved in variable and murky flows now found itself bathed by clean, 46 °F water year-round. The result was predictable: today four species of native fish cling tenuously to survival under the protection of the Endangered Species Act and non-native plants have driven out much of the river's natural flora. Conservation had unintended environmental consequences. Unfortunately, Boulder/Hoover was not an anomaly, only a beginning.

The massive Grand Coulee Dam acted as the Pacific Northwest counterpart to Hoover, and salmon paid the environmental price for the dam's cheap hydropower and irrigation. Congress had authorized a study of the Columbia River system in 1925, which seemed a vast, untapped, and untamed resource. The result was a report recommending 10 dams along the Columbia's main stem, from its mouth to the Canadian border. The worsening Depression, which hit its nadir in 1932, combined with the election of Franklin Roosevelt that same year, meant that such an ambitious agenda was now feasible. Thus, in 1933, Congress authorized the Army Corps of Engineers (another reclamation arm of the federal government) and the Bureau of Reclamation to build the Bonneville Dam on the Washington/Oregon border and Grand Coulee Dam, respectively.

Bonneville's completion in 1938 paid some heed to the dam's potential for environmental destruction. Such a mighty plug, located 40 miles upstream from Portland could wreak havoc on the river's $10 million annual salmon catch, so in response to public outcry, the dam's overall structure incorporated the latest in fish ladder technology. Engineers designed a switch-backing water stairway/ladder to facilitate fish passage and allow spawning salmon effectively to scale the dam. While mature fish were mostly able to navigate this new barrier, spring smolts (young salmon) were not. These small fry depended on the Columbia's strong currents to sweep them downstream, tail first, and out to sea. But the slackwater pool behind the dam meant that the young ones had to turn around and swim, using up their scant energy reserves and also making them much more vulnerable to hungry predators. Moreover, the top entrance of the fish ladder was not easy for the little fish to find, so they often ended up either lost and milling across the length of the dam, which again made them easy prey, or getting sucked through the power-generating turbines. So long as Bonneville was the only dam on the Columbia, however, the fish ladder solution proved reasonably effective. But Bonneville was just the first of many and Coulee was no Bonneville.

Coulee was an engineering marvel, like Boulder/Hoover, and "the biggest thing on earth," boasted one booster. Congress authorized it in 1933, and the Bureau of Reclamation completed it in 1942 – like Boulder/Hoover, swiftly and under budget. Grand Coulee Dam provided irrigation and cheap hydropower to the central Washington region and promised to make the arid interior of that state into an apple and hops garden. But unlike Bonneville, Coulee made no provision for fish passage. At 550 feet in height and a stunning 5200 feet in length (the equivalent of 12 city blocks and more than three times the size of Hoover), this concrete leviathan was literally a dead end for fish, blocking spawning salmon from access to more than 1000 miles of habitat and bringing the extirpation of all anadromous species above the dam (an estimated loss of more than 1 million fish annually). In 1941, when the gates closed on the so-called Eighth Wonder of the World, tens of thousands of steelhead, Chinook, and sockeye that had surmounted more than 600 miles of Columbia River obstacles and challenges swam in bewildered circles at its base, cut off from their ancient spawning redds by the latest extractive industry of the West.

These were the costs of conservation and reclamation. And at the time, most Americans were willing to accept or ignore these environmental losses and celebrate the economic profits. Contemporary folk singer and labor activist Woody Guthrie paid homage to these dam wonders in his iconic songs "Roll On Columbia" and "Grand Coulee Dam," singing about the mighty river's power "turning our darkness to dawn." Guthrie celebrated the new reality that "at Bonneville now there are ships in the locks" and that Grand Coulee Dam, "the mightiest thing ever built by a man," could now "run the great factories and water the land." Today, there are 14 major dams on the Columbia River. Above Coulee, the river is salmon-less. For perspective, law scholar Charles Wilkinson observed that "the 1214-mile-long river, which drains an area larger than France and whose annual discharge into the ocean is more than twice that of the Nile, is now a series of placid, computer-regulated lakes." By the 1970s, a similar fate had befallen almost all of the West's major rivers, including the Colorado.

In the Southwest, the Colorado River serves as the wellspring of the region's "hydraulic society." The federal government manages the mighty river according to the so-called "Law of the River," a suite of compacts and agreements among and between Mexico and the seven states with straws in its waters. The foundation of this entangled bureaucracy is the Colorado River Compact (CRC), which some have called the western equivalent of the Constitution. Signed in 1922, during this formative interwar era, the CRC defines the (often strained) relationships and water allocations between the upper basin states (Colorado, Wyoming, Utah, and New Mexico) and the lower basin states (Arizona, Nevada, and California). Over the years, the CRC has been a lightning rod of contention particularly because the upper basin states supply the water that the lower basin states suck dry. In 1922, the CRC used an estimated annual river flow of 17.5 million acre-feet as the basis for allocation. Each basin received 7.5 million acre-feet annually, Mexico received 1.5 million acre-feet annually, and the "surplus" could be divided among the lower basin states (with everyone understanding what this really meant: California).

And the fighting began. California refused to ratify the CRC until Congress authorized the Boulder Canyon Dam project (among others benefitting California); Arizona wanted to know exactly who was getting exactly what in the lower basin or it would refuse to ratify, etc. Finally, in 1928, six of the seven states (all except Arizona) ratified and the draw-downs began in earnest. California, which adds not a drop to the Colorado River, nevertheless took the biggest drink, 4.4 million acre-feet annually, which never sat well with the other lower basin states. And significantly, for the long-term management of this resource, the 17.5 million acre-feet estimated annual flow has proved an inflated prediction rather than an accurate annual flow. Yet the once mighty river's tamed water was the elixir the arid West craved if it was to realize its potential as the nation's breadbasket.

This new grand-scale cultivation the Colorado made possible was perhaps most remarkable in California. By 1930, the Golden State was home to fully half of the entire West's population (5.5 out of 11 million). Blessed by its geography, California benefits from a weather pattern called the Pacific High – a high-pressure system that parks just off the west coast and diverts incoming storms northward, bathing the Golden State in sunshine from March through October. This fortuitous climate condition also happens to occur precisely in what environmental scientist Garrison Sposito has called "the richest agricultural region in the history of the world": the Central Valley. Cradled between the Sierra Nevadas and the Coastal Range, the Central Valley encompasses the Sacramento and San Joaquin watersheds, stretching 500 miles from Redding south to Bakersfield and varying in width between 60 and 100 miles. The late-nineteenth-century twin perfections of the transcontinental railroad and refrigerated boxcars had sent California produce coursing across the continent. New Yorkers savored "Sunkist" oranges and "Sun-Maid" raisins during the long, dreary winter months and, by the 1920s, California was producing more than 200 commercially grown crops in the thirsty and arid West. Much of this early agricultural success was the result of tapping into underground water resources. But as drought threatened the state in the late 1910s and early 1920s, an all-too-familiar "tragedy of the commons" crisis began to develop. Over-pumping depleted the resource and by the 1930s, desperate farmers turned once again to the federal government. It had the perfect solution: reclamation.

The Central Valley Project (CVP) began as a state effort in 1933, but the nation's economic collapse rendered California too cash-poor to continue and so the federal government came to its rescue in 1935. Beginning in 1937, under the Bureau of Reclamation's oversight, dam and irrigation projects began to rise from the valley floor, starting with the 48-mile-long Contra Costa Canal east of San Francisco. The project continued the following year with the erection of Shasta Dam on the Sacramento River (just north of Redding), the "keystone" of the whole CVP. By the twenty-first century, the massive plumbing project incorporated 20 dams and reservoirs, 11 power plants, 500 miles of canals, and managed water for approximately one-third of California's 9 million farmable acres. As one proud CVP workman proclaimed, "Mister, we're moving the rain!" In addition to salvaging the drought-threatened farms of the Valley, the "golden faucet," as Worster has called the CVP, would also bring 3 million newly irrigated acres on-line. The beneficiaries of this federal subsidy were mostly corporate agribusinesses. As analysts Edwin Wilson and Marion Clawson write, "this degree of concentration of land ownership is rarely encountered in the United States."

As with Hoover and Grand Coulee, this hydraulic "progress" in the name of conservation came at a disastrous environmental cost. Four species of native salmon that had called the rivers of the Central Valley home for tens of thousands of years found themselves cut off from their primordial redds by the massive concrete slabs that generated power for cities and provided navigation, irrigation, and flood control. The destruction of riparian zones along the rivers, loss of sedimentation, alteration of stream flows and temperatures, and the inundation of Native archeological sites were also added to the ledger. And perhaps most ironically, the rapid expansion of arable lands inspired by the flood of cheap, federal water accelerated the depletion of the Valley's groundwater aquifers as zealous corporate growers out-planted the water supply. This "tragedy of the commons" cost-reckoning was not on the minds of contemporary California farmers or the Bureau of Reclamation, however. As Worster concludes, "together these groups could proudly say that they had forced the earth to obey their wishes, that they had turned 'waste' into wealth, and never mind what or whom that wealth was for."

The most dramatic ecological repercussion of the West's heedless economic boosterism, however, was the Dust Bowl, arguably the single greatest environmental disaster in American history. Between 1931 and 1937, an estimated 100 million acres of the wind-whipped, over-tilled soils of the Great Plains blackened skies as far away as Washington DC and New York City and blanketed ships hundreds of miles out in the Atlantic with dust. It also bankrupted thousands of homesteading farm families who had answered the siren call of agricultural demand during the booming war years and revealed the folly of federal policies that encouraged the cultivation of previously unplowed prairie lands. The Dust Bowl was a calamity borne of hubris and unfettered agricultural expansion during the Great War, but it had a long history behind it.

In 1819 and 1820, explorer Stephen Long carried out a federally sponsored scientific expedition to the Great Plains (and the heart of the future Dust Bowl) and concluded that "it is almost wholly unfit for cultivation, and of course uninhabitable by a people depending upon agriculture for their subsistence." Indeed, the region's only benefit, Long conceded, was as a "barrier to prevent too great an extension of our population westward" and his maps identified the entire area as the "Great American Desert." The federal government ignored its own experts. Four decades later, Congress passed the original Homestead Act of 1862 (granting 160 acres, the average size of a Virginia farm) to encourage settlement on western lands, and then followed it with the 1909 Enlarged Homestead Act (granting 320 acres per adult) to entice settlers onto the more marginal, un-irrigable lands of the Great Plains. Thousands answered the call.

Similar to the demise of the buffalo discussed in Chapter 3, the causes of the Dust Bowl were complex and intertwined. Like a bullseye centered over western Kansas, the affected area radiated into eastern Colorado and New Mexico and down across the panhandles of Texas and Oklahoma (see Figure 7.2). Reclamation projects may have slaked thirsty settlements in other parts of the West, but these farmers were counting on rainfall to water their ambitious crops. They shouldn't have. Farmers who flocked to the Plains to grow "wheat to win the war" planted intensively and aggressively, failing to practice crop rotation or fallow their stressed soils. Their efficient plows cut deeply into the prairie soil, tearing out deep-rooted bunch grasses that anchored the topsoil and preserved moisture. Once farmers harvested their shallow-rooted wheat for market, they failed to plant cover crops to protect the exposed soil. Unregulated grazing of cattle further eroded the public domain. And then the specter of drought, always a major factor on the Great Plains, reappeared in the 1930s, when these overworked, exposed, marginal soils were at their most vulnerable. The result was disaster. Great roiling dust storms picked up the precious top soil and carried it away in black blizzards of choking dust. As one farmer lamented, "We're through... Our fences are buried, the house is hidden to the eaves, and our pasture, which was kept from blowing by the grass, has been buried and is worthless now."

Worster has argued that this epic environmental collapse was the inevitable consequence of unfettered capitalism, unwise federal policies (the Enlarged Homestead Act), and above-average rainfall totals that lured settlers onto untenable homesteads, dooming them to failure and the land to destruction. Other environmental historians have suggested that it was not over-plowing that was the major catalyst for the so-called Dirty Thirties, but drought, and that as awful as it was, the "black rollers" that could reduce visibility to just a few feet were part of the natural cycle of the plains and had occurred before in the region's longue durée/deep time history. As with Pleistocene megafauna extinctions and the near extinction of the bison, the answer likely lies at the nexus of these explanations, in the complicated interactions between humans and their environment.

The destruction of the Dust Bowl launched hundreds of thousands of Americans on a westward trek to California, Oregon, and Washington in a desperate search for jobs, much like the Joad family in John Steinbeck's *The Grapes of Wrath* (1939), but it also inspired some more environmentally

THE DUST BOWL

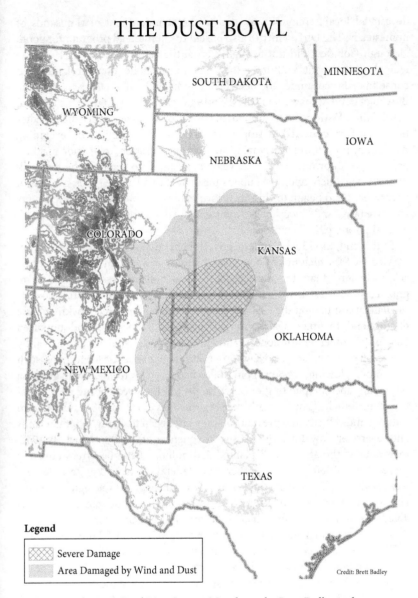

Figure 7.2 The Dust Bowl Map. Source: Map drawn by Brett Badley and reproduced with permission.

conscious interactions with the land. The 1920s marked the population high point on the western Great Plains; the region has been in steady decline ever since. The combination of the Great Depression and the Dust Bowl devastated local economies and led to the abandonment of thousands of homesteads. The Dirty Thirties also busted the homestead program for good, although Congress did not formally repeal the act until 1976. In 1934, the federal government withdrew the remaining public domain lands and consolidated them under the new Taylor Grazing Service, which became the Bureau of Land Management (BLM) in 1946 when it merged with the General Land Office. Within a year, more than 65 million acres fell under the jurisdiction of the Service tasked "to stop injury to the public grazing lands [excluding Alaska], by preventing overgrazing and soil deterioration, to provide for their orderly use, improvement and development, [and] to stabilize the livestock industry dependent upon the public range." By the end of the 1930s, the federal government had begun to shift its priorities away from free land enticements and giveaways and toward better management and conservation of the West's natural resources and environment.

To this end, in 1935, the federal government created the Soil Conservation Service (SCS), which linked a healthy economy to a healthy environment by acknowledging that "the wastage of soil and moisture resources on farm, grazing, and forest lands … is a menace to the national welfare." Like its regulatory companion the Grazing Service, which monitored stockmen's use of rangelands to protect against overgrazing, the SCS supervised and supported farmers by implementing conservation practices designed to maintain healthy and productive landscapes. New conservation-style wise *use* techniques, such as contour plowing, strip cropping (alternating crops to maximize growing potential), and the planting of cover crops and hundreds of miles of windbreak shelterbelts (north–south running treelines along the 98th meridian to reduce wind velocity and prevent soil erosion) began to restore blighted lands and reverse or slow down the worst consequences of the Dust Bowl. By 1942, for example, the agency had planted 220 million shelterbelt trees covering more than 18 000 miles. Another new federal agency, the Resettlement Administration, bought out failed homesteads throughout the region, eventually amassing nearly 9 million acres. This program not only removed unsuitable lands from cultivation, but also became the foundation for a new category of public lands: the national grasslands (managed by the US Forest Service).

The SCS produced mixed results, however. The SCS's scientific agronomy had the potential to make real in-roads into people's understanding about the fragility of the natural environment and to encourage questions about long-term sustainability that conservation efforts often failed to consider. Instead, the unfortunate lesson that many learned from the Dust Bowl was that technology could provide a "fix" even for a disaster of this magnitude. Rather than accept that the High Plains were poorly suited ecologically to raising wheat and grain crops, for example, farmers used new SCS techniques and technology to continue farming *in spite* of the environment. Fickle rainfall had always been a hazard, but technology came to the rescue on this front, too. By the late 1930s, farmers realized that there was water everywhere on the Great Plains, it was just hidden underground in the massive Ogallala Aquifer, one of the largest subsurface water tables in the world. Newly minted V8 engine pumps lifted this precious commodity to the surface and effectively washed away Great Plains aridity with arching tut-tut sprinklers of precious "rain" (without any consideration for sustainability). SCS-supported shelter belts halted soil erosion, to be sure, but the exotic fast-growing trees planted *in* the shelter belts (such as Russian olive and saltcedar) out-competed native vegetation and fundamentally altered prairie plant and animal communities. Worster laments that a region that had once teemed with biological diversity like an American Serengeti was now "no more interesting than a parking lot."

Ironically, then, even an event as epic as the Dust Bowl failed to capture the long-term ecological attention of the nation. The resolution of this crisis was a continued emphasis on western extraction and a conservation effort, especially at the federal level, to "control" and "harvest" wild nature, whether by damming the mighty Columbia and Colorado rivers or instructing farmers in the art of contour plowing. Americans were not humbled by the Dirty Thirties, but challenged. By the 1940s, many felt they had won the "war" against the environment. The mighty weapon of technology seemed invincible. As Guthrie sang, "These mighty men labored by day and by night, matching their strength 'gainst the river's wild flight, through rapids and falls they won the hard fight, so roll on, Columbia, roll on." In 1930, the population of the entire American West was just 30 million people, about the same as the single eastern state of New York. Yet by the early 1940s, more than $40 million in federal funds had flowed onto the Great Plains alone, and that federal largesse yielded approximately $37 million in farm benefits – hardly a savvy return on investment. The many had and would continue to subsidize the few in order to extract wealth from the West and make this arid region "bloom." Roll on, indeed.

Suggested Reading

Bernard Baruch, "American Industry in War: A Report of the War Industries Board," in *American Industry in the War: A Report of the War Industries Board* (Washington DC: Government Printing Office, 1921), 61, 63–67, 69, 98–100. www.enotes.com/topics/american-industry-war-report-war-industries-board (accessed February 4, 2016).

Ken Burns, *The Dust Bowl*, two-part/four-hour documentary (PBS, 2012).

Jeffrey P. Cohn, "Resurrecting the Dammed: A Look at Colorado River Restoration," *Bioscience*, Vol. 51, No. 12, 998–1003. http://bioscience.oxfordjournals.org/content/51/12/998.full (accessed February 4, 2016).

Geoff Cunfer, "The Southern Great Plains Wind Erosion Maps of 1936–1937," *Agricultural History*, Vol. 85, No. 4 (Fall 2011), 540–559.

Mark Fiege, "The Weedy West: Mobile Nature, Boundaries, and Common Space in the Montana Landscape," *Western Historical Quarterly*, Vol. 36 (Spring 2005), 22–47.

Guy Fringer, *Olympic National Park: An Administrative History* (Seattle: National Park Service, 1990), 34–54. http://npshistory.com/publications/olym/adhi.pdf (accessed February 4, 2016).

Stephen Johnson, Gerald Haslam, and Robert Dawson, "Chapter 1: An Overview," in *The Great Central Valley: California's Heartland* (Berkeley: University of California Press, 1993), 4–25.

Tom McCarthy, *Auto Mania: Cars, Consumers, and the Environment* (New Haven: Yale University Press, 2009).

Frederick Simpich, "More Water for California's Great Central Valley," *National Geographic*, Vol. 90 (November 1946), 645–664.

Joseph E. Taylor, III, "El Niño and Vanishing Salmon: Culture, Nature, History, and the Politics of Blame," *Western Historical Quarterly*, Vol. 29, No. 4 (Winter 1998), 437–457.

Magner White, "We're Moving the Rain," *Saturday Evening Post*, Vol. 212, No. 44 (April 1940), 18–19, 36–42.

8

Booming the West

"We abuse land because we regard it as a commodity belonging to us," wrote forester-ecologist Aldo Leopold in 1948. "When we see land as a community to which we belong, we may begin to use it with love and respect." This simple yet profound conclusion formed the foundation of his "land ethic" and it would become, in time, a bedrock of the environmental movement in America. The primary tenet of Leopold's land ethic was that economic considerations alone were *not* the most important. "A thing is right when it tends to preserve the integrity, stability, and beauty of the biotic community," he explained. "It is wrong when it tends otherwise." Leopold's beliefs derived from a lifetime spent observing the world around him at his various postings throughout the West as a US Forest Service ranger. Leopold had not begun his career as a man concerned about the costs of development and resource consumption. Indeed, he had actively advocated for and participated in the "eradication" of "varmint" species like wolves during his early years in Arizona and New Mexico. But his experiences throughout the West began to reveal the great interconnectedness of all species and their environments.

In perhaps his most famous essay, "Thinking Like a Mountain," Leopold acknowledged his earlier role in facilitating the extermination of wolves in the West and articulated the true costs of his shortsightedness:

> In those days we had never heard of passing up a chance to kill a wolf. In a second we were pumping lead into the pack, but with more excitement than

Losing Eden: An Environmental History of the American West, First Edition. Sara Dant.
© 2017 John Wiley & Sons, Inc. Published 2017 by John Wiley & Sons, Inc.

accuracy: how to aim a steep downhill shot is always confusing. When our rifles were empty, the old wolf was down, and a pup was dragging a leg into impassible slide-rocks.

We reached the old wolf in time to watch a fierce green fire dying in her eyes. I realized then, and have known ever since, that there was something new to me in those eyes – something known only to her and to the mountain. I was young then, and full of trigger-itch; I thought that because fewer wolves meant more deer, that no wolves would mean hunters' paradise. But after seeing the green fire die, I sensed that neither the wolf nor the mountain agreed with such a view.

Leopold's epiphany was an insight into what ecologists call a "trophic cascade": a situation where the removal of one species ripples, or cascades, through the food chain or ecosystem. In Leopold's case, the removal of the West's wolves produced an eruption in their prey species, deer in particular. Without the balance that wolves provided, exploding deer populations devoured every leaf and blade, denuding entire mountainsides and leaving the south-facing slopes wrinkled under the weight of their trails. In time, overpopulated deer herds collapsed, too. "I now suspect," Leopold concluded, "that just as a deer herd lives in mortal fear of its wolves, so does a mountain live in mortal fear of its deer."

When he died in 1948, Leopold was at the vanguard of what would become the environmental movement of the 1960s. In 1949, his thoughtful and thought-provoking essays, such as "Thinking Like a Mountain," appeared in the posthumously published *A Sand County Almanac*, which became a handbook and manifesto for later activists. He was among the first to ask the simple question: at what practical and moral cost do we alter the world around us to suit human comforts and needs? In the years between 1945 and 1960, his was a lonely lament and oft-ignored query, in part because the post-war period of "go-go" development in the West seemed almost universally positive. The thought of questioning such progress rarely entered mainstream public consciousness. The United States emerged from World War II more powerful than any nation had ever been, and her citizens reaped the rewards of success in a booming, consumer-oriented economy. Ironically, this emphasis on consumption opened American minds to a greater acceptance of conservation and preservation ideas, but in a way that continued to define natural resources and parks as commodified consumer goods. Leopold's own experiences in the environments of the West shaped his concerns, and by the end of the first six decades of the twentieth century, they would assume a far greater influence. But that day was still in the future.

Between 1945 and 1960, the land-as-commodity idea prevailed and the federal government's role in shaping both the environment and the economy of the twentieth century West accelerated dramatically. The Pacific Theater in World War II significantly expanded federal presence and influence in the region in the form of airplane manufacturing and ship building plants, military installations, and research facilities. The decades following the war continued this trend as massive federal funding coursed into the region for Cold War weapons development, power production, and transportation and recreation infrastructure. Indeed, by 1958, federal expenditures exceeded tax revenues in all but three of the 11 western states. In other words, western states got more money *from* the federal government than they contributed *to* it in taxes, etc. Uncle Sam also owned more than half the land in the Rocky Mountains and Great Basin, and its land management agencies subsidized the West's developing economies. Moreover, in the 15 years after the war the population west of the Mississippi River boomed, from 32 million to 45 million, and by 1962, California, with 19 million by itself, surpassed New York, becoming the most populous state in the union. The extensive influence of the federal government in the West during this period erased the last vestiges of colonialism and dependency, and ushered in a new era of financial stability and economic and industrial leadership. Federal largesse ensured that this part of the country fully participated in the burgeoning prosperity of the 1950s. In these heady, pro-development times, few heeded Leopold's admonitions or questioned the long-term costs to ecosystems and human health.

In the post-war period, expansionism did not remain confined to traditional extractive endeavors such as farming, mining, timber harvest, and petroleum drilling, the familiar components of western "progress." For example, between 1945 and 1960, the American West became central to the development of the most environmentally destructive innovation humans have thus far imagined and created: the atomic bomb (see Figure 8.1). Work on the top secret effort known as the Manhattan Project, began in 1939 and much of the research and development occurred at Los Alamos, New Mexico, near Santa Fe. Here scientists worked to convert radioactive uranium – much of it mined in Utah, New Mexico, and Colorado – into the most powerful explosive devices ever built. They succeeded. On July 16, 1945, the United States Army conducted the first full-scale detonation test, known as Trinity, in the deserts of Alamagordo, New Mexico. It billowed an iconic mushroom cloud 7.5 miles into the sky, scoured out a crater 250 feet wide, and incinerated the surrounding sand into glass. With the blast, the United States ushered in the atomic age, and in less than a month, it unleashed these weapons of mass destruction on the cities of Hiroshima (August 6) and Nagasaki (August 9), Japan, with the hope of bringing a swift end to World War II in the Pacific. It did. The resulting deaths of 200 000 Japanese people, most of them civilian, and the threat of a third bomb (which the United States did not have) was powerfully persuasive. The Japanese emperor surrendered to the Allied Powers on August 15, 1945, and the most destructive war in the planet's history finally came to a close.

Figure 8.1 April 15, 1955, atomic test at the Nevada Test Site. Source: Reproduced with permission of the National Nuclear Security Administration, Nevada Field Office.

But once released, the atomic genie failed to return to its bottle and the environmental consequences were high. In the aftermath of World War II, the United States and the Soviet Union engaged in a high-stakes competition for the allegiance of countries across the globe called the Cold War. This freezing of diplomatic relations manifested itself in many ways, but atomically, it led to an all-out arms race. In 1945, the United States was the only country in the world with an atomic bomb and this monopoly elevated it to elite super-power status. Thus, in 1947, to maintain this atomic advantage, the federal government folded the Manhattan Project into the newly created United States Atomic Energy Commission and charged it with maintaining nuclear superiority. Bigger, better, more powerful weapons like the hydrogen bomb were the solution. And the country demonstrated its nuclear might regularly at the Nevada Test Site, located about 65 miles northwest of Las Vegas. Between 1951 and 1992, the United States detonated more than 1000 bombs. In the 1950s, these military tests were also tourist attractions; visitors sat in bleachers wearing "protective" glasses and watched mushroom clouds, often visible for 100 miles in every direction, roil into the skies like a mighty firework display.

But these mushroom clouds bore a sinister cargo. As the smoke and ash dispersed in the wind, radiation rained down, spreading sickness and related cancers to unsuspecting "downwinders" – people living in the nuclear fallout zones, which included 5 counties in northern Arizona, 6 counties in central Nevada, and 10 counties in southern Utah. Within a few years, reports surfaced of a "significant excess" of leukemia deaths suffered by children in Utah who had been exposed to the fallout during the 1951–1958 period. Abnormally high rates of other cancers, thyroid diseases, and genetic defects also emerged in these same areas and the Nevada Test Site remains one of the most radioactively contaminated sites in the United States to the present day. Ultimately, in 1963, the Partial Test Ban Treaty limited signers to underground testing after this date, to prevent further fallout hazards, but for many, the damage had already been done. In 1990, Congress passed the Radiation Exposure Compensation Act, which provides monetary compensation for workers involved in the actual testing as well as for individuals who have contracted cancer or other radiation-related diseases.

Nevadans and Utahans were not the only victims in the atomic West. In 1943, the United States had also built a nuclear production complex at Hanford in Washington state. Like the Nevada Test Site, Hanford became a major source of radioactive soil, water, and air pollution. Hanford discharged water used to cool the super-heated nuclear reactors that manufactured plutonium (used in both the Trinity test and the Nagasaki bomb) directly into the Columbia River. Its reactors released radioactive isotopes into the air, resulting in contamination plumes that reached the Washington and Oregon coastal waters and spread downwinder symptoms throughout the Pacific Northwest and Canada. One downwinder recalled that one of his earliest childhood memories was "many hospital visits and surgeries, being paralyzed and in [an] iron lung. Then, starting school with crutches and braces, and with sores all over my body, my teeth rotting out. My hair fell out twice. Waiting for the births of cows and sheep, praying that they would not be deformed ... cows with two heads, 6 or 7 feet, some without eyeballs and so on." The 75 000 square miles surrounding the Hanford Reactor remains the most contaminated nuclear site in the country and its fallout has continued to plague the food chain of the entire region, appearing in beef, cow's milk, fish (especially salmon), and human breast milk.

In addition to inspiring and funding the West's atomic evolution and revolution, the federal government continued to engineer the western environment to facilitate settlement and power production. Environmental historian Donald Worster has called the West's extensive and extravagant waterworks a "hydraulic society," one dependent upon large-scale water relocation via irrigation and dam infrastructure. Historians Richard Etulain and Michael Malone put it more simply: "every major river of the West came, to a greater or lesser extent, under the control of the dam builders and water pumpers." During the Great Depression, the Bureau of Reclamation (and the other federal dam-building agency, the Army Corps of Engineers) had been busy harnessing the West's mightiest rivers for power, irrigation, storage, and flood control. Behemoth construction projects such as the Hoover and Grand Coulee dams had brought jobs and cheap hydropower to the region during the depths of economic collapse. As a result, the public viewed these dams positively as symbols of American ingenuity and prosperity, and the federal agencies that built them as economic saviors. World War II's acceleration of western industrial and commercial development had also ramped up power demands and the call for more dams grew to a crescendo. The Bureau, along with the Army Corps of Engineers, was ready and willing to build.

The Bureau of Reclamation quickly realized that the best way to ensure full compliance with the 1922 Colorado River Compact allocations, which divvied up the annual flow among eight western states and Mexico, was to store as much of the river as possible behind major dams along its serpentine course (see Figure 8.2). Their grand dam plan was the Colorado River Storage Project (CRSP) – a 10-dam mega-project that would simultaneously solve the desperate needs of thirsty farmers in the upper basin, who had barely survived the Great Depression, and keep the spigot on full blast for California's burgeoning agricultural economy. Without such development, the *Salt Lake Tribune* cautioned its readers, Utahns were "likely to awaken to find their water in California." In June of 1950, to thwart this unthinkable outcome, the Bureau proposed and the Secretary of the Interior approved construction of a dam at Echo Park in Utah's Dinosaur National Monument "in the interest of the greatest public good." It was classic conservationism.

Established in 1915, Dinosaur National Monument lies on the northern border of Utah and Colorado. President Franklin Roosevelt had significantly expanded the monument in 1938 to encompass both its scientifically important dinosaur bone quarry and its scenic splendor. One reporter described the area as "seven or eight Zion cañons strung together, end to end; with Yosemite Valley dropped down in the middle of them." In spite of these

100th
Meridian

Legend

▫ Dams

— Rivers

▦▦▦ 100th Meridian

Credit: Brett Badley

U.S. Department of the Interior - Bureau of Reclamation - Maps for Reclamation Dams - http://www.usbr.gov/projects/maps.jsp

Figure 8.2 Bureau of Reclamation Dams in the American West. Source: Map drawn by Brett Badley and reproduced with permission.

superlatives, the monument languished during the 1930s and 1940s; its remote location meant that visitors rarely made the trek to explore its rivers and canyons and Congress spent no money to encourage them. But not everyone ignored Dinosaur. Federal hydropower generated by the proposed Echo Park dam would benefit residents across four neighboring states, sparking economic growth, while flood control measures promised to tame the wild Green River. These benefits would come at the cost of a free-flowing river, however.

The Bureau's proposal unleashed a major battle between dam advocates and opponents, as both sides sensed that Echo Park would act as a test case for the sanctity of the National Park System. Several other reserves faced similar pressure for development. For preservationists in particular, the prospect of flooding Echo Park rekindled painful memories of the loss of the Hetch Hetchy Valley in Yosemite National Park some 40 years earlier. The Director of the National Park Service, Newton Drury, protested that such a dam would flood a monument set aside for preservation and resigned rather than oversee its construction. Olaus Murie, president of the Wilderness Society, echoed John Muir's laments regarding the fate of Hetch Hetchy when he wrote that an un-dammed Dinosaur Monument was essential "for our happiness, our spiritual welfare, for our success in dealing with the confusions of a materialistic and sophisticated civilization."

Led by the Sierra Club and the Wilderness Society, a coalition of nearly 80 national and more than 200 state organizations joined the campaign to block the Echo Park Dam. Through a barrage of media – coffee-table books, photographs, and articles – preservationists touted the scenic beauty of Dinosaur, describing the sinuous canyons and quiet places that the dam's reservoir would inundate. In 1950, *Harper's* columnist and native Utahan Bernard DeVoto argued, "No one has asked the American people whether or not they want their sovereign rights, and those of their descendants, in their own publicly reserved beauty spots wiped out. Thirty-two million of them visited the national parks in 1949. More will visit them this year. The attendance will keep on increasing as long as they are worth visiting, but a good many of them will not be worth visiting if engineers are let loose on them." Perhaps the most compelling publication, however, was a photographic collection edited by noted western writer Wallace Stegner entitled *This is Dinosaur: Echo Park Country and Its Magic Rivers.* The publicity generated a blizzard of mail that ran 80-1 against the dam and forced congressional representatives to remove the dam from the Colorado River Storage Project authorizing legislation. Indeed, when the CRSP became law in April of 1956, it contained a provision that specifically prohibited the violation of national monument and park boundaries with dams and/or their reservoirs.

The Echo Park controversy was a seminal moment in the history of wild lands preservation as it established the developmental inviolability of the nation's parks and monuments and presaged the later 1964 passage of the Wilderness Act. But the preservationists' victory carried a high price, unknown to them at the time. In saving Echo Park, they had agreed not to oppose the rest of the CRSP, which would go on to build a number of other dams including one in Glen Canyon. Like Echo Park, Glen Canyon was virtually unknown in 1956. Its supine canyons and scenic wonders along the Utah–Arizona border had attracted few visitors. But the Glen Canyon site remained in the final CRSP bill and once dam construction began that same year, the Sierra Club hurriedly tried to compensate, issuing yet another illustrated book entitled *The Place No One Knew: Glen Canyon on the Colorado*. It was too little, too late. A decade later, when the dam's floodgates closed, much of Glen Canyon slipped quietly under the rising waters of Lake Powell. The dam became the most important link in the CRSP, conserving 64% of the project's total water storage and generating 75% of its power output. In 1958, Congress established the Glen Canyon National Recreation Area (NRA), which in 2014 attracted more than 2.4 million visitors, pumped nearly $175 million into the local economy, and sustained 2218 jobs. But the environmental costs had been high. The Sierra Club's leader, David Brower, considered the loss of Glen Canyon the major failure of his life and "the biggest sin I ever committed," and the episode reminded preservationists of the costs of bargaining away places no one knew.

In neighboring Idaho, private power development also led to environmental problems. The 1958 "Oxbow Incident" involved the Idaho Power Company's horribly failed attempt to maintain viable salmon runs by transporting migrating salmon around the Oxbow Dam, under construction on the Snake River. The sheer bulk of the dam presented a formidable obstacle to the spawning fish, so Idaho Power proposed an audacious solution to fulfill its obligation to preserve the salmon runs: it would scoop up the migrating salmon with skimmers, load them into trucks, haul them around the dam, and then redeposit them in the river. This expensive fish-out-of-water proposal that prioritized the economy over the environment failed. Disaster struck the fall 1958 Chinook salmon and steelhead run when malfunctioning traps, poorly organized trucking – with fish caught on the Idaho side of the river, while the transport trucks waited on the Oregon side – and the isolation of most of that year's run in an unaerated pool below the dam led to what historian William Ashworth called "one of the greatest anadromous fish disasters in history." In its December 1958 report on the "Oxbow Incident," the US Fish and Wildlife Service estimated a loss of about 4000 adult Chinook salmon and steelhead. It also estimated "that 50 percent of the 14,000 salmon which were collected and transported around the project did not survive to spawn. The success of the 3,700 steelhead trout which were passed remains to be determined." In addition to the fish tragedy, "the monetary loss from [the salmon's] failure to spawn was literally incalculable." Furthermore, the summary report on the "Oxbow Incident" concluded that these "losses could have been avoided, and that there is little justification for sacrificing this valuable living fish resource to a desire to expedite … the hydroelectric power development of the project." The drama of thousands of dead salmon drew national attention to the shortcomings of technology. The next year, when the federal Army Corps of Engineers opened hearings on the revision of their original development plan for the Columbia River system in the wake of the "incident," they drew an audience with a clear concern for "the fish problem."

In January of 1961, the Idaho State Department of Fish and Game added another voice by compiling a summary report that detailed the impact of dams on salmon. The conclusions were stunning: a decline of more than 50% in the numbers of fall Chinook that reached the spawning grounds on the Middle Snake in 1958 and 1959 as compared to 1957; downstream migrant salmon and steelhead mortality rates as high as 78% in 1959; and the "apparent failure of most of the million fall chinook downstream migrants estimated to have entered the Brownlee Reservoir in 1959 to either pass through the reservoir or to be attracted to and trapped by the artificial outlets or skimmers." The causes for the dramatic losses to the salmon and steelhead populations were many and varied. Two other dams on the Columbia River (downstream from the Snake) further complicated fish passage, McNary Dam (1953) and the Dalles Dam (1957), as did the Ice Harbor Dam on the lower Snake (1961). The fall 1957 runs also sustained "considerable loss," in the words of the Assistant Secretary of the Interior, due to a malfunctioning fish trap at Brownlee Dam. Further losses occurred as a result of the above-discussed "Oxbow Incident" in 1958. Many of the downstream migration facilities at both dams, most notably the fish "skimmers" at Brownlee, failed in both 1957 and again in 1958, during the height of the downstream migration. Thousands of other smolts died as they passed through the dam turbines.

Idaho Power eventually agreed to "compensate" for the salmon and steelhead that its dams exterminated by building an anadromous fish hatchery below Oxbow – technology to the rescue once again. But at what cost? True enough, the Echo Park Dam controversy and the Snake's salmon slaughter began to sour the public on big dams, but not before significant damage had been done. Today, for example, the more than 400 dams that riddle the Columbia River Basin block fish access to an estimated 40–60% of original salmon and steelhead habitat. Hatchery fish also introduce entirely new problems into the ecosystem: they "stray" rather than return home to their natal spawning grounds, displace wild stock and contaminate them with diseases, and are less productive overall. The environmental consequences radiate out from this loss in a trophic cascade that is incalculable.

Development won the day throughout the West during the 1950s. The Colorado River Storage Project ultimately led to the building of six major dams on the Colorado River and its tributaries, the Green, San Juan, and Gunnison rivers, and to numerous other mammoth water management projects throughout the upper basin states. One of the largest of these projects, the Central Utah Project (CUP), which allows Utah to develop its 1922 CRP allocated share of Colorado River water, has quadrupled in costs compared with the initial estimates. Yet it is the extensive "hydraulic society" of the West that makes possible the lush lawns, emerald golf courses, air conditioning, and Las Vegas fountains that both residents and tourists demand in such an arid environment. Water projects also grow the lettuce, tomatoes, cotton, almonds, roses, and other mass-produced agricultural goods that flow from central California and the deserts around Phoenix to stock the nation's grocery stores with fresh fruits and vegetables 365 days a year. Historian Marc Reisner complained "that despite heroic efforts and many billions of dollars, all we have managed to do in the arid West is turn a Missouri-size section green – and that conversion has been wrought mainly with nonrenewable ground-water." But in the period between 1945 and 1960, few people questioned the costs of such amenities and simply enjoyed their seeming success at making the desert bloom.

In addition to bombs and dams, the federal government's extensive influence over the western environment was also evident in its development of the interstate highway system. Not surprisingly Americans' love affair with the automobile directly coincided with the rapid expansion of the nation's roads. After the war, as industry spanned from Atlantic to Pacific and drivers took to the open roads for recreation and tourism, the need for an efficient transcontinental transportation network became readily apparent. In response to these demands, President Dwight Eisenhower championed a massive federally funded public works program to knit the country together. Authorized in 1956, the Interstate Highway System was inspired by the highly efficient German Autobahn, which Eisenhower had experienced (and appreciated) first-hand during his tenure as Supreme Commander of the Allied Forces during World War II. Eisenhower initially called for the construction of 41 000 miles of "broader ribbons across the land," linking the nation's major cities in an interconnected network. Funding for the massive road-grid derived from federal fuel taxes, so that user fees directly paid for the majority of construction and maintenance costs. And conveniently, East–West-running Interstates are numbered evenly and increase from South to North, while North–South-running Interstates have odd numbers and increase from West to East.

The Interstate fundamentally changed the nation and shaped the American West in key ways. First of all, it prioritized the automobile as the primary mode of transportation, both for individuals and commerce. Cheap, federally funded and maintained roads revolutionized interstate commerce as businesses moved away from track-bound, although more energy-efficient, freight trains to infinitely adaptable long-haul trucks. Individuals and families also relied more and more on the automobile to get them to far-off destinations like grandma's house back in Michigan, but also increasingly to work, the

grocery, school, church, the movies, and to their refuge from the city: the suburbs. Between the war's end and the mid-1960s, rail passenger traffic declined
by half, while total track mileage declined each year and big corporations
bought out smaller independent railroads. The conversion to automobile and
long-haul truck primacy was unstoppable.

The rise of the automobile and the Interstate Highway system also facilitated suburbanization in the West, as elsewhere in the country, which allowed
people to live outside the cities and directly contributed to urban sprawl. Post-
war affluence enabled emerging middle class (usually white) city dwellers to
flee blighted downtowns for the safety and open spaces of the suburbs.
Nowhere was this phenomenon more pronounced than in California. During
World War II, hundreds of thousands of people had flocked to the sunny state
in search of reliable, high-paying defense industry jobs. The resulting
population boom clogged the existing transportation system, and so by 1947,
California had committed itself to an extensive state freeway development
program. Easy access to the sprawling lands lying outside of southern
California's especially congested and crowded cities, combined with low-
interest-rate government home-loan programs such as the GI Bill, spawned a
great white flight to single-family housing in the new satellite communities
that radiated out from older urban centers. Los Angeles was the poster child.
Today, the city's metropolitan area, which urbanist William Whyte character-
izes as "an unnerving lesson in man's infinite ability to mess up his environment," extends across nearly 4900 square miles. But sprawl is not unique to LA
(statistically, it isn't even in the top 20 worst cities); metropolitan expansion
around cities such as Phoenix, Las Vegas, Denver, Seattle, Albuquerque, and
Salt Lake is also daunting. Aldo Leopold had earlier decried such unsustainable development, observing that "bureaus build roads into new hinterlands,
then buy more hinterlands to absorb the exodus accelerated by the roads."

Home and garden magazines such as *Sunset* and *House Beautiful* touted
and celebrated energetic post-war western suburbanization, however. One
article extolling the iconic low-to-the-ground, long-eaved "ranch" house style
as the essence of "California living," for example, encouraged readers to "try
to visualize the social values that such a house represents." By the 1950s, the
California ranch rambler accounted for nine out of every 10 new houses.
Garages replaced front porches, and families prioritized privacy by erecting
fences and hedges to shield them from the prying eyes of curious neighbors
and strangers. Curvilinear streets and cul-de-sacs replaced older grid systems
and created mini-communities of homogeneous, similarly valued, one-story
homes, each with its own lawn and backyard (see Figure 8.3). Mixed-use
neighborhoods – those with shopping, service, restaurants, theaters, offices,
and healthcare all mixed in together – disappeared, ensuring that every
household had to get into a car and drive to meet even their most basic

Figure 8.3 Suburbanization, curvilinear streets, and urban sprawl became standard features of the post-war West, as this 2015 image of Albuquerque, New Mexico, demonstrates.

subsistence needs. Suburbanization was also directly responsible for the emergence of the two-car family; in 1956 there were more cars than households in America and the station wagon became the virtual symbol of the suburban phenomenon and a way to "keep up with the Joneses." Indeed, by the 1950s, more Americans lived in suburbs than in cities, and each year they spent more time and drove more miles in their cars.

Unfortunately, westerners' love affair with their automobiles and suburbanization also brought about the rapid collapse of urban mass transit, and no company worked harder to facilitate the end of the trolley and cable car era in the West than automobile manufacturer General Motors (GM). Between 1936 and 1950, as historian Tom McCarthy has shown, GM converted 45 cities over to its bus lines, National City Lines. The conversion was so thorough and swift that by 1955, "88 percent of the nation's electric streetcar network was gone." Buses, however, were an ineffective solution – they were often inconvenient, expensive, and soon forsaken, as GM hoped they would be, for the automobile. Unlike the bus (and railroad), cars take passengers exactly where they want to go. As McCarthy concludes, "urban mass transit worked for millions, especially as routine transportation between home and workplace, but it simply could not compete with the multifaceted allure of the automobile." As the car became a status symbol, an obvious icon of success and a measure of the "good life" for many Americans, public transportation increasingly seemed "second class." Advertisers played into this value system by provocatively asking "why be part of the ten-cent common herd?" Automobiles were the golden ticket to freedom and upward social mobility.

Regardless of the cultural caché that car ownership imparted, the environmental impact of such an automotive acceleration was significant. Between 1945 and 1960, Americans drove a lot more cars a lot farther. The number of passenger cars speeding along the nation's highways soared from 25.8 million to 61.7 million, and the annual mileage driven nearly tripled, from 200 billion to 587 billion miles. Gasoline consumption followed a predictably similar trajectory and, even as late as 1954, nearly 80% of it came from the West, primarily Texas, Oklahoma, and California. Thus, at every stage of what environmental historians call the product life cycle – raw material extraction, manufacturing, consumer use, and disposal – the automobile exerted an ever-expanding influence. Every year, for example, five million defunct automobiles ended up in junkyards. Unfortunately, according to McCarthy, the "golden decade" of the automobile coincided directly with the "dark ages" of its environmental impact. The acceleration of raw material extraction and mining, proliferation of automobile factories, consumption of fossil fuels, pollution of the air, and desertion of old cars – these were the costs of the nation's auto mania. Aldo Leopold had felt this personally and lamented the "loss" of his beloved White Mountain in Arizona earlier in the 1920s, vowing never to return: "I prefer not to see what tourists, roads, sawmill, and logging railroads have done for it, or to it."

For most westerners, the automobile's most obvious effect in this four-phase product life-cycle was smog – the choking smoky fog (thus, "smog") that hovered over car-intensive cities and suburbs like Phoenix, Las Vegas, Salt Lake City, and Los Angeles. Indeed, by the 1940s, Los Angeles had become so synonymous with the phenomenon that it earned the nickname "Smog Town." As it turned out, the same sunny marine climate that was so ideal for year-round agriculture was also ideal for trapping car and industry emissions. Smog results from temperature inversions – warmer air at low elevation with cooler air above, which traps smoke and other pollutants because there is no circulation. Los Angeles experiences these conditions on 340 or more days out of every year, on average, as its bowl-like geography, with ocean on the west and mountains on the east, provides a perfect smog-collecting trap. As McCarthy has argued, for a city and an area renowned for its clean air and healthy environment, "dirty air struck at Southern California's very identity and posed a direct threat to one of the central tenets of the region's marketing" – it was a breach of climate contract. By 1949, for example, automobile-produced smog in Los

Angeles County damaged leafy crops such as lettuce and spinach, costing farmers there hundreds of thousands of dollars. In 1954, heavy smog shut down the city's schools and industries for much of October.

Californians were not about to leave their cars at home, however, so the onus for solving the problem rested on automobile manufacturers, who began developing the catalytic converter to trap noxious emissions. In the 1950s, though, the auto industry deemed the device too expensive for commercial use and consumers failed to demand change. The catalytic converter would have to wait until the 1970s. The reason was simple, writer Thomas Hine argues: Americans failed to question the environmental costs of their automobile habit because after the deprivation of war, they experienced an "outright, thoroughly vulgar joy in being able to live so well … [and] the sense that a new car [was] an achievement worth celebrating." US automakers gladly joined in the celebration by offering cars with increased horsepower, fueled by gas-guzzling, growling V8 engines, and ever-more dazzling refinements such as chrome tailfins. In their Cadillac-catatonia, few consumers wondered what happened to the chemicals that made their cars so shiny (discharged directly into local rivers, streams, and lakes) or what the environmental costs of open-pit iron mines, offshore oil wells, and junked Fleetwoods and Eldorados might be. As Hine concludes, "in some part of his being, every American wanted a Cadillac."

Oblivious to the long-term ecological effects of their auto-lust, post-war Americans and their touring cars took to the open road and new Interstates and visited national parks, monuments, forests, and recreation areas in record numbers. The end of World War II and onerous wartime rationing liberated people from concerns about "over there," and they set out to explore the nation's scenic wonders in a frenzy of recreation travel and adventure. Tourism ignited the West's economy as busted-out mining towns transformed into ski resorts, campgrounds proliferated, and families loaded their station wagons with bologna- and cheese-filled ice chests and set out to "see the USA in your Chevrolet." By 1950, historians Malone and Etulain calculate, "nearly two-thirds of all Americans took vacations, and four-fifths of them went by car." After dramatic declines during the war years, the national parks experienced an explosion in visitorship. In 1940, an American population of 130 million had enjoyed 22 million acres of national parks; only two decades later, the population had swelled to 183 million, but the park system still languished and suffered visibly from overuse and disrepair. By 1960, most parks experienced a doubling of their pre-war tourist numbers, and major parks such as Yosemite, Yellowstone, and the Grand Canyon logged well over a million visitors annually. Open spaces and public lands constituted yet another commodity that fulfilled rapacious post-war consumer demand. Leopold had anticipated this auto excess when he wrote, "everywhere is the unspecialized motorist whose recreation is mileage, who has run the gamut of the National Parks in one summer."

By 1956, deferred maintenance and the parks' basic inability to adequately handle and serve the crush of new tourists finally prompted the National Park Service to implement Mission 66, an aggressive 10-year plan to modernize, develop, and generally spruce up the national parks' infrastructure by their 50th anniversary in 1966. The most notable amenity added under this program was the visitor center, now a foundational institution at every park, but Mission 66 also included improved roads, employee housing, interpretive displays, and utilities. The West continued to provide a disproportionate share of its scenic splendor to the federal system through additions such as Grand Teton (1950) and Petrified Forest (1958) national parks, but also through newer federally managed recreation areas like Coulee Dam/Lake Roosevelt (1946) and Glen Canyon (1958). In 1951 the parks had hosted 37 million visitors. By 1956, when Mission 66 began, the numbers had exploded to more than 60 million, and by the program's conclusion in 1966, visitorship had more than doubled again to 133 million.

Such intense pressure on the parks came at a cost: Americans were loving their parks to death and in many cases ruining the very scenery that had justified park protection. As Leopold had predicted, "mass-use involves a direct dilution of the opportunity for solitude ... when we speak of roads, campgrounds, trails, and toilets as 'development' of recreational resources, we speak falsely in respect of [solitude]." The key, he concluded, was for humans to begin to recognize their membership in an integrated community, not just with other humans, but with the entirety of the world around them. "In short," Leopold had argued, "a land ethic changes the role of *Homo sapiens* from conqueror of the land-community to plain member and citizen of it. It implies respect for his fellow-members, and also respect for the community as such."

In the wake of world war, American affluence contributed to a surge in outdoor recreation and a corresponding sense that "quality of life" now included beautiful places in which to recreate and contemplate. As historian Samuel Hayes has demonstrated, "evolving environmental values were closely associated with rising standards of living and levels of education." "Success" and "progress," in the form of industrialization and a vibrant economy, had produced unintended and increasingly unacceptable consequences such as atomic radiation, dammed rivers, declining species, pollution, sprawl, and overcrowded public spaces. Surely a people who had triumphed over fascism could have it all, economic prosperity *and* a healthy environment. Or, as Hayes said simply, "beauty, health, and permanence." In 1949, Leopold's assertions that "conservation is a state of harmony between men and land" garnered too few adherents, but in little more than a decade, with the environmental costs of the heady development-centric decade of the 1950s beginning to mount, Leopold's conservationist consciousness began to evolve into the modern environmental protection movement.

Suggested Reading

Sara Dant Ewert, "Evolution of an Environmentalist: Senator Frank Church and the Hells Canyon Controversy," *MONTANA: The Magazine of Western History*, Spring 2001, 36–51.

Jared Farmer, "Glen Canyon and the Persistence of Wilderness," *Western Historical Quarterly*, Vol. 27, No. 2 (Summer 1996), 210–222.

Steven M. Fountain, "Ranchers' Friend and Farmers' Foe: Reshaping Nature with Beaver Reintroduction in California," *Environmental History*, Vol. 19, No. 2 (April 2014), 239–269.

Sarah Alisabeth Fox, *Downwind: A People's History of the Nuclear West* (Lincoln: University of Nebraska Press, 2014).

Samuel P. Hays, *Beauty, Health, and Permanence: Environmental Politics in the United States, 1955–1985* (New York: Cambridge University Press, 1987).

Jim Klein, *Taken for A Ride*, public transit documentary, New Day Films, 1996.

Aldo Leopold, *A Sand County Almanac* (New York: Ballantine Books, 1986).

Eric Loomis, "When Loggers Were Green: Lumber, Labor, and Conservation, 1937–1948," *Western Historical Quarterly*, Vol. 46, No. 4 (Winter 2015), 421–441.

David B. Louter, "Wilderness on Display: Shifting Ideals of Cars and National Parks," *Journal of the West*, Vol. 44 (Fall 2005), 29–38.

Tom McCarthy, *Auto Mania: Cars, Consumers, and the Environment* (New Haven: Yale University Press, 2009).

Gregg Mitman, "In Search of Health: Landscape and Disease in American Environmental History," *Environmental History*, Vol. 10, No. 2 (April 2005), 184–210.

Linda Nash, "The Fruits of Ill-Health: Pesticides and Workers' Bodies in Post-World War II California," *Osiris*, Vol. 19 (2004), 203–219.

National Park Service, "2014 National Park Visitor Spending Effects: Economic Contributions to Local Communities, States, and the Nation," April 2015. www.nature.nps.gov/socialscience/docs/VSE2014_Final.pdf (accessed February 6, 2016).

Susan Rhoades Neel, "Newton Drury and the Echo Park Dam Controversy," *Forest and Conservation History*, Vol. 38, No. 2 (April 1994), 56–66.

Eliot Porter, *The Place No One Knew: Glen Canyon on the Colorado*, 25th Anniversary Edition (Layton: Gibbs Smith, 2000).

Bob H. Reinhardt, "Drowned Towns in the Cold War West: Small Communities and Federal Water Projects," *Western Historical Quarterly*, Vol. 42, No. 2 (Summer 2011), 149–172.

Mark Reisner, *Cadillac Desert: The American West and Its Disappearing Water* (New York: Penguin Books, 1993). See also: *Cadillac Desert: Water and the Transformation of Nature*. Complete 4 Tape VHS Set, PBS Video, 1997.

Daniel Simberloff, "Integrity, Stability, and Beauty: Aldo Leopold's Evolving View of Nonnative Species," *Environmental History*, Vol. 17, No. 3 (July 2012), 487–511.

Smart Growth America, "Measuring Sprawl 2014," April 2014. www.smartgrowthamerica.org/documents/measuring-sprawl-2014.pdf (accessed February 4, 2016).

Ian Stacy, "Roads to Ruin on the Atomic Frontier: Environmental Decision Making at the Hanford Nuclear Reservation, 1942–1952," *Environmental History*, Vol. 15, No. 1 (July 2010), 415–448.

Wallace Stegner, *This Is Dinosaur: Echo Park Country and Its Magic Rivers*, Reprint (Lanham: Roberts Rinehart Publishers, 1985).

Paul S. Sutter, "Driven Wild: The Problem of Wilderness," *Forest History Today* (Spring 2002), 2–9. www.foresthistory.org/publications/FHT/FHTSpring2002/DrivenWild. pdf (accessed February 6, 2016).

John L. Thomas, *A Country in the Mind: Wallace Stegner, Bernard DeVoto, History, and the American Land* (New York: Routledge, 2000).

Washington State Department of Health, "An Overview of Hanford and Radiation Health Effects," 2004. http://web.archive.org/web/20100106001013/http://www.doh.wa. gov/hanford/publications/overview/overview.html (accessed February 4, 2016).

9

Building Consensus

How much can one person really do? If the purpose of environmental history is to examine the "role and place of nature in human life," as historian Donald Worster argues, then what about the role and place of an individual? It is hard to imagine the environmental movement, for example, without the lives of John Muir, Aldo Leopold, or Rachel Carson to make it accessible, comprehendible, and memorable – *human*. This chapter demonstrates how one individual shaped the environmental history of the West and the nation between 1960 and 1980: Senator Frank Church, a Democrat from Idaho. Without Church, Idaho certainly would not have the rich public lands it enjoys today, and the West and the nation would also have been poorer. Significantly, Church's environmental contributions to wilderness, wild and scenic rivers, forests, and land conservation are evident not only in the legislation he succeeded in passing but also in the *way* he went about passing these laws. As Sierra Club advocate Doug Scott recalled, Church "did not come across as a crusader for wilderness, but rather as a quieter, careful workman who crafted the deft compromises and accommodations." If studying the past helps clarify the present, the Senate career of Frank Church provides an illustrative and instructive window into this critical era of environmental fluorescence (see Figure 9.1).

Church's tenure in the US Senate aligns with a period of unprecedented federal environmental protective legislation. Presidents John Kennedy, Lyndon Johnson, and Richard Nixon presided over nearly a decade and a half

Losing Eden: An Environmental History of the American West, First Edition. Sara Dant.
© 2017 John Wiley & Sons, Inc. Published 2017 by John Wiley & Sons, Inc.

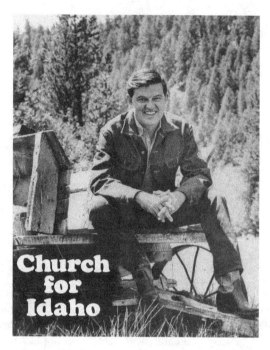

Figure 9.1 Church for Idaho Campaign Poster. Frank Church (D) served as Idaho's senator from 1957 to 1981 and helped craft some of the most influential state and national environmental legislation passed during that era. Source: Reproduced with permission of the Frank Church Papers, Boise State University Library.

of landmark congressional lawmaking that focused national attention on preservation – protecting nature from exploitation – and established some of the most far-reaching and powerful laws affecting plant and animal species, air and water, and public lands ever. During this remarkable stretch of years environmental bipartisanship flourished. Today, the Wilderness Act bitterly divides advocates and opponents; in 1964, by contrast, the House of Representatives passed it by a whopping 373-1 majority. In 1973, the House passed the now-controversial Endangered Species Act in a landslide 355-4 vote. Even Nixon, not known for environmental advocacy, jumped on the green bandwagon for a short ride. In 1972, he proclaimed that our "environmental awakening must mature finally into a new and higher environmental way of life." Church's Senate career powerfully illustrates the critical role of the individual in the machinations of environmental politics. His ability to galvanize consensus ensured that measures remained bipartisan and popular, a win–win model of environmental legislation. This "green pork" ideal, where everyone "wins" politically, not only worked during the heyday of environmental legislation of the 1960s and 1970s, but it also has the potential to maintain the fragments of bipartisan political consensus by providing a powerful model for twenty-first century environmental cooperation.

Church's support and affinity for the environment grew out of his deep appreciation for the wild Idaho of his youth. Born in 1924, Church was a third generation Idahoan who spent his boyhood recreating with family and friends throughout the scenically spectacular and sparsely populated state. "I never knew a person who felt self-important in the morning after spending the night in the open on an Idaho mountainside under a star-studded summer sky," he liked to tell people. When he took office in 1957, he was only 32 years old. He was green, certainly, but not necessarily in the environmental sense. His 1956 senatorial campaign had promised "to build your Idaho" by attracting industry and economic development to this natural resource-rich, cash-poor state. But Church was also a quick study, and his tenure on the Senate Interior Committee especially began to reveal another way to calculate land values – one that moved beyond board-feet of timber and kilowatt-hours of power to an appreciation of the intrinsic wealth of nature in its pristine state. He pioneered a way to value land beyond its extractive capabilities. Church came to understand that unbounded economic development was not only an unrealistic goal for Idaho, the West, and the nation, but also an undesirable one, and for these reasons he championed some of the most important pieces of conservation legislation passed during the heyday of the environmental movement: the Wilderness Act, the Wild and Scenic Rivers Act, and the Land and Water Conservation Fund Act. As a pragmatic politician, Church was also keenly aware that not all Americans shared his conservation zeal, including many of his own constituents. Yet instead of trying to out-shout those who opposed him, Church pioneered a model of consensus and cooperation that incorporated competing concerns and demands, and accomplished environmental ends through diplomatic negotiation and compromise. During his Senate career from 1957 to 1981, he successfully mediated conflicts between natural resource users and protection proponents, demonstrating that economic development/conservation and environmental preservation are not mutually exclusive objectives.

By the late 1950s, a growing public awareness of environmental degradation had begun to coalesce into a powerful movement to legislate change. While its sources were myriad, this nascent "environmentalism," as it would come to be called, drew strength from the confluence of a thriving economy and rising standards of living, the revival of conservationism and the emergence of ecology as a "legitimate" science, and widespread concern about the "costs" of atomic energy and rampant industrialization. The outdoor recreation boom exemplifies this confluence. It had begun in the 1920s, accelerated during the 1930s, and exploded following World War II. Americans who felt secure economically and enjoyed the benefits of industrial technology wanted to add what remained of wilderness spaces and nature to their "quality of life" calculus. Television brought the great outdoors into suburban living rooms nightly, and terms such as "wetlands" and "wilderness" supplanted "swamp" and "wasteland" as the national lexicon evolved to incorporate this new appreciation. Furthermore, as population expanded, production and consumption increased, and urbanization threatened to gobble up the countryside, the environmental toll finally registered with a growing portion of the general public. Americans were loving nature to death and recreation "supply" failed to keep up with demand. In addition to Sierra Club members and bird fanciers, hunters and sportsmen, fishers and families joined the swelling chorus calling for a new biocentric environmental ethic – a belief that humans are no more important than other life – first suggested by Aldo Leopold.

In the fall of 1961, Church found himself suddenly thrust into the limelight of one of the most contentious bills in the Senate at the time: the Wilderness Act. Congress had been debating federal protection for wilderness areas since 1956. The final version of the act stated that "a wilderness, in contrast with those areas where man and his own works dominate the landscape, is hereby recognized as an area where the earth and its community of life are untrammeled by man, where man himself is a visitor who does not remain." Church was keenly aware that such a definition incited strong opposition among natural resource interests, like the Idaho timber industry, who feared the designation would block extraction, so he had avoided publicizing his support of the measure, preferring instead to work behind the scenes. But Church's hopes of quietly voting "yea" evaporated when the wilderness bill's original sponsor suffered a gallbladder attack on the eve of the Senate floor debate and asked Church to take control.

Church's measured and thoughtful presentation assured timber, livestock, and other user interests that wilderness designations would not "lock up" valuable natural resources. Instead, wilderness could become its own valuable resource: "wilderness areas will become a mighty magnet for the tourist trade … few industries have as much potential for us." Public lands-laden western states would bear the brunt of the wilderness designations, he acknowledged, but they would also be "its chief beneficiaries," not "rich easterners" as detractors alleged. "It is in the West alone that a person can still escape the clutter of roads, signposts, and managed picnic grounds," he argued, unlike in the crowded East. Moreover, federal agencies had already set aside the proposed wilderness areas included in the pending bill as national parks and monuments, wildlife refuges and ranges, or Forest Service Primitive Areas. The wilderness legislation would not change this situation and so would have "no adverse effect on anyone."

Much of the credit for the Senate's overwhelming support for the bill (78-8) that year went to Church, but trouble in the House of Representatives forced Church and other supporters to reintroduce the bill in 1963. Finally, in 1964, a joint House and Senate conference committee, which included Church, met to iron out points of contention. On September 3, President Lyndon Johnson signed the bill into law, immediately incorporating just over 9 million acres, the vast majority from the West, into a new National Wilderness Preservation System. Secretary of the Interior Stewart Udall listed Church as "one of the two or three people in Congress" deserving the greatest credit for its passage, while his brother, Arizona Representative Morris "Mo" Udall (D), stated simply that without Church "there would have been no Wilderness Bill."

Church's advocacy for the Wilderness Act had been a political risk in conservative Idaho, but by the late 1960s he believed that most of his Idaho constituents would support environmental legislation as long as they did not view it as a threat to their livelihood. "If it is really a choice of conservation or their job, they'll take their job," he observed, "but as long as it is sensible conservation and propaganda about loss of their jobs that they can sort out, they'll take conservation." Economy and environment *can* coexist.

Significantly, that September 3, 1964, Wilderness Act morning in the Rose Garden of the White House bore witness to President Johnson signing not one but two remarkable pieces of environmental legislation: the well-known Wilderness Act and the far-lesser-known Land and Water Conservation Fund (LWCF) Act. "It is with a great deal of pride and pleasure and hope for the future," Johnson proclaimed, "that we enact into law today by signing these bills some of the most far-reaching conservation measures that a farsighted nation has ever coped with." His assessment of their future significance was prescient. By the 1960s, the growing strength of the environmental movement began to translate public concerns about the ecological costs of unbridled post-war expansion into federal protective legislation. The two acts followed a similar legislative path to eventual bipartisan success, and together they formed a symbiotic relationship that ensured their mutual success. Church played a similar role in the passage of both.

In the early twentieth century, support for both measures drew on an emerging national consensus that the federal government was the best guardian of the nation's last, best places. Wilderness, parks, monuments, preserves, habitats, estuaries, and ecosystems all existed within a political system that enshrined private property and landholder rights. Environmental protection needed both law and land to succeed. Too often, private resource users had proved poor stewards of the nation's grazing lands, forests, rivers, and open spaces, environmental advocates observed. Economic success brought ecological destruction. Earlier Progressive-era reformers had argued that public ownership and management seemed to offer the best "solution" to the "problem" of environmental degradation. In this nationalist spirit, protection proponents encouraged the use of federal dollars to convey private lands back into public hands, reversing the older trend embodied by the Homestead Act. After World War II, as supporters continued to press for the preservation and protection of the nation's natural wonders, their focus remained fixed on place.

The fates of wilderness and the LWCF had long been inextricably intertwined, and the cooperative bipartisan effort that finally led to successful wilderness protection depended heavily on the politics of the LWCF. Officially called the "Land and Water Conservation Fund Act of 1965," the measure's objective was "to assist in preserving, developing, and assuring accessibility to all citizens" to the nation's outdoor recreation resources. More specifically, the LWCF had two primary purposes: to provide funding for the management and acquisition of federal lands, including the purchase of private inholdings and the augmentation of existing wilderness areas, parks, and forests, and to provide matching grants to states for recreation planning, land acquisition, and facility development of projects such as urban parks and municipal playgrounds. To accomplish this goal, Congress organized the LWCF as a federal "trust fund" that could accumulate revenues up to an established annual ceiling. The LWCF was popular and palatable, constituting a kind of "green pork" environmentalism that created a win–win situation for legislators who could pick and choose the projects they wished to fund to ensure that they benefitted local interests and voters.

One vexing but predictable problem soon emerged: as wildlands disappeared under urban sprawl, those that remained experienced soaring property values. The more rare the resource – park inholdings (privately owned land within a national park, forest, etc.), for example – the higher the price. Private landowners, even those with conservation sympathies, often concluded that the market favored commercial sale and/or development, since the federal government was a notoriously miserly bidder. Moreover, if the federal government proposed to condemn the land, or acquire it at below market value for the "public good," it met fierce opposition on numerous fronts for assaulting sacred private property rights. The LWCF sought to finesse this onerous private property issue, particularly in the West, by asserting that the federal government was the best long-term steward of these last open spaces, and that it was willing to pay current fair-market prices for them. The creation of this mighty fund was a cooperative, bipartisan effort that drew "yeas" from both sides of the aisle, and became (and remained until 2015) the principal source of federal monies for recreation lands. Those who wanted to preserve wilderness or parks out of preservationist idealism or in the name of ecological science often found pragmatic reasons to cooperate with those who saw tourism dollars in pristine wilderness spaces (even if they fought over some details of legislation).

Like its wilderness cousin, the LWCF grew out of recommendations contained in the 1962 report of the Outdoor Recreation Resources Review Commission, a bipartisan congressional commission tasked to assess the nation's outdoor recreation potential. In 1962, the original LWCF bill proposed to derive revenue from user fees at federal recreation areas, sales of surplus federal lands, a tax on motorboat fuels, and an annual levy on the use of recreation boats. This provision quickly drew the ire of recreation boat owners, who flooded Congress with telegrams of protest. In November of 1963, the LWCF gained a powerful new ally, however, when Lyndon Johnson, thrust suddenly into the nation's highest office following the assassination of Kennedy, vowed to continue the work Kennedy had begun. Conservation figured prominently in his agenda.

Johnson was not the charming and charismatic individual that Kennedy had been, but he was a far more experienced and skilled politician. By the following year, he had begun to sketch the outlines of his Great Society – broad-reaching social welfare programs that he hoped would not only forge consensus and enrich the impoverished but also improve every American's quality of life. At the heart of Johnson's liberalism was his belief that the federal government existed for the public good. Harkening back to his predecessor Franklin Roosevelt, Johnson insisted that government had a responsibility to uphold the well-being of its citizens. "The Great Society rests on abundance and liberty for all," Johnson maintained, which meant leveling the playing field and providing every American with equal access to the American Dream and a healthy environment. For Johnson, that dream included "natural splendor": "once man can no longer walk with beauty or wonder at nature his spirit will wither and his sustenance be wasted." Thus the LWCF fit Johnson's vision for an act that could "create new concepts of cooperation, a creative federalism, between the National Capital and the leaders of local communities."

Frank Church concurred and managed the LWCF bill in the Senate at the same time that he was shepherding the Wilderness bill, calling the LWCF a vital supplement to the "precious resource" of wilderness. "Daily, as the cities stretch their concrete tentacles farther and farther into the countryside, as superhighways chew through woods and hills," Church argued, the states found it more difficult and more expensive to set aside recreational opportunities "for the use and enjoyment of all the people." The LWCF would change all of this, permitting states to play a pivotal role in the development of outdoor recreation. Furthermore, under the LWCF's provisions, states could transfer funds to counties and cities, thus ensuring local control over recreation development. Wilderness bill critics who had railed against federal control in the West found this local control provision in the LWCF bill reassuring – a kind of political tit for tat that facilitated the ultimate passage of both pieces of legislation. On August 12, 1964, the LWCF's bipartisan support was manifest as the bill passed the Senate by a lopsided 92-1 vote. Johnson praised the bipartisanism on display that September 3 morning: "I think it is significant that these steps have broad support not just from the Democratic Party, but the Republican Party, both parties in the Congress." Furthermore, he added, "this reflects a new and a strong national consensus to look ahead, and, more than that, to plan ahead; better still, to move ahead." Church's efforts to craft compromise allowed local and national interests to align, a rare occurrence in the experience of many westerners.

Since 1968, the Fund's major source of revenue derived from the mineral leasing receipts generated by oil and gas drilling on the Outer Continental Shelf (OCS) (see Figure 9.2). This shrewd political move not only provided a lucrative well-spring of money, but it also assuaged a great deal of congressional guilt by allowing mineral exploitation to fund land and water conservation. The law stipulated that 60% of the monies from the LWCF be available to the states, while the federal government's four land management agencies had access to the other 40%. Significantly, the law also contained a formula that set aside fully 85% of federal funding for acquisitions *east* of the 100th meridian. This provision not only allayed some western senators' fears

Figure 9.2   Frank Church accepts a pen from President Lyndon Johnson, who just signed the 1968 amendment to the Land and Water Conservation Fund Act authorizing the use of Outer Continental Shelf oil monies as a major funding source for federal, state, and local conservation. Source: Reproduced with permission of the Frank Church Papers, Boise State University Library.

of a "federal land grab," but also ensured adequate spending on what Church called "the section of the country where land is most desperately needed for recreational purposes." Thus the LWCF allowed federal agencies to buy inholdings in wilderness, park, and forest areas - "out there" - but it also built urban parks, baseball diamonds, swimming pools, and playgrounds where most Americans actually *lived*. An impressive fusion of conservation and preservation. The legacy of this unique fund was and is impressive. For more than half a century, the LWCF acted as the principal federal revenue source for new recreation lands, providing billions of dollars to federal land managing agencies and to state and local governments for the purchase of millions of acres in nearly every state in the union. Moreover, the LWCF encouraged both state and federal agencies to cooperate with non-profit organizations and private companies to facilitate land and water conservation. This "local control" mechanism placated states' rights advocates (especially in the West), and was central to the fund's continued popularity. Unfortunately, in 2015, despite broad bipartisan support, the LWCF fell victim to far-right opposition, led by Utah Representative Rob Bishop, and Congress failed to reauthorize it. Both acts, however, exemplified the kind of positive, consensus-based environmental legislation Church advocated during his tenure in the Senate.

At the same time that Church was embroiled in the wilderness and LWCF debates, he also grappled with a dam controversy on the Snake River, a potential hydro-electrical powerhouse for Idaho. Competing proposals pitted public and private power companies against one another in a race to put a plug in Hells Canyon. As Church later recalled, the early Hells Canyon controversy "was not about whether or not a dam would be built but rather where it would be built and who should build it." Church's efforts to balance environment and economy meant that he initially supported federal development. But one of the public dam proposals threatened to block the state's famed "river of no return," the Salmon River, home to 30% of the total anadromous fish spawn in the Columbia River basin and more than half of all its spring and summer Chinook. That was a cost Church was unwilling to pay. The economic gains did not justify the ecological losses.

Thus, in March 1965, drawing on his involvement with the Wilderness and LWCF Acts, Church introduced the National Wild Rivers bill, designed to protect sections of some of the nation's scenic rivers from economic development. Calling the bill "a working partner to the wilderness bill," Church believed the wild rivers bill would eventually take its place alongside the "landmark" wilderness bill as "another first for America." Yet, while Church believed the wild rivers proposal provided an important companion to the wilderness bill, he emphasized their differences. Most importantly, he noted, the wild rivers bill did "not seek to create corridors of wilderness through which these rivers will flow." Rather, the philosophy of multiple use generally would prevail, allowing grazing, timber harvest, mining, and road building to continue. Church considered the wild rivers system "an essential weapon" in the fight to save Idaho's dwindling salmon and steelhead runs. For water, this meant moving away from an older conservation/reclamation agenda that characterized unharnessed rivers as "wasted" commodities. "Once a dam is built," he argued, "a wild river is lost forevermore." He hoped that in Idaho and elsewhere, conservation could be "the companion of development," predicting that outdoor recreation "could be the most valuable money-earner in the whole Idaho economy in another ten years." Sometimes, the best dam was no dam.

On October 2, 1968, Church's Wild and Scenic Rivers proposal became law. In its final form, the new system included three categories for river preservation, a concession designed to please almost everyone and ensure maximum river corridor protection. The most restrictive category was "wild river." Designed to protect the "vestiges of primitive America," these rivers would be "free of impoundments and generally inaccessible except by trail, with watersheds or shorelines essentially primitive and waters unpolluted." The second category, "scenic river," protected those rivers "still largely primitive and shorelines largely undeveloped, but accessible in places by roads." The third and least restrictive designation, "recreational river," protected rivers that were "readily accessible by road or railroad that may have some development along their shorelines, and that may have undergone some impoundment or diversion in the past." In other words, untouched river areas remained untouched, and those with existing access remained open for recreation and even development. The law immediately designated eight rivers, more than half in the West including the Salmon, for inclusion in the Wild and Scenic Rivers system. It also harkened back to Church's original goal by not only prohibiting the Federal Power Commission from licensing dams or other projects on any river within the system, but also blocking licensing on "study" rivers (potential Wild and Scenic River additions) for a five-year period following enactment or during congressional consideration of a river's inclusion into the system. Lack of inclusion did not leave rivers vulnerable or unprotected. In the previous century, under Theodore Roosevelt, the user-oriented notion of conservation that called for the greatest good for the greatest number had sufficed. But by the mid-twentieth century, a growing national ecological awareness began to reveal that this philosophy could lead to the irreversible disruption of some of the planet's most basic life systems. Much of this concern arose in response to biologist Rachel Carson's classic work, *Silent Spring*.

In 1962, Carson wrote that "for the first time in the history of the world, every human being is now subjected to contact with dangerous chemicals, from the moment of conception until death." Her specific target was the country's dramatically expanded use of pesticides, and the powerful dichlorodiphenyltrichloroethane (DDT) in particular, which by the late 1950s had fully supplanted all other pest control methods. A modern miracle to many, these chemicals promised to increase agricultural production and eradicate pesky insects, though few understood the ecological repercussions that massive spraying campaigns entailed. As Carson saw it, these chemicals "should not be called 'insecticides,' but 'biocides.'" Her seminal contribution to the raising of national environmental consciousness was her compelling explanation of the interrelatedness of all life. "As crude a weapon as a cave man's club," she argued, "the chemical barrage has been hurled against the fabric of life – a fabric on the one hand delicate and destructible, on the other miraculously tough and resilient, and capable of striking back in unexpected ways." In the West, her exposé all but ended the United States Forest Service's (USFS) indiscriminate aerial DDT spraying for moths and other forest pests and ultimately brought an end to federally sanctioned strychnine bait poisoning of coyotes. Carson's warning helped launch a national movement of protest and reform in which the preservation of nature became integral to the question of the quality of life.

Carson's thinking influenced Church. Her biographer, William Souder, contends that the publication of *Silent Spring* "was a cleaving point – the moment when the gentle, optimistic proposition called 'conservation' began its transformation into the bitterly divisive idea that would come to be known as 'environmentalism.'" By the late 1960s and early 1970s, Senator Church also believed the term "conservation" had become an anachronism with little relevance or meaning for modern society and began to call for change. In an April 1969 speech before the Northwest District Conference of the National Recreation and Parks Association in Coeur d'Alene, Idaho, Church outlined the horizons of an environmental ethic he called the "New Conservation." Noting that Theodore Roosevelt had sounded the call to conservation more than 60 years earlier, Church recounted the "remarkable achievements" the nation had made in the field: land and water use measures, national forests and national parks, the Wilderness and Wild and Scenic Rivers acts, and the 1968 National Trails System Act. Characteristically, Church illustrated this progress with examples from Idaho, noting that "the Wilderness Act insures that the future will not witness the ruination of our great primitive areas," nor the defilement of the Salmon and Clearwater rivers. Yet, he also insisted, "I want to go beyond the immediate conservation targets in Idaho and focus instead upon the larger challenge which confronts the country as a whole." The challenge, Church argued, was for conservationists to move beyond the "limited concept" articulated by Roosevelt, to the mission of the New Conservation: "a healthy and habitable environment for man." This big-picture approach sought to integrate the biocentric land ethic first expressed by Aldo Leopold into mainstream environmental protection without negatively affecting economic development.

In outlining the battle ahead, Church drew heavily from new environmental studies that had begun to assess the costs of boundless American expansion. Obviously inspired by *Silent Spring*, Church's New Conservation speech recounted the toll that pesticides, herbicides, and "other poisons" had exacted as they coursed through soil, air, and water systems of the nation and the world. He questioned whether these chemical miracles were inherently beneficial, warning that insufficient attention had been paid to the "long-term consequences on our whole environment." Humans had to learn to cooperate with nature, Church explained, and the New Conservation "must point the way toward redressing the imbalance which now exists between man and the whole of his environment." Church believed this imbalance had reached "crisis proportions" in four areas – water pollution, air pollution, noise pollution, and the recreation boom – which if left unchecked might make humans themselves an endangered species. Church quoted the Sierra Club's David Brower, concluding that all life on earth was "part of an incredibly complex interwoven blanket," yet "the rending of our life fabric goes on." Truly, he argued, conservation "has become a matter of life and death."

Church's use of Brower's rhetoric was an important indication of the senator's transition in thinking about the natural environment, beyond rivers and dams. By the late 1960s, Brower and the Sierra Club had adopted an aggressive, proactive, national approach to environmental activism, perhaps most evident in their efforts to block two proposed dams in the Grand Canyon. As discussed in Chapter 8, in 1956, in the early phase of the wilderness fight, Brower and other conservationists had conceded to the damming of Glen Canyon, just upstream from the Grand Canyon, as the necessary price to save Echo Canyon in Dinosaur National Monument from a similar watery fate. It was a decision Brower bitterly regretted. A decade later, a Bureau of Reclamation proposal to dam the Grand Canyon seemed a cinch for congressional approval since it enjoyed the official backing of both President Johnson and Secretary of the Interior Stewart Udall. The commissioner of the Bureau, Floyd Dominy, had touted the many benefits of the dam, including the enhanced ability of tourists to enjoy the Grand Canyon from motorboats.

None of them anticipated the battle Brower was willing to wage. In June of 1966, the Sierra Club countered the Bureau's vision of motorboats in the Grand Canyon with a blistering, full-page, Brower-designed advertisement in the *New York Times* and the *Washington Post*. It provocatively asked, "should we also flood the Sistine Chapel so tourists can get nearer the ceiling?" Costing $15 000, the ad described the proposed dams and warned that "there is only one simple, incredible issue here: this time it's the Grand Canyon they want to flood. *The Grand Canyon*." Oppositional mail poured into congressional offices. Ironically, when the Internal Revenue Service subsequently revoked the Sierra Club's tax exemption for attempting to influence legislation, it freed the organization to take an even more vigorous opposing stance and membership soared. Brower's tactic worked. In February of 1967, Udall announced that the Johnson administration had changed its mind about the Grand Canyon dams, and in 1968, Congress killed the proposal. As Brower later remarked, "If we can't save the Grand Canyon, what the hell can we save?" The days of big dams were numbered.

Church specifically and Congress in general benefitted directly from the support of increasingly powerful, popular, and influential civic groups like the Sierra Club, National Wildlife Federation, the Wilderness Society, the Nature Conservancy, and Friends of the Earth. Their lobbying both influenced and bolstered legislative initiatives. As Church's New Conservation became an element of the new politics, and at the urging of the Sierra Club, the senator focused his attention on the heretofore unassailable USFS. At issue was the agency's increased reliance on even-age management, or clearcutting, to keep pace with industry demands to expand the allowable cut in anticipation of a national housing shortage. The term clearcutting refers to the timber industry practice of harvesting all trees regardless of size in one operation, and then attempting to establish a new stand – either from advanced reproduction or through natural seeding, stump sprouting, or direct seeding and planting – that results in a uniform, single-species, same-aged "forest" (see Figure 9.3). Occasionally in the 1960s and 1970s, logging companies bulldozed terraces into steeply sloped hillsides to make it easier to replant trees after clearcutting. This practice radically altered the topography of the landscape, caused significant ecological changes, and in effect turned natural forests into tree farms. By 1971, clearcutting accounted for more than half of the total volume of wood removed from national forests annually. Critics charged that the USFS was abandoning its multiple-use mandate and caving in to the timber industry. The agency maintained that clearcutting was an efficient, economical, and effective management tool, which naturally favored high-yield, shade-intolerant tree species such as Douglas-fir. This mantra of old conservation efficiency rang hollow in the dawning era of environmental preservation, however, and Church pounced.

In the summer of 1971, Church scheduled congressional oversight hearings into the clearcutting practice. Though the USFS had produced several internal reviews of its forest management practices, criticism of the agency continued to mount, and was particularly acute regarding the Bitterroot National Forest in Montana and several national forests in Wyoming. One damning report in 1970, known as the "Bolle Report," charged that "multiple use management, in fact, does not exist as the governing principle on the Bitterroot National Forest." Instead, the USFS was engaging in non-sustainable "timber mining," where clearcutting and terracing could "not be justified as an investment for producing timber." This negative publicity illuminated the

Figure 9.3 Clearcuts, Lewis and Clark National Forest, Montana, by W.E. Steuerwald. Source: Reproduced with permission of USDA Forest Service.

agency's inability to balance soaring demands for forest resources with the post-World War II population explosion and the current boom in outdoor recreation. Calling Church's quest for answers "welcome," one editorial writer posited that "perhaps policies that were acceptable a few years ago, when forest products were abundant and competition for the use and enjoyment of national forest and wilderness areas between industry and 'recreation' was easily accommodated, are outdated."

Testimony at the Church hearings revealed the tremendous biological toll that clearcutting exacted from the land. As professional forester Gordon Robinson affirmed, clearcutting caused increased water run-off, which upset the watershed values of the forest. Heavily eroded soils leeched of important nutrients made timber replanting and reproduction more difficult, which resulted in the widespread use of chemical defoliants to keep down competing vegetation. Even more alarming was that the loss of nutrients associated with clearcutting could so deplete the soil that after two cuts there would be "permanent eradication of productivity for saw timber production." Furthermore, clearcutting's promotion of monoculture forestry also created a perfect medium for epidemic disease, since many tree fungus parasites were often virulent during only one stage of tree development. "Infection is direct and rapid" in forest stands comprised of one dominant tree species, he noted, leaving absolute devastation in its wake.

Beyond these biological considerations, clearcutting came under fire during the Church hearings as a short-sighted management technique that sacrificed forest health to economic concerns. Testimony revealed a number of cases in which the USFS had grossly overestimated the amount of commercial timber in a timber sale "working circle" area – in one case by nearly 800%. The disparity meant that to reach the timber quota specified in their contract with the USFS, contractors had to rely on clearcutting, instead of selective harvesting, to recoup the difference. Moreover, though there had been no significant increase in national forest acreage since 1950, the annual allowable cut had risen by more than 264%. The USFS had increased its inventory by shortening cut rotation cycles, combining working circles, and embracing clearcutting. Much of the increase in annual timber sales consisted of "marginal species of timber growing on steep unstable soils." This steep-slope clearcutting frequently caused landslides, with the potential to foul pristine endangered salmon and trout streams in Pacific Coast states and Alaska. A Federal Water Quality Administration official testified that sediment in streams increased as much as 7000 times in improperly harvested clearcuts, prompting a stunned Church to ask him to repeat his findings. Finally, in addition to the ecological devastation, Robinson concluded, "clearcut areas have lost their recreational values for many years to come."

While Church's concerns and questions regarding clearcutting won the approval of New-Conservation-minded witnesses, both the USFS and the timber industry had an opportunity to present their perspectives before and during the oversight hearings. Members of the Industrial Forestry Association pointed out that the nation's forests had built more than 40 million homes in the past quarter-century, while the management of timber constituted the fourth largest business in the country, and played a vital role as a barometer of the health of the economy. Their statements clearly indicated that changes in USFS policy would have broad economic ramifications. To the USFS's credit, Chief Edward Cliff noted that the agency's own reports reflected its on-going effort "to attain and maintain both a high level of timber productivity and a quality environment." Both Church and the subcommittee noted, however, that the USFS's testimony presented clearcutting mainly within the context of timber management, failing to incorporate the broader perspective of suitable environmental policy. "A large piece of clearcut land has obviously usurped other uses," Church argued, and "logging has become the dominant use."

In March of 1972, Church's Senate Subcommittee on Public Lands issued a new set of guidelines to regulate the practice of clearcutting on public lands. Commonly referred to as the Church Report or Church Guidelines, the document sought balance between economic and environmental concerns by calling for a periodic review and adjustment of allowable harvest levels on federal forest lands to ensure that they remained suitable for timber production and received satisfactory funding for intensified management practices. Although the guidelines did not eliminate clearcutting as a management tool, they severely restricted its use: "It can be applied judiciously and with expertise with favorable results, or it can be applied carelessly with unfavorable, even calamitous results." After explicitly stating that clearcutting should not be used in environmentally sensitive areas, the Church Report went on to caution that the method was only appropriate when "it is determined to be silviculturally essential" and should be "blended as much as possible with the natural terrain." And finally, the Church Report stated that federal timber sale contracts should contain requirements "to minimize or avoid adverse environmental impacts of timber harvesting," even if that meant lower net returns to the national treasury. The following day, USFS Chief Cliff pronounced the guidelines "sound" and pledged that the agency would abide by them. In a private letter to Church, he added that the guidelines were "a clear expression of Congressional and public concern" which represented "a desirable and constructive policy statement for future Federal forest land management." Compromise in the best sense, cooperation, and pragmatic politics form the core of Church's legislative legacy. He later wrote that it had always been his policy "to attempt to consider and reconcile the legitimate concerns of the timber industry, environmentalists, and the Forest Service."

This ability to forge consensus out of conflict was also evident in Church's continuing efforts to protect wilderness. In June of 1976 and again in 1977, Church introduced the Endangered American Wilderness Act to preserve "remnants of the wilderness upon which we founded our society and culture." The bill specifically sought protection for western tracts excluded by the USFS's so-called "sights and sounds" doctrine – a "purity" standard invoked for areas that were too close to major urban centers such as Albuquerque, Salt Lake City, and Tucson. Since the late 1960s, the USFS had been engaged in a process known as the Roadless Area Review and Evaluation (RARE) to determine which of its lands were suitable for inclusion in the National Wilderness Preservation System. The horribly flawed process, which failed twice (RARE I and RARE II), resulted in the agency classifying a number of western roadless areas as multiple-use lands unsuitable for wilderness protection. Church and many environmental organizations like the Sierra Club thus deemed them "endangered" by logging, mining, and mechanized recreation. As the senator argued, "it was not the intent of Congress that wilderness be administered in so pure a fashion as to needlessly restrict their customary public use and enjoyment."

The Endangered American Wilderness bill enjoyed widespread bipartisan congressional support despite predictable opposition from various natural resource user interests, and both the Senate and the House passed the measure by overwhelming majorities in February 1978. In its final form, the act designated 17 wilderness areas in 9 western states, incorporating 1.3 million acres into the national wilderness system. Congress also used the act to admonish the USFS publicly, charging that undeveloped national forest lands were "not being adequately protected or fully studied for wilderness suitability by the agency responsible for their administration." In the face of such negligence, the law reads, Congress "finds and declares that it is in the national interest" to protect these "endangered areas" as wilderness.

USFS reform and a national commitment to wilderness designation were part of Church's larger goal of compelling the federal government to "assume a leading role" in the fight against environmental degradation. He continued to back up his occasionally fiery rhetoric by building congressional support for some of the decade's most innovative environmental protection laws including the Clean Air Act and its amendments, the Clean Water Act and its amendments, the Clean Lakes Act, the creation of the Environmental Protection Agency, the Pesticide Control Act, the Endangered Species Act, and numerous land use planning and wilderness acts. When he spoke out against air pollution's "biggest offender," the internal combustion engine, which he predicted "may well be outlawed or die of its own unpopularity," Church sponsored legislation requiring the federal government to buy only those vehicles which operated on unleaded fuels. He also urged the nation to move cautiously in its love affair with nuclear power. "We have not given enough concern to the environmental problems which attend the production of atomic power," he insisted as he fought to ensure that the Atomic Energy Commission received adequate funding to develop atomic reactor safety programs and improve atomic waste disposal methods. Beyond these regulatory acts, Church also cosponsored legislation to expand significantly citizens' rights to sue the federal government to protect the environment, giving the courts greater authority to review actions by federal agencies.

As political reporter Jon Margolis put it, in a democracy, "everyone sitting around the table has to get something, meaning everyone has to give something." That democratic ideal is bound up in the legislation Frank Church helped to pass. Over the course of his four Senate terms, from 1957 to 1981, Church often wrestled with balancing the conflicting demands for resource use and preservation, of economy and environment, in Idaho, the West, and the nation. As he once conceded, "getting action in Congress depends upon lining up the votes. I work in a political forum, where success usually depends on some measure of accommodation. I try to be effective without compromising end objectives." Church both shaped and was shaped by a national sentiment that increasingly counted a healthy environment as an integral part of the good life and a measure of a higher standard of living. The senator also established a kind of symbiotic relationship with environmental organizations such as the Sierra Club: he needed their more radical positions to make him appear moderate in an increasingly conservative Idaho, while they needed him to craft the political compromises necessary to achieve environmental protection. This partnership set the tone for their long and fruitful cooperation, and together they translated grassroots activism into concrete legislation that helped build the foundation of the modern environmental movement. In the end, however, Church did not embrace environmental concerns because they were fashionable, but because he genuinely believed they were right. Church's tenure fortuitously coincided with a moment in time when environmental legislation found broad support in both Congress and the general public. But in 1980, a growing national conservative movement culminated in the simultaneous election of the Republican Ronald Reagan to the White House and the defeat of Church, ushering in an era of environmental backlash.

Suggested Reading

LeRoy Ashby and Rod Gramer, *Fighting the Odds: The Life of Senator Frank Church* (Pullman: Washington State University Press, 1994).

Frederica Bowcutt, "Tanoak Target: The Rise and Fall of Herbicide Use on a Common Native Tree," *Environmental History*, Vol. 16, No. 2 (April 2011), 197–225.

Rachel Carson's Silent Spring, directed by Neil Goodwin, PBS Documentary, DVD, June 26, 2007.

William Cronon, "The Trouble with Wilderness; or, Getting Back to the Wrong Nature," in William Cronon, ed., *Uncommon Ground: Rethinking the Human Place in Nature* (New York: W. W. Norton & Co., 1995), 69–90.

Sara Dant, "LBJ, Wilderness, and the Land and Water Conservation Fund," *Environmental History*, Vol 19, No. 4 (October 2014), 736–743. Reprinted in *Forest History Today*, Vol. 20, Nos 1 and 2 (Spring/Fall 2014).

Sara Dant, "Making Wilderness Work: Frank Church and the American Wilderness Movement," *Pacific Historical Review*, Vol. 77, No. 2 (May 2008), 237–272.

Sara Dant Ewert, "Evolution of an Environmentalist: Senator Frank Church and the Hells Canyon Controversy," *Montana: The Magazine of Western History*, Spring 2001, 36–51.

Sara Dant Ewert, "Peak Park Politics: The Struggle Over the Sawtooths, from Borah to Church," *Pacific Northwest Quarterly*, Summer 2000, 138–149.

John P. Herron, "The Call in the Wild: Nature, Technology, and Environmental Politics," in Jeff Roche, ed., *The Political Culture of the New West* (Lawrence: University Press of Kansas, 2008), 310–331.

Andrew G. Kirk, *Counterculture Green: The Whole Earth Catalog and American Environmentalism* (Lawrence: University of Kansas Press, 2007).

Ed Marston, "Floyd Dominy: An Encounter With the West's Undaunted Dam-builder," *High Country News*, August 28, 2000.

Richard M. Nixon, "Special Message to the Congress Outlining the 1972 Environmental Program," February 8, 1972. www.presidency.ucsb.edu/ws/?pid=3731 (accessed February 8, 2016).

Adam Rome, "The Genius of Earth Day," *Environmental History*, Vol. 15, No. 2 (April 2010), 194–205. Also, Adam Rome, *The Genius of Earth Day: How a 1970 Teach-in Unexpectedly Made the First Green Generation* (New York: Hill and Wang, 2014).

William Souder, *On a Farther Shore: The Life and Legacy of Rachel Carson* (New York: Broadway Books, 2012).

Adam M. Sowards, "William O. Douglas's Wilderness Politics: Public Protest and Committees of Correspondence in the Pacific Northwest," *Western Historical Quarterly*, Vol. 37, No. 1 (Spring 2006), 21–42.

Paul S. Sutter, *Driven Wild: How the Fight against Automobiles Launched the Modern Wilderness Movement* (Seattle: University of Washington Press, 2005).

Paul S. Sutter, "Driven Wild: The Problem of Wilderness," *Forest History Today*, (Spring 2002), 2–9. www.foresthistory.org/publications/FHT/FHTSpring2002/DrivenWild.pdf (accessed February 6, 2016).

James Morton Turner, *The Promise of Wilderness: American Environmental Politics since 1964* (Seattle: University of Washington Press, 2013).

10

Environmental Backlash and the New West

"We will mine more, drill more, cut more timber," vowed James Watt, whom President Ronald Reagan selected as his Secretary of Interior in 1981. With these nine terse words, Watt effectively announced the shattering much of the environmental consensus that had developed over the previous two decades and ushered in what an *LA Times* editorial called his "outrageous reign of error." The environmental tide had definitely turned; James Watt was no Frank Church. Born and raised in Wyoming, Watt developed an early and powerful affinity for natural resource users and business interests. In 1976, he initiated the Mountain States Legal Foundation, a law company "dedicated to individual liberty, the right to own and use property, limited and ethical government, and the free enterprise system." This "government-is-the-problem" philosophy attracted the attention of newly elected President Reagan, who offered Secretary Watt a chance to impose his vision – "to follow the Scriptures which call upon us to occupy the land until Jesus returns" – on the nation's public lands.

For Watt, "occupation" was synonymous with exploitation. Watt may have been Secretary of the Interior for less than three years, but in that short time, he and his allies in government and business reversed the environmental politics represented by Frank Church and revived a nineteenth-century throw-back vision of unbridled exploitation of natural resources (see Figure 10.1). Preservationists had to change tactics to defend the gains they had made in the 1960s and 1970s, rather than build on them. Watt and Reagan

Losing Eden: An Environmental History of the American West, First Edition. Sara Dant.
© 2017 John Wiley & Sons, Inc. Published 2017 by John Wiley & Sons, Inc.

Figure 10.1 This January 8, 1981, self-professed "prescient" editorial cartoon by Steve Greenberg anticipated the polarizing influence of soon-to-be-confirmed Secretary of Interior James Watt. Source: Reproduced with permission of Steven Greenberg.

also left behind a deeply polarized political climate. "I never use the words Democrats and Republicans," Watt proclaimed. "It's liberals and Americans." Prior to Watt, environmental initiatives had been largely bipartisan, in the vein of Church, but after Watt and Reagan, they struggled to rediscover that cooperative spirit. During the 1980s, user groups, including sportsmen, co-opted classic Theodore Roosevelt/Gifford Pinchot "conservation" into "Wise Use," a cleverly named movement advocating private property rights and reduced government regulation of and control over public lands. Environmentalists countered by digging in their heels and refusing to compromise on preservation efforts. The resulting clash between utility and stewardship – between profit and protection – produced bitter environmental controversies, harked back to the early 1900s, and destroyed the bipartisan political consensus of the 1960s and 1970s. As Watt's brief tenure in Interior symbolizes, an anti-environmental backlash roared to life in the West and across the nation in the 1980s, leaving a deep divide between preservation and development advocates that endures to the present.

It is hard to know where to begin with Watt. In his reign at the Department of Interior, he essentially threw open nearly the entire US coastline for offshore oil and gas drilling, including areas known to be unprofitable. He bragged openly about leasing "a billion acres" of coastal waters. In 1983, Watt presided over an Alaskan land swap that gave away $400 million in federal lands and subsurface oil and gas in exchange for a less-attractive/extractive $6 million tract. But that's not all. As part of the swap deal, Watt granted the private Arctic Slope Regional Corporation, a for-profit Alaska Native (primarily Iñupiat Eskimos) corporation, exclusive rights to drill a test well in the Arctic National Wildlife Refuge, such that it alone retains the data from that well, even to the exclusion of the federal government itself. This policy means that today a private corporation knows more about the oil and gas potential of these federally protected lands than the federal government does.

Wherever he could, Watt eliminated or redirected funding away from data collection, analysis, and research that might support federal protection and instead prioritized resource leasing and exploitation – profit. He bought no new park lands. He quadrupled the area of coal mining on public lands. Despite the historic non-development precedents set in Dinosaur National Monument and Grand Canyon National Park, he believed that neither park nor wilderness designations offered real environmental protection. Had Watt remained in office, he ultimately intended to lease public lands containing an estimated 17 billion tons of coal, including deposits adjacent to Chaco Culture National Historical Park and the imminent Bisti Bandlands Wilderness in New Mexico. He also pushed for oil and gas seismic testing in the Bob Marshall Wilderness of Montana. Even when Watt appeared to support public lands, as when he pumped more than $200 million into national park improvements (restrooms, visitor centers, etc.), he did so by slashing that same amount *out of* the parks' land acquisition budget. Better bathrooms make better parks? More like development trumps protection.

Watt also assiduously avoided enforcing protective environmental legislation such as the Endangered Species Act (ESA) and the National Environmental Policy Act's Environmental Impact Statement requirements. He vigorously whittled away at the Federal Land Policy and Management Act, the 1976 law mandating the Bureau of Land Management's (BLM) retention and management of public lands. As Secretary, Watt also actively sought to sell off what he believed were "excess" federal properties to the states, as part of his "Assets Management Program," the first round of which would have auctioned off approximately 2.5 million acres were it not for his ouster. Before he left, however, he did manage to slash the BLM's land use planning budget by 25% and effectively derailed the production of quality Resource Management Plans by discouraging new data collection and research, in effect leaving the agency uninformed about its own lands. He also gutted many wilderness study areas by excising 1.5 million acres from wilderness consideration before environmental organization lawsuits finally stopped him. For Watt, economic development constituted his agency's sole purpose. In New Mexico, for example, environmental advocates pressed for the above-mentioned Bisti Badlands Wilderness designation, which they got in 1984, in order to protect these desolate and strange rock formations and fossils from Watt's rapacious reach.

And finally, for more than two decades, Watt held the record as the Secretary who protected the fewest species under the Endangered Species Act in United States history – holding out for 382 days before his first listing. Secretary Dirk Kempthorne (from Idaho), George W. Bush's Interior appointee, eventually eclipsed him by going for more than two years without listing a single species. As wilderness advocate Bill Cunningham from the Montana Wilderness Association summed up Watt's legacy, "I can't remember a single instance where Secretary Watt took an ecosystem approach to park management."

Watt's tenure was not an anomaly, however. His actions mirrored and reflected Reagan's politics and found support among increasingly conservative members of Congress and state governments in the West. It was no coincidence, for example, that the 1980 "Reagan Revolution" helped unseat the four-term Church with a well-coordinated "Anybody But Church" (ABC) campaign. Watt's term also coincided with the emergence of more radical environmental organizations like Earth First!. Founded in 1979, Earth First! activists engaged in more confrontational tactics, such as logging road blockades and tree-sitting (to prevent logging), that alienated some traditional supporters. Their "No Compromise in Defense of Mother Earth" slogan also distanced them from Church-style consensus as surely as Watt's tactics did, and helped widen the political gap.

In the end, Watt's Interior exit came courtesy of Watt himself. Public outrage forced his resignation in 1983 after a bigoted quip in which he proclaimed that his agency's coal leasing advisory panel was diversified. "We have every kind of mixture you can have," he said. "I have a black, I have a woman, two Jews, and a cripple. And we have talent." Yet as Watt's Interior predecessor, Cecil Andrus, marveled: "The astonishing thing about it was that his personal insensitive feelings brought about his eviction. It wasn't this administration's plunder of the natural resources that brought him down." In 1983, Congress blocked some of Watt's worst initiatives by placing a moratorium on the agency's environmentally destructive and unprofitable coal leases to private developers. Similar congressional restraints on offshore oil and gas drilling followed, effectively shutting down the Department of Interior's two major programs under Watt. In 1985, a federal judge also struck down Watt's decision to allow strip mining in national parks. Watt's mine–drill–cut mantra had gone too far. The Natural Resources Defense Council characterized Watt as one of the two most "intensely controversial and blatantly anti-environmental political appointees" in American history. The other was his contemporary, fellow Reagan appointee Anne Gorsuch (Burford), director of the Environmental Protection Agency. In 2008, *Time* magazine listed Watt as the sixth worst cabinet appointee *ever*.

Yet Watt's anti-environmental stance resonated with many westerners. Between 1979 and 1981, one of the most contentious political skirmishes in the American West was in many ways an anti-wilderness crusade: the Sagebrush Rebellion. The campaign represented a legally dubious effort on the part of several western states to "reclaim" federal lands within their borders in order to expand their sovereignty and tax base. According to Rebel logic, the states owned the forests and ranges within their borders first and the federal government had wrongly usurped them, dictating from far-away Washington, policies that had little relevance or benefit to local constituents. Put more simply, in neo-West-as-colony rhetoric, the states essentially griped that since the federal government owns more than half of all the land in the West, states "lose" revenue income because they can neither tax nor sell these acres. The Rebels argued that if the federal government relinquished its control over the public domain, western economies would flourish. Armed with bullhorns and bulldozers, this take-back-the-land movement found powerful allies in Watt and Reagan, who once urged a Salt Lake City crowd to "count me in as a Rebel."

The rebellion actually began in 1979 when the Nevada state legislature, looking to shore up its ailing economy, passed a bill asserting its right to both own and manage the 49 million acres of federal holdings within its borders. Sagebrush dotted much of the BLM-held land that ranchers utilized for grazing and some that the agency was considering for wilderness designation, thus "Sagebrush Rebellion." The claim was largely symbolic, since the states never actually owned the original land and the federal government had no intention of surrendering its sovereignty. Nonetheless, the act captured the love–hate relationship western states have long carried on with the federal government, the West's dominant landlord.

The Rebellion had a special resonance in Utah, where two-thirds of the state falls under federal control. Senator Orrin Hatch (R) readily proclaimed his support for the movement – a "second American Revolution," he argued. It would counter the influence of "selfish" and "radical" environmentalists, whom he derided as "dandelion pickers" and "a cult of toadstool worshippers," determined to "lock up" the state's valuable natural resources. Such vitriol created deep divisions and provoked Utah's environmental community to join in the chorus of opposition that labeled the rebellion the "sagebrush ripoff." In August of 1979, Hatch backed up his fiery rhetoric by introducing a bill in the US Senate calling for the "return" of the West's federal lands to their "rightful" state owners. Utah legislators attempted the same land coup as Nevada the following year when they introduced the Public Lands Reclamation

Act of 1980, going so far as to stipulate 15-year jail sentences for BLM officials trying "to assert jurisdiction over public lands." The bill sailed through both houses of the state legislature, but before Governor Scott Matheson would sign it, legislators had to excise the criminal penalties for federal land managers. Matheson, too, believed that the act was largely symbolic, designed, as he later said, to increase "public involvement in the public land planning process at the state level." In other words, the western states wanted greater influence over the public lands within their borders.

The Sagebrush Rebellion ignited what historian Jedediah Rogers has called a "brushfire through the West" and "embattled ranchers, miners, and other rural people, who felt that the federal government was an insensitive landlord and environmental legislation did not serve local interests, fanned its flames." For many, wilderness designations represented the crux of the problem as they most severely restricted traditional "Old West" land uses: mining, grazing, timbering. This pattern of restriction was especially evident in rural Grand County, Utah, home to the town of Moab, where federal land ownership stood at 90% – country that writer Edward Abbey proclaimed "the most beautiful place on earth." The conflagration got especially hot over Negro Bill Canyon, located just a few miles northeast of Moab. In late 1978, despite numerous mining claims in the canyon, the BLM designated it a Wilderness Study Area (WSA) and closed off motorized access with boulders. Defiant locals arrived with bulldozers to challenge the BLM for control. In the summer of 1980, on July the 4th no less, Grand County commissioners themselves authorized a bulldozed "upgrade" of the canyon's "road," which was little more than a Jeep trail. To ensure their position was crystal clear, the commissioners festooned the ceremonial road grader with an American flag and a sticker proclaiming "I'm a Sagebrush Rebel." The bulldozer brigade, too, was largely for show, for when faced with a federal lawsuit, the Rebels agreed to restore the area to its pre-July 4 condition. However, by the end of the year, in a conciliatory gesture, the BLM dropped an estimated 1.25 million acres in the Negro Bill Canyon area from the WSA.

Bulldozers proved to be bad PR in the end. Organizations like the Sierra Club and the Wilderness Society led a national effort to discredit the rebellion. They distributed brochures, gave public talks, lobbied state legislators, worked phone banks, and made radio and television appearances in order to rally the environmental opposition. Their own experiences on the receiving end of derogatory jabs such as "tree-huggers" and "granola lovers" in previous decades motivated their efforts to inextricably link Sagebrush Rebels with "bulldozer diplomacy." Although they failed to halt the passage of Utah's Public Lands Reclamation Act of 1980, they succeeded in keeping environmental issues on the front burner, which in turn paved the way for more controversial organizations such as the newly formed Southern Utah Wilderness Association (SUWA) to challenge emerging threats from the administration of President Reagan.

In the end, the Sagebrush Rebellion languished due to the more states' rights friendly, laissez-faire attitude that Reagan and his pro-development Secretary of the Interior Watt brought into the federal government. Rebellion seemed less necessary with Reagan and Watt in control. Without a villainous federal windmill to tilt at, the rebels switched off their dozers and moseyed on home. Yet the movement's legacy has been long-lasting. In 2014, for example, a 20-year, on-going dispute between Nevada cattle rancher Cliven Bundy and the BLM escalated into an armed stand-off as federal officials began rounding up Bundy's cattle for non-payment of grazing permit fees. Bundy's claim that he doesn't "recognize the United States government as even existing," attracted large crowds of supporters and militia groups to southeastern Clark County, Nevada, forcing the BLM to halt the round-up "because of our serious concern about the safety of employees and members of the public." As of early 2016, although Bundy still owed more than $1 million in back grazing fees, the BLM's efforts to seek a solution "administratively and judicially" had been a failure. In January of 2016, Bundy's son Ammon led an armed militia take-over of a federal bird refuge in Oregon to demand that the federal government surrender its lands "to get the logger back to logging, to get the rancher back to ranching, to get the miner back to mining." When law enforcement officials finally ended the weeks-long standoff, one Bundy follower was killed and nearly a dozen were arrested, including Ammon and later Cliven. As Rogers concludes, the Sagebrush Rebellion "served to polarize, alienate, and entrench, not bring together." Unfortunately, the polemics of groups like the Sagebrush Rebels as well as Earth First! had pushed pragmatic environmental politics to the margins.

The Sagebrush Rebellion represented the opening salvo in the larger Wise Use movement, a perverse play on words that used classic conservation terminology to camouflage exploitational and developmental intentions. The Wise Use movement was (and is) comprised of a savvy and environmentally antagonistic collection of developers, states' rights advocates, resource users, and private property interests. Its supporters sought to counter campaigns for wilderness, expanded parks, and public lands by dismantling environmental regulations and eliminating federal restrictions on development. The genesis for Wise Use was a 1988 Reno, Nevada, conference that outlined a comprehensive Wise Use Agenda calling for, among other elements, the opening of "all public lands to mining and energy production," assertion of "states' sovereign rights in matters pertaining to water distribution and regulation," intensified logging, timber harvesting, and grazing in the national forests and on all public lands, weakening of the Endangered Species Act, and protection of private property rights against environmental protection laws. Taking their cues from environmental activists and cleverly employing conservation rhetoric, Wise Users mimicked their foes. They lobbied Congress, packed and testified at public hearings, organized fundraising and letter-writing drives, used savvy PR campaigns, and boycotted programs that advocated environmental protection. Often well-funded by resource and extractive industries, like timber and mining corporations, Wise Use groups nevertheless portrayed themselves as grassroots champions of rural values and nature-loving lifestyles – a masquerade that many environmental organizations endeavored to expose.

A current, more benign example of a Wise Use group is the Blue Ribbon Coalition (BRC), which boasts "members in all 50 states." Its self-stated purpose is "to keep your land open for use, whether you recreate on a mountain bike, snowmobile, motorcycle, personal watercraft, ATV, four-wheel drive, horse, or your hiking boots." BRC's seemingly inclusive website, "sharetrails.org," ominously warns that "radical environmentalists" are seeking "to lock up millions of acres" in northern California and southern Oregon as part of an "Ancient Forest National Park" proposal. Joining forces with "Stop Land Grab," the BRC argues that such a park "would result in colossal loss of recreational access, private property rights and local input into federal lands decisions," and encourages its members to attend a panel discussion and fundraiser sponsored by Stop Land Grab. In another missive about wilderness proposals in Utah, the BRC urges its membership to attend and testify at public meetings: "Wilderness activists, resource companies, mountain bike clubs, hikers, equestrians, climbers and canyoneers are all viewing this as an opportunity, and you should too!" Bulldozers were out, participatory democracy was in. Like their environmentalist counterparts, Wise Users began to work within the system.

The Wise Use movement illustrates the ongoing tension between economy and environment, and continues the century-long dialogue about development versus preservation in the West. The increasingly radical voices in these debates echo the rhetoric of the past, but in a transformed context, with a much more powerful preservationist coalition than in John Muir's time. Nowhere was this late-twentieth-century fissure more evident than in Oregon, where Wise Use and the Endangered Species Act collided over the fate of a nocturnal predator called the northern spotted owl (see Figure 10.2).

The genesis of the controversy was the 1973 Endangered Species Act (ESA), which stipulates, among other requirements, that once the government lists a species, its protection becomes primary, reducing all other concerns, even those of private property holders, to secondary. Essentially, under the ESA, preservation trumps profit. In 1990, the US Fish and Wildlife Service listed the northern spotted owl as threatened. The most immediate consequence was a blanket protection, including a court-ordered ban on logging, for the ecosystem the owls called home: the last remaining old-growth forests of Oregon, Washington, and California. While most of the owls inhabited federal lands, significant numbers also resided on state and private property. The

Figure 10.2 Spotted owls in a Pacific Northwest old growth forest. Source: Reproduced with permission of Jason Mowdy.

monster trees in these ancient stands also happened to be the bread and butter of the region's flagging timber industry, which already faced serious economic challenges from automation and international competitors like Canada. The superficial result seemed to be a classic environment versus economy brawl, one that drove the wedge between environmental advocates and resources interests even deeper.

In one corner were ESA proponents, who pushed for the spotted owl's protection because of its role as an "indicator species," a species that acts as a barometer for the health of the entire ecosystem that it inhabits. Northern spotted owls are intolerant of habitat disturbances. In Pacific Northwest old-growth forests, the red vole is similarly sensitive to habitat health, but it's neither cute nor countable. The spotted owl is both. In addition to being charismatic and visually appealing, a definite bonus for eliciting sympathetic public support for protection, the medium-sized fluffy brown owl is relatively easy to find and thus count. Quite simply, if you "whoo" in the forest, the spotted owl will "whoo" back. By 1990, the owl's numbers were plummeting as ever more vigorous logging efforts turned to valuable old-growth timber to sustain the traditional extractive local economy. As recently as 2015, scientists estimated that the owl's entire population in the Pacific Northwest numbered fewer than 4000 individuals.

In the opposite corner from owls and advocates sat the multi-billion dollar timber industry and the numerous small towns and rural families that depended upon logging for their livelihoods. For them, the owl acted as an indicator species, too; it indicated that their extractive way of life was in serious jeopardy. Both the logging industry and the US Forest Service estimated the owl's protection would cost 30 000 jobs in economically hard-pressed communities. Anti-owl bumper stickers blossomed throughout the Pacific Northwest – "Save a logger, eat an owl" and "I Like Spotted Owls – Fried" – and it was not uncommon to see a cute little stuffed owl effigy smashed into the grilles of logging trucks thundering out of Pacific Northwest forests.

For both sides, the spotted owl became the simplified totem of a much more complicated and nuanced struggle. In the polarized political climate ushered in by Watt, rational Church-like consensus became as endangered and rare as the spotted owl. Environmentalists were not wrong to assert that old-growth forests and the ecosystems they supported were in grave jeopardy. By 1990, old-growth acreage had diminished to just 10% of its original range. Biologists predicted that at the current cut rate, old-growth forests themselves would go extinct within 10–30 years. At that point, the majestic giants would disappear as would all the species that thrived in this particular environmental niche, while loggers and logging towns would still face the same economic dead-end dilemma. Save the last ecological remnants now, ESA advocates argued, before we lose it forever. It was a fair and rational argument.

But this argument ignored the human costs associated with protection. What about the third- and fourth-generation logging families that depended on these same forests to pay their mortgages and send their kids to school? "Move." "Get a different job." "It's inevitable." These insensitive responses of owl zealots overlooked the reality that people are also part of nature – that the old-growth forest was their ecosystem, too. Both people and owls were in danger/endangered. As environmental historian William Cronon admonishes, "if we are to solve those problems, we need an environmental ethic that will tell us as much about using nature as about not using it … [and create] a middle ground in which responsible use and non-use might attain some kind of balanced, sustainable relationship."

In reality, the spotted owl did *not* cause timber industry woes, but it became an easy and effective symbol/target for both sides. Increased automation that replaced humans with machines, decades of clearcutting, and cheap wood from Canada and elsewhere that flooded the timber market and drove down prices constituted the real culprit. Pacific Northwest mills and logging operations could not compete and so they began shutting down. Old-growth harvests functioned as their economic Hail Mary. The most rational business executives and workers ultimately understood that even if they cut down every last colossal conifer, they could only temporarily stave off impending industry crisis. From 1947 to 1964, for example, long before the spotted owl controversy, the number of Pacific Northwest logging jobs had declined by 90%. Once the towering cedars, firs, hemlocks, and spruces disappeared for good, families and corporations alike would face the same hard retooling choices. Old-growth was not timber's salvation; at best it offered only a temporary reprieve to a traditional extractive industry facing fundamental reorganization if it wished to survive into the twenty-first century. Frustrated lumberjacks found blaming the spotted owl and "radical environmentalists" a simpler solution, however, and both provided more obvious targets for regional protests and rallies.

By the early twenty-first century, the spotted owl controversy mostly subsided as expanding global timber demand raised hopes and economic revenues in the Pacific Northwest's logging towns and communities. As one Oregon timber industry representative remarked in 2010, 20 years after the spotted owl's listing, "It's interesting that in spite of everything that's happened to our industry, we're still the second-biggest industry in the state, behind high tech. But with that being said, our industry is not what it used to be. Hundreds of mills closed, and tens of thousands of people lost their jobs, and those jobs haven't been replaced."

On the ecological side of the ledger, northern spotted owl numbers continue to decline by 3–7% each year, but the primary culprit is no longer intensified logging. Instead, competition from invasive barred owls, which are bigger, more aggressive, and less ecologically sensitive, is causing the spotted owl to "circle the drain" in some parts of its range. The US Fish and Wildlife Service, the agency charged with protecting endangered species, now faces a perplexing problem: do you kill one owl to save another? As forest biologist Eric Forsman admits, "You could shoot barred owls until you're blue in the face, but unless you're willing to do it forever, it's just not going to work." Like most environmental problems, this one defies simple solutions. Yet, as of 2015, spotted owls remained threatened (and under consideration for "endangered") under the ESA, many Pacific Northwest timber towns remained economically threatened, and environmental consensus remained out of reach as evidenced by the flurry of lawsuits both sides continued to file.

President Bill Clinton added fuel to the Wise Use fire in September of 1996, when he used the powerful 1906 Antiquities Act to create the nearly 1.9 million acre Grand Staircase –Escalante National Monument (GSENM) in southern Utah, the largest national monument in the system. It was a bold and controversial stroke, worthy of Theodore Roosevelt. Clinton gave the state's governor and congressional representatives only 24 hours' advance notice, knowing that his actions would ignite a firestorm of criticism, especially within Utah. The president was not mistaken. In fact, Clinton tried to avoid the heat by announcing the GSENM dedication not in Utah, but at the Grand Canyon in

Arizona – a state he desperately needed to win (and did) in his 1996 re-election campaign. Utah's Senator Hatch gave voice to the opposition of local ranchers, farmers, developers, and gas, coal, and oil extractors whose economic development prospects for this section of Utah's back country were suddenly cut off when he decried the creation of the new monument as "the mother of all land grabs."

The GSENM derives its name from early Spanish explorer Father Silvestre Vélez de Escalante (who never actually saw his namesake river) and an early geological survey of the region that described as a "great stairway" the unique, candy-colored sandstone cliffs that ascend through the park from the Sonoran Desert into coniferous forests. The monument is situated in the heart of scenic southern Utah, adjacent to Bryce Canyon National Park and Glen Canyon National Recreation Area, and is divided into three areas: the Grand Staircase, the Kaiparowits Plateau, and the Canyons of the Escalante. Significantly, the BLM manages the monument – a first for the agency – rather than the National Park Service, which has contributed to the GSENM's polarizing presence. The BLM's long-standing contentious relationship with local ranchers and mechanized recreationists stems from the agency's efforts to manage its arid holdings in southern Utah by attempting to strike a balance between environmental stewardship and economic utility. The result has been a running battle between BLM officials and monument vandals in yet another clash between protection and development.

The GSENM further reveals the fractured environmental consensus brought on by Watt and his allies. Although Clinton's designation certainly shored up his electoral numbers in the region, it also directly responded to the wilderness/Sagebrush controversies mentioned above. The monument's protection not only ensured that management of sensitive potential wilderness areas would preserve their integrity, but it also effectively blocked the massive Andalex coal mine, which had set its sights on the remote and lucrative Kaiparowits Plateau. The rugged, isolated, pinyon-juniper-dotted plateau, sprawling over 1600 square miles, holds hundreds of archeological sites, dinosaur fossil beds, a diverse and complex high-desert ecosystem, and 5–7 billion tons of recoverable coal. The original proposal to build a 3000-megawatt coal-fired power plant fed by the plateau's fossil fuel resources emerged in 1965, but its unfortunate timing coincided with the fight over Glen Canyon Dam, which drew negative attention to extractive resource use in scenic but remote areas. The escalating costs to withdraw the region's coal reserves finally killed the project in 1975. But in 1991, Andalex Resources revived the plan. It proposed the extraction of 14 000 tons of coal every two days (2.5 million tons per year), hauled by 300 trucks per day (24-7), on $75 million taxpayer-subsidized roads through Glen Canyon National Recreation Area, two WSAs, the Paiute Indian reservation, and several small towns. Andalex anticipated that the entire project would potentially attract 1400 new residents, directly employ more than 450 people, and pump more than $12 million into the state's coffers.

Environmentalists blanched at the blatant development calculus. An attorney for the Southern Utah Wilderness Alliance said simply, "there are no substitutes for the wilderness value of this area." To develop or not to develop, that was the question. Clinton's designation of the GSENM provided one answer: not here. Edward Abbey had always argued that "the idea of wilderness needs no defense, it only needs more defenders." For the Kaiparowitz, this defender was Clinton. Nevertheless, to assuage offended constituencies and redress potential economic losses, the 1998 Utah Schools and Lands Exchange Act swapped out state lands and mineral rights within the monument for other federal lands in Utah and gave the state an additional $50 million. This generous federal compensation that attempted to bridge the economy/environment chasm seldom merits mention by those still angered by Clinton's act.

While many aspects of the monument's creation and management could start a fight in an empty bar, the most controversial issue affecting GSENM and other parts of the West remains Revised Statute 2477 (RS 2477), a one-sentence power-house left over from the nineteenth century. Congress passed RS 2477 in 1866, a time when the federal government actively promoted western settlement, access to mineral deposits, and the transfer of public lands into private hands (e.g. the 1862 Homestead Act). The act declared that "the right-of-way for the construction of highways over public lands, not reserved for public uses, is hereby granted." The 1976 passage of the Federal Land Policy Management Act repealed RS 2477, but provided a loophole big enough for southern Utahans to drive a bulldozer through. "Nothing in this Act, or in any amendment made by this Act," FLPMA states, "shall be construed as terminating any valid lease, permit, patent, right-of-way, or other land use right or authorization existing on the date of approval of this Act." Road rights prevailed.

Therein lies the rub: what exactly constitutes a "highway" or road? Landowners, wilderness advocates, recreation users, and agency managers all have their own definitions and they rarely agree. In 2000, in obvious homage to the Wise Use/Sagebrush Rebellion ideology, Utah informed the Department of Interior that it intended to pursue legal authority over 25 000 "roads," some of which it admitted were no more than off-road-vehicle tracks and dry stream-beds (see Figure 10.3). The challenge was not a hollow one, however. Relying on the clause in the 1964 Wilderness Act that stipulates that "there shall be no commercial enterprise and no permanent road within any wilderness area designated by this Act," anti-wilderness crusaders mounted their earth movers to plow "roads" through wilderness study areas in the hope that such scars would nix designation. In GSENM, for example, local rights

Figure 10.3 An example of a questionable state "road" claim under RS 2477 in a disputed wilderness study area of the Dirty Devil River in southeastern Utah. Source: Reproduced with permission of Ray Bloxham/Southern Utah Wilderness Alliance.

activists and several Utah counties protested vehemently that under RS 2477, pre-existing "roads" gave them title and access to roads crossing the newly declared monument thus negating federal authority.

In 2003, seeking to avoid tens of thousands of court cases and endless legal skirmishes, the State of Utah and the Department of Interior signed a Memorandum of Understanding (MOU) outlining a fair process for determining the validity of RS 2477 road claims. In 2010, as evidence of the possibility for successful resolution under this compromise solution, the federal government recognized the validity of one RS 2477 claim and relinquished quiet title to the GSENM's Skutumpah Road to Kane County. The county, not the federal government, controlled the road. However, in 2012, under conservative Governor Gary Herbert, the state resumed its lawsuits-for-roads tactic and claimed victory in March of 2013, when, after tens of thousands of dollars had been spent on opposing sides, the courts granted the state title to 89 miles of road out of the 35 000 miles Herbert intends to pursue. In response, the Utah Wilderness Coalition dug in its heels and upped the ante on its 2013 Citizens' Proposal to demand protection for 9.1 million wilderness acres throughout the state. In such cases, the vastness of the gulf that still separates the two constituencies seems insurmountable. Watt's wedge politics endure.

Yet for all of the division and shouting that followed in the wake of Reagan's assumption of the presidency, there were some positive developments in western environmental history in the late twentieth century. One was the return of the wolf. Interestingly, the "land ethic" of Aldo Leopold, a man once committed to eliminating wolves, played an important role in their restoration. Former Secretary of Interior (under Clinton) Bruce Babbitt explained the connection, "In January 1995 I helped carry the first grey wolf into Yellowstone, where they had been eradicated by federal predator control policy only six decades earlier. Looking through the crates into her eyes, I reflected on how Aldo Leopold once took part in that policy, then eloquently challenged it. By illuminating for us how wolves play a critical role in the whole of creation, he expressed the ethic and the laws which would reintroduce them nearly a half-century after his death." Babbitt, like so many others, had come to appreciate the "trophic cascade" so deftly predicted by Leopold – the rippling effect through an entire ecosystem that the elimination of keystone species (one that has a disproportionate impact on its environment) like wolves produced. It sent the whole delicate balance careening toward ill-health and degradation. Wolf reintroduction reversed the decline, restoring not only the individual species but also the health of the larger ecosystem.

The US Fish and Wildlife Service first listed the gray wolf as endangered in 1974, one year after passage of the Endangered Species Act. Wolf numbers had plummeted to just 20 breeding pairs exiled in northern Minnesota and a few on Isle Royale, Michigan, as a result of predator control programs, loss of habitat, and the destruction of their traditional prey base (bison, elk, even beavers, etc.) In addition to providing a last minute save from extirpation in the contiguous 48 states, federal ESA wolf protection also allowed for capture-and-release as well as captive breeding programs to begin to rebuild populations for reintroduction into their former habitats. The Mexican gray wolf, for example, is a smaller relative found in the American Southwest. The rarest subspecies of gray wolf, the Mexican wolf had all but disappeared from the wild by the 1970s, when biologists captured the last four wild males and last wild female in Mexico and initiated a captive breeding program to maintain the wolf's genetics sufficiently to thwart its disappearance. In 1980, coincidentally, a wild gray wolf pack from Canada – the Magic Pack – crossed into Glacier National Park in Montana and began to reestablish the canids' historic role in the western environment. A decade and a half later, Secretary Babbitt helped restore wolves to Yellowstone and their populations have continued to expand ever since. From a low of fewer than 300 individuals, wolves now number more than 4000 in the lower 48 states. Although they once ranged from Atlantic to Pacific, gray wolves now make their limited home in the West in the mostly forested lands of Montana, Idaho, and Wyoming, while small populations of Mexican gray wolves fight extinction in Arizona and New Mexico. In a hopeful development, however, in 2015 at least six Mexican wolf packs had produced 28 pups in their recovery area.

The restored presence of wolves in an ecosystem has had a profound effect. As the US Fish and Wildlife Service discovered, "within two years of the [Yellowstone] wolf reintroduction, researchers found that wolves had killed half the coyotes in the area, forced elk to become more vigilant, and provided many opportunities for scavengers to share their kills. Because there are fewer coyotes, rodents and small animals such as fox may be more plentiful, a boon for predators like hawks and bald eagles." The tendency of wolves to hunt weak, diseased, and physically impaired prey also moderates the health of other species, and acts as a check on their prey populations, encouraging "survival of the fittest" among deer, elk, and other wildlife. Additionally, the presence of wolves in the park helped restore beaver populations, which had become extirpated in Yellowstone, as well as red foxes, and the health of aspen and willow stands. In a classic trophic cascade, wolf predation on elk meant fewer hungry mouths lingered along the park's rivers and mowed down the willows. Willows are a primary food source and building material for beavers. With elk on the move, willow stands recovered, and so, too, did beavers. Wolves, it turns out, even help to fatten up grizzly bears. Recent scholarship demonstrates that in Yellowstone, wolves' control of the park's elk population has predictably lessened the elks' consumption of berry-producing shrubs, which in turn leaves more berries for the bears. Echoing the earlier sentiments of Aldo Leopold, ecologist Robert Beschta concluded that "as we learn more about the cascading effects they have on ecosystems, the issue may be more than having just enough individual wolves so they can survive as a species. In some situations, we may wish to consider the numbers necessary to help control overbrowsing, allow tree and shrub recovery, and restore ecosystem health."

In the age of Wise Use and environmental polarization, however, wolf reintroduction was not without significant controversy. Major opposition around Yellowstone and in nearby Idaho arose primarily from ranchers and hunters, who feared the return of this effective predator would negatively affect livestock and big game populations. Furthermore, in the states' rights mindset of the West, wolf reintroduction represented yet another example of the heavy hand of the federal government imposing its will on voiceless locals, who nevertheless had to bear the financial consequences of bureaucratic decisions from far-off Washington DC. In an effort to mediate the environment versus economy dispute and acknowledge and offset ranchers' concerns, the environmental organization Defenders of Wildlife established a "wolf compensation fund" that to date has paid more than $1.4 million to private livestock owners for predation losses. Further compromise emerged when the US Fish and Wildlife Service agreed to reintroduce wolves in both Yellowstone and Idaho as "non-essential experimental populations," which significantly relaxed the strict ESA-mandated protection requirements.

In spite of the political contests that swirled around them, gray wolves flourished. By 2013, their population in the northern Rocky Mountain states stood at more than 1600 adult wolves divided among more than 320 packs, marking the 11th year that western wolves exceeded recovery goals stipulated in their ESA listing. As a result, in 2013, the US Fish and Wildlife Service federally delisted the gray wolf (but not the Mexican wolf) from the ESA and turned over their management to the states. This policy change was also controversial, as Idaho, Montana, and Wyoming have conservative, powerful anti-wolf constituencies. All three states proposed and began to utilize sport hunting as a means of managing their wolf populations. Wyoming went a step further and regionally classified some wolves as "Trophy Game Animals" and others as "Predatory Animals" in order to legalize year-round wolf hunting. These actions in turn aroused the ire of wolf advocates, who feared a return to the eradication/bounty policies of the early twentieth century that ultimately landed wolves on the ESA list to begin with. In September of 2014, in light of these developments, a federal judge reversed wolf delisting in Wyoming, ensuring that the politics of wolves would remain contentious in the West.

In many ways, these continued clashes between developers and preservationists, Sagebrush/Wise Use proponents and ESA/public lands advocates in the post-Watt West erupted with such force during the last two decades of the twentieth century because the West itself had been evolving from extractive to attractive. The "New West's" financially "attractive" powerhouses of tourism, service industries, and technology supplanted "Old West" resource-based extractive economies founded on mining, ranching, agriculture, timber, and salmon, with the notable exception of the recent oil fracking boom in North Dakota. While neither fluid nor foregone, this Old West/New West transition varied widely across the region, and the result often manifested as Old West politics and politicians railing against New West ideas and values about nature that threatened traditional western ways of life. In-migration from the rest of the country exacerbated these differences. By 2000, California and Texas alone comprised nearly 20% of the nation's population, while states like South Dakota, Kansas, and Wyoming expanded minimally, and North Dakota actually lost population until the fracking boom. Newcomers with little sense of the historic West were often less sympathetic to entrenched extractive industry, as exemplified in the spotted owl controversy. Moreover, new westerners gravitated to the cities, where these natural resource industries played less important roles in the local economy. For these New West urban and suburbanites, wolves and wilderness, not cattle and mines, constituted the nostalgic remnants of the Wild West/Old West that they longed to protect.

Perhaps the most striking example of this New West economy is Las Vegas, a glittering jewel set in the arid Nevada desert. Between 1980 and 2000, the Clark County population, which includes suburban Las Vegas and "the Strip," exploded from 463 087 to 1 375 765 around an economy based on tourism and gaming, which in turn fuels its service and consumer sectors. Founded as a railroad town and a conduit for extractive mining goods at the beginning of the twentieth century, Las Vegas expanded with the construction of Hoover Dam during the Great Depression. But the legalization of gambling in 1931 boomed the city's "attractive" economy and made Las Vegas a true tourist destination – as did atomic bomb test viewing parties. By the turn of the twenty-first century, one-fifth of all the city's jobs were gaming related and Las Vegas boasted the highest rate of new job growth in the country, disproportionately focused on New West gaming, hospitality, and construction. Old West natural resources, agriculture, and mining employed just over 3000 people in the county out of a labor force of nearly 895 000, for example, and just 28 500 worked in manufacturing. New West "arts, entertainment, recreation, accommodation, and food services," by contrast, employed nearly 263 000.

Historian Samuel Hayes argues that the shift to a New West economy also affects attitudes about environmental protection. "Those areas with a long history of urbanization where urban demands had influenced the course of politics for many years," he observes, "provided the strongest environmental support, and those where rural and raw-material-producing influences persisted well into the twentieth century had the lowest." In the post-Watt West, this shift has meant that the "attractive" Pacific Northwest and California usually lead the way in environmental protection and legislation, while the still somewhat "extractive" Mountain West states and Arizona lag behind, and the Great Plains remain actively resistant.

That new westerners sought out the environmental amenities that Old West industries threatened – open spaces, public lands, unmarred views, abundant wildlife, clean air, and free-flowing rivers – only exacerbated enmity. With their imported dollars, they built trophy homes where urban areas and wildlands meet and buried the bones of the Old West under sprawling decks and four-car garages. Red Lodge, Montana, is a good example. This former busted-out mining town boomed again as a blue-ribbon trout fly-fishing destination because of its environmental amenities. Park City, Utah, found that its ghost town mining skeletons provided a rustic and "colorful" backdrop for downhill skiing and the independent Sundance Film Festival. And the uranium extractive frenzy that had once made Moab, Utah, roar, gave way to mountain bikers and Jeep enthusiasts who flock to the spectacularly attractive red and rimrock country in adjacent Arches and Canyonlands national parks. These newcomers often have both the time and money to devote to environmental activism and they have become a powerful constituency that frequently aligns itself in direct opposition to traditional mining, ranching, logging, and prospecting interests. Even in largely extractive Montana, the state's constitution, for example, guarantees all of its citizens "the right to a clean and healthful environment." The new tourist industries offered jobs in many areas where extractive industry had declined, although these service oriented jobs typically paid less and came with fewer benefits or protection by a labor union than the mining, oil, and timber jobs of the past – a "devil's bargain," according to historian Hal Rothman.

Watt and other Reagan appointees shared the view that environmental values and protection were neither deeply nor widely held by the American public, but were instead the agenda of a few "radical" activists who had temporarily (they hoped) captured the public imagination. Watt's appointment vigorously tested this theory and revealed that, while deep divides still partition the American West, the question had shifted from *whether* to *which* species and natural environments should be protected and how. Westerners, it turned out, were unwilling to sell off wholesale the last best places just to save a few cents on their utility bills. Certainly each side had strong opinions about the appropriate means for achieving both a healthy economy *and* environment, but in the end, open dialogue proved the only way to achieve this balance. Watt was not the answer. As the American West entered the twenty-first century, the region faced on-going Old West/New West challenges to be sure, but the specter of accelerating global climate change now threatened to disrupt traditional ecosystems and imperil the health of the many species, including humans, who call it "home." The West would have to reconcile environment and economy, the cultural and political divides that shaped how westerners thought about them, and rediscover its center.

Suggested Reading

George Cameron Coggins and Doris K. Nagel, "'Nothing Beside Remains': The Legal Legacy of James G. Watt's Tenure as Secretary of the Interior on Federal Land Law and Policy," *Boston College Environmental Affairs Law Review*, Vol. 17, No. 3 (Spring 1990), 473–550. http://lawdigitalcommons.bc.edu/cgi/viewcontent.cgi?article=1533&context=ealr (accessed February 8, 2016).

William Cronon, "The Trouble with Wilderness; or, Getting Back to the Wrong Nature," in William Cronon, ed., *Uncommon Ground: Rethinking the Human Place in Nature* (New York, Norton, 1996). The essay also can be found on Cronon's website: www.williamcronon.net/writing/Cronon_Trouble_with_Wilderness_1995.pdf (accessed February 8, 2016).

Michael J. Dax, *Grizzly West: A Failed Attempt to Reintroduce Grizzly Bears in the Mountain West* (Lincoln: University of Nebraska Press, 2015).

Robert A. Goldberg, "The Western Hero in Politics: Barry Goldwater, Ronald Reagan, and the Rise of the American Conservative Movement," in Jeff Roche, ed., *The Political Culture of the New West* (Lawrence: University Press of Kansas, 2008), 13–50.

Marcus Hall, "Repairing Mountains: Restoration, Ecology, and Wilderness in Twentieth-Century Utah," *Environmental History* Vol. 6, No. 4 (October 2001), 584–610.

Brian Leech, "Protest, Power and the Pit: Fighting Open Pit Mining in Butte, Montana," *Montana: The Magazine of Western History*, Summer 2012, 24–43.

Michael McCarthy, "The First Sagebrush Rebellion: Forest Reserves and States Rights in Colorado and the West, 1891-1907," in Harold K. Steen, ed., *The Origins of the National Forests: A Centennial Symposium* (Durham: Forest History Society, 1992). www.foresthistory.org/Publications/Books/Origins_National_Forests/sec13.htm (accessed February 8, 2015).

William Ripple, "Of Bears and Berries: Return of Wolves Aids Grizzly Bears in Yellowstone," Oregon State University Press Release, July 29, 2013. http://oregonstate.edu/ua/ncs/archives/2013/jul/bears-and-berries-return-wolves-aids-grizzly-bears-yellowstone (accessed February 8, 2016).

Jedidiah S. Rogers, "The Volatile Sagebrush Rebellion," in Brian Q. Cannon and Jessie L. Embry, eds, *Utah in the Twentieth Century* (Logan: Utah State University Press, 2009), 367–384.

Jedediah S. Rogers, *Roads in the Wilderness: Conflict in Canyon Country* (Salt Lake City: University of Utah Press, 2013).

Hal K. Rothman, *Devil's Bargains: Tourism in the Twentieth-Century American West* (Lawrence: University Press of Kansas, 1998).

Jeffrey C. Sanders, "Animal Trouble and Urban Anxiety: Human-Animal Interaction in Post-Earth Day Seattle, *Environmental History*, Vol. 16, No. 2 (April 2011), 226–261.

Ellen Stroud, "Troubled Waters in Ecotopia: Environmental Racism in Portland, Oregon," *Radical History Review*, Vol. 74 (Spring 1999), 65–95.

James Morton Turner, "'The Specter of Environmentalism': Wilderness, Environmental Politics, and the Evolution of the New Right," *The Journal of American History*, June 2009, 123–148. www.journalofamericanhistory.org/teaching/2009_06/article.pdf (accessed February 8, 2016)

Craig Welch, "The Spotted Owl's New Nemesis," *Smithsonian*, January 2009. www.smithsonianmag.com/science-nature/the-spotted-owls-new-nemesis-131610387/?sessionGUID=1db28138-d648-7354-3720-c4932ea9a752&no-ist=&page=1 (accessed February 8, 2016)

Thomas R. Wellock, "The Dickey Bird Scientists Take Charge: Science, Policy, and the Spotted Owl," *Environmental History*, Vol. 15, No. 3 (July 2010), 381–414.

"What Watt Wrought," *High Country News* article collection, October 31, 1983, 10–14. https://www.hcn.org/external_files/40years/blog/WattWroughtArticles.pdf (accessed February 8, 2016).

Richard White, "'Are You an Environmentalist or Do you Work for a Living?': Work and Nature," in William Cronon, ed., *Uncommon Ground: Rethinking the Human Place in Nature* (New York: W.W. Norton & Co., 1995), 171–185.

Michael Wise, "Killing Montana's Wolves: Stockgrowers, Bounty Bills, and the Uncertain Distinction between Predators and Producers," *Montana: The Magazine of Western History*, Vol. 63, No. 4 (Winter 2013), 51–67.

Epilogue

Sustainability and the "Triumph of the Commons"

In 1950, physicist Enrico Fermi posed a deceptively simple question about extraterrestrial life to his lunchmates at the Los Alamos National Laboratory in New Mexico: "where is everybody?" In the vastness of the universe, he observed, with billions of other galaxies, some billions of years older than our own, there are almost certainly planets capable of supporting life. Surely at least some of them have experienced intellectual evolution sufficient to support interstellar travel … even earth-bound humans are exploring these possibilities. If so, then extraterrestrial galactic colonization or visitation should "only" take a few tens of millions of years. Yet, as far as we know, no one has come. Why not? Are we alone? This inexplicable dilemma has become known as the Fermi Paradox.

Scientists have spent the past several decades debating solutions to the Fermi Paradox. Explanations range from the simple – we're unique in all the universe – to the bizarre – there are aliens among us, we just don't recognize them. But the theory that most focus on is some variation of "The Great Filter," which argues that life, especially intelligent life, at some stage of development hits an evolutionary wall beyond which it can't survive to engage in interstellar travel – a developmental dead-end. In the last half of the twentieth century, nuclear warfare seemed the mostly likely candidate for human self-destruction on earth, but the real peril may be far more insidious: technological overreach. In other words, the rapid pace of resource extraction and consumption facilitated by ever-improving technology may so imperil

Losing Eden: An Environmental History of the American West, First Edition. Sara Dant.
© 2017 John Wiley & Sons, Inc. Published 2017 by John Wiley & Sons, Inc.

the ecological balance of the planet – through global climate change, species elimination, and food and water shortages – that human extinction becomes inevitable. For centuries, human populations have transformed their natural environments through innovations such as the wheel, irrigation, and genetic modification, yet history is rife with examples of environmental overreach, as in ancient Mesopotamia or more recently in the American West Anasazi cultures. Resource abundance devolved into resource scarcity and accompanying salinization of soils, deforestation, erosion, loss of species abundance, and exotic invasions. Time and again, when humans have exceeded the carrying capacity of their surrounding environment, they have paid with cultural decline and then scattered. But there is nowhere left on earth to scatter to today. Something is preventing interstellar travel; is it possible for a planet bound species to evolve technologically *without* destroying itself? The riddle of Fermi's Paradox provides a cautionary prospective for considering the present and future West.

At the beginning of the twenty-first century, the greatest environmental threat to the West, the nation, and the world is global climate change, aka global warming. The long-term rise in temperatures – big-picture change over a century or more – rather than short-term variation, defines global climate change. It may well be our species' "Great Filter." Although the planet's climate has always been in flux, cycling between ice ages and warmer epochs, what distinguishes recent trends is the *rate* of change. In the past, even minor temperature variations occurred over millions or even tens of millions of years; now scientists measure them in decades. To track these cycles, scientists use an index of global average temperatures, and they indicate a steady and disconcerting increase since the 1880s. The principal cause of this warming trend is the rise in carbon dioxide emissions and other heat-trapping greenhouse gases released during the Industrial Revolution. The primary source: the burning of fossil fuels. Since this time, the earth has warmed by approximately 1.5 °F. Although this sounds like a minuscule shift, the earth's ecosystems function much like finely tuned instruments and even small changes can produce major consequences. Some of these include:

- rising sea levels that would imperil the nearly 40% of Americans who live along the nation's coasts;
- more extreme weather events: hotter summers, colder winters, more frequent and powerful tornados and hurricanes, wildfires, torrential rains and floods;
- more extreme, longer-lasting periods of drought, irreparable alteration of species habitats, accelerating extinctions, and shifting plant and animal ranges;
- earlier and farther animal migrations as many species seek out higher elevations;
- disruption of food and water supplies.

The list is daunting, some of the consequences of global climate change are already evident, and the possibilities yet to come are frightening. Because the American West is at the vanguard of these environmental shifts, the need to develop a long-term sustainable relationship between people and nature in this region has become urgent. "Humans are literally cooking their planet," warned atmospheric scientist Jonathan Overpeck after 2014 became the hottest year on record since record-keeping began in 1880. The average global temperature that year was 58.24 °F, fully 1.24 °F higher than the twentieth-century average. The year 2015 smashed that record, registering a whopping 0.29 °F warmer than 2014. So far, 15 of the warmest 16 years on record have occurred in the twenty-first century.

Aridity defines the American West, and the region's water worries have intensified as high temperatures and parching drought have evaporated the hydraulic systems essential for making the desert bloom. Since 2004, the Colorado River Basin alone has lost an estimated 17 trillion gallons of water – enough to quench the thirst of more than 50 million households for a year – and the vast majority of that loss has been in groundwater. Groundwater is especially critical because both farmers and municipalities utilize it as an essential "reserve" to compensate for years when rainfall fails to replenish more traditional irrigation sources. The consequences are far-reaching; as senior water cycle specialist Jay Famiglietti concluded: "combined with declining snowpack and population growth, this will likely threaten the long-term ability of the basin to meet its water allocation commitments [outlined in the Colorado River Compact] to the seven basin states and to Mexico."

Hoover Dam's Lake Mead, the largest human-made reservoir in the country, acts as a barometer for the Colorado Basin, which some have called "the most over-allocated in the world." In 2014, lake levels were 139 feet below capacity, leaving a wide, white bathtub ring around the reservoir that directly slakes the thirst of more than 20 million westerners. If it falls just 30 feet more, Lake Mead will be at "dead pool," a condition that prevents water from flowing out of the dam and through its turbines – no water and no power. By mid-2015, the lake was down another 5 feet. Some scientists have predicted that Mead faces a 50% chance of falling below dead pool by 2017 and an equal chance of completely drying up by 2021. The city of Las Vegas, which draws 90% of its water from the reservoir, was in no mood to wait for doomsday. In December of 2014, workers completed construction of a nearly $1 billion "third straw" project, and the state authorized an additional $680 million for pumps that will siphon trapped dead pool waters directly to this desert oasis and maintain the lush mirage. Glen Canyon Dam and Lake Powell face a similar fate, the loss of which would cut power to more than 350 000 homes and the air conditioners that make life in Phoenix tolerable.

For California, 2015 was a particularly grim year. Coming off a winter where the Sierra snowpack was "the worst in a century" according to Jeff Anderson, a federal snow surveyor, California confronted unprecedented water shortages across the state as drought there became a declared "national disaster." A persistent high pressure had parked off the coast since the winter of 2013–2014 and shoved all of the Golden State's moisture northward into Alaska and Canada. Climate scientist Daniel Swain called it the "Ridiculously Resilient Ridge," or "Triple R." New studies show that California and parts of the West may be in for a 1000-year "megadrought" (lasting for decades or longer) that could exceed even the worst conditions in the region's deep history. When Governor Jerry Brown announced the first mandatory water restrictions in California's history, designed to reduce "potable [drinkable] urban water usage" by 25%, he acknowledged that daily lawn watering was "going to be a thing of the past." So, too, may car washing. Currently, no city in the country has more car washes than Los Angeles, and no state has more than California. As water prices rose, some of them switched to reclaimed or recycled water to stay in business (and avoid restrictions), but many have not. Another major economic concern is tourism. Only about a third of California's 866 golf courses irrigate with non-potable water, and the prospect of brown golf "greens" has managers concerned. Additionally, homeowners who paid premium property prices to live next to the fairways complain about plans to convert fringe areas into more drought tolerant landscaping. Water worries also menace the state's lucrative recreation industry centered around lakes, pools, and spas. Significantly, Brown's restrictions did not extend to the agriculture industry, which immediately raised suburban howls of protest, since farms use about 80% of the state's water supply and contribute about 2% to the state's economy. As the world's breadbasket, however, California cannot afford to dry up and blow away. Since 2010, "epic" drought has cost the state in excess of $5 billion, and those figures will only continue to rise. In November of 2014, voters passed Proposition 1 to provide more than $7 billion for massive new public works projects. But more dams and reservoirs are not the answer.

Elaborate hydraulic schemes are no match for prolonged drought. If the West is to weather a new era of aridity aggravated by climate change, it will have to embrace a far more sustainable relationship with its natural environment. As Governor Brown said simply, "It's a different world. We have to act differently." Weather patterns and forest densities mean that the Southwest will be at the forefront of observable climate change effects. As Nevada water official Scott Huntley observed, "It's not just urban conservation that's needed. We need to conserve it across the spectrum of all water uses." The 1450-mile Colorado River sates the water demands of 40 million westerners and produces 15% of the entire country's food, yet the allocation rates outlined in the 1922 Colorado River Compact grossly oversubscribed the average annual flow of this liquid lifeline. Climate change studies predict that rising temperatures alone will further reduce current lower flows by 5–35%; reduced rainfall/drought would only increase these losses. As legal adviser Bradley Udall remarked, "Nineteenth century water law is meeting twentieth century infrastructure and twenty-first century climate change, and it leads to a nonsensical outcome." More dams and even desalinization, which is both expensive and energy intensive, cannot overcome this reality, but other kinds of technology may catalyze change.

The real solution to the West's water woes is conservation. States and cities across the West have committed to recycling sewage effluent for irrigation and incentivized xeriscaping (landscaping with drought-tolerant plants) through rewards programs and "cash for grass" payments. Water recycling constitutes a (small) element of California's Proposition 1 designed to encourage municipalities to retrofit golf courses, parks, offices, and even homes with "purple pipe" carrying non-potable but clean water for lawns, toilets, and landscaping. In late 2014, San Diego voters agreed to spend $3 billion on equipment to purify enough water to slake the thirst of one-third of the city. In Arizona, farmers minimize run-off and erosion by employing laser leveling techniques to ensure that their fields are truly flat, while Washington and California hop fields and vineyards utilize drip irrigation to deliver precise water dosages and minimize evaporation losses. Simple shifts from alfalfa to wheat and even cotton cultivation would save more than 250 000 acre-feet, and more efficient region-wide irrigation would add another million acre-feet to this total. California's corporate agribusiness currently ships much of its agricultural wealth to China, effectively exporting the region's most precious commodity. The West will have to reconsider this unsustainable trade relationship in the light of climate change. In Colorado, for example, the New Belgium Brewing Company does its part to conserve the river's flow by recapturing and reusing wastewater, donating a portion of its proceeds to non-profit conservation organizations, and initiating the Save the Colorado campaign dedicated to promoting sustainable river utilization – proving that sometimes drinking beer actually can save water. And in December of 2014, California, Arizona, and Nevada signed a historic agreement to add collectively as much as 3 million acre-feet of water to Lake Mead by 2020, primarily through conservation efforts. The results are beginning to trickle in: Las Vegas residents use 30% less water than they did a decade ago, while Phoenix denizens have reduced their water habit by 27% over the past two decades – a feat Albuquerque has also matched, and El Paso uses less water per person (130 gallons/day) than any other city in Texas. In the end, as southern Nevada water official John Entsminger concluded, "we're all going to have to use less water."

The West's prolonged twenty-first century drought also has implications for the region's forests. Since the turn of the century, average annual

Figure E.1   Between 2002 and 2003, the one-two punch of drought and bark beetles caused a massive regional die-off of piñon trees across the American Southwest, one of the many consequences of global climate change. Source: Reproduced with permission of Dan Flores.

temperatures have risen faster in the Rocky Mountains than in the United States as a whole. In the past 15 years, climate change here has unleashed a triple threat of heat and drought stress, ferocious wildfires, and tree-killing insects that has decimated tens of millions of trees – the equivalent of the entire state of Colorado. Over the past decade, for example, New Mexico has experienced a stunning decline in its coniferous forests including its especially hard-hit official state tree, the piñon pine (see Figure E.1). The state simply no longer receives enough moisture to support the existing biomass and so new ecosystems – drier, more savannah-like grasslands – are emerging. In California's Sequoia National Park, the namesake trees, called by some "the immortals" because of their extreme longevity, are also dying. One survey of the Sierra Nevada forests in the spring of 2015 estimated the death toll at more than 10 million trees, including sequoias, in the previous year alone. Hotter summers combined with lower mountain snowpack and reduced runoff will dramatically alter and reduce the forests that filter our air and transform carbon dioxide into life-supporting oxygen.

These stressed and declining forests in turn amplify wildfire risks. Wildfire season in the West now typically stretches across seven months, fully two months longer than in the past. Although fire is a natural process that keeps forests ecologically balanced, much of the West is overgrown and overly dense due to human intervention, which long protected timber commodities at the expense of forest health. As these forests shed conifers in record numbers, they build up a tinderbox of dead and dying fuels that erupt into raging conflagrations. California's 2015 *annus horribilis*, for example, recorded more than 6300 wildfires. In nearby Washington, the largest fire in the state's history, the Okanogan Complex, blackened more than 250 000 acres and was growing by more than 26 square miles *per day*. On average, the Rocky Mountain West now endures 18 large fires *every year*, an increase of nearly 75% since the 1980s.

In addition to drought stress and wildfires, the West's forests, from Mexico to the Yukon, are under siege by the pine bark beetle, which has chewed its way through scores of millions of acres. These highly specialized members of the weevil family are actually native to the West and have co-evolved with pines as an essential player in overall forest health: they cull weak trees and ensure the survival of the fittest pines. What makes their recent outbreaks remarkable is, again, their scale. Warmer temperatures mean that some populations of mountain pine beetles now produce two generations per year, dramatically boosting the bugs' threat to lodgepole and ponderosa pines. Milder winters fail to kill them off. Writer Dan Baum notes that at times the swarms are "so intense that you can scoop them out of the air with a baseball cap." And dehydrated trees cannot produce beetle-repelling resins. The US Forest Service estimates that southern Wyoming and northern Colorado lose 100 000 beetle-infested trees *a day*. At this level of population density, the beetles no longer serve as mere forest product recyclers; instead they become prime timber predators, taking out even healthy trees overwhelmed by the pest invasion.

As with water in the West, the key to overall forest health will be a focus on sustainability. Although climate change will continue to exert a disproportionate influence, ecologist Craig Allen has prescribed "a radical rethinking" of water management in the forests to include irrigating the forests, more aggressive tree thinning efforts, mulching to retain soil moisture, and the use of drought-tolerant native species to stabilize the biomass. Promising research is also exploring non-toxic repellants to thwart beetle expansion. In particular, scientists have been able to use the beetles' own pheromones, or scent signals, against them in some cases. When a tree has reached its carrying capacity of beetles, the living put out a "no vacancy" pheromone that repels further colonization. The US Forest Service is currently using this new pheromone-mimicking strategy to protect high-value pines in places like trailheads and ski areas. But different beetles require different chemical processes, so there is a constant battle to stay one step ahead of the bugs. Scientists may ultimately have to concede, however, that this dramatic forest thinning is evolutionarily essential. As forest pathologist Diana Six observed, "The beetles are taking out trees adapted to past conditions that aren't doing well, and they're leaving behind some that are better-adapted, but didn't grow as well 50 years ago."

Range shifts for both plant and animal species are a normal part of adaptation, but this accelerated rate of global climate change is too rapid to allow for evolution and ecosystem reorganization. Plants and animals simply can't keep up. The US Geological Survey reports, for example, that New Mexico will lose at least 50 birds to range shifts and decline: bright blue piñon jays will struggle for survival as the state's piñon forests disappear; wild turkeys and ducks will face severe restrictions to their summer and winter ranges; and songbirds such as rosy finches may also vanish, making Rachel Carson's warning of a Silent Spring seem eerily prescient. In California, 16 of the state's 23 butterfly species have shifted their migration patterns and now arrive earlier, which may throw off their historical breeding, pollination, and feeding patterns. Western cutthroat trout and already endangered salmon, which rely on glacier-fed cold water streams for survival, face an even more grave future as fewer mountain ranges are able to maintain year-round snows, and their rivers warm up. In the Great Basin, scientists project that habitat fragmentation caused by just a 3 °F temperature increase (the region is currently at plus 2 °F) will lead to an extinction rate of between 20 and 50%, with alpine and subalpine zones suffering the disproportionate effect as they essentially disappear. If temperatures continue to rise, federal studies indicate that 20–30% of the plant and animal species thus far evaluated at the national level risk extinction, a rate 10 000 times greater than in the deep geological past. Beyond that, some international studies indicate that, if left unchecked, global climate change will eliminate as many as one-third of all plants and *half* of all animals in the places they now inhabit.

One indicator of overall environmental health in the West, as well as the nation, is the humble honeybee. Although an "exotic" species introduced to the Americas during the Columbian Exchange, the honeybee has become the foundation upon which much of the West's floral health – and by extension human health, is based. Because of their intimate and symbiotic relationship with plants, bees function as sensitive ecosystem monitors, a western version of the diagnostic "canary in a coal mine." As writer Hannah Nordhaus observed, honeybees "are the glue that holds our agricultural system together." Although they are not native to the Americas, their busy attention to flowering plants accounts for one out of every three mouthfuls of food Americans consume each day. In 2006, these essential insects began experiencing a catastrophic population decline – 30–90% mortality – that scientists have labeled "colony collapse disorder" (CCD). This phenomenon, where the entire worker bee population simply disappears despite the presence of an otherwise healthy hive structure (queen, comb, brood, honey), has proved a mystifying and maddening malady. The death toll is stunning – losses in the order of one-third of all honeybee colonies nationwide *every year*. Scientists are stumped. Parasitic mites, pathenogenic fungi, and pesticides, particularly a relatively new class of poisons known as neonicotinoids that attacks the central nervous system, are the primary culprits, but there are no definitive connections. As with bison demise and the Dust Bowl, the ultimate answer to the CCD riddle may not be one saboteur but many, the convergence of a perfect storm of stresses. What scientists do know is that since the 1940s, the number of viable bee colonies in the nation has contracted by half. The plight of the honeybee may be symptomatic of our own environmental fate.

The economics of these plant and animal range shifts and disappearances is sobering. In addition to food and water crises and fouled air no longer filtered by the planet's biota, these changes threaten the very livelihoods of citizens and revenue generators in local, state, regional, national, and international economies. In New Mexico, for example, bird watchers and hunters contribute millions of dollars to the state's economy. No birds, no tourist dollars. In California, bees make or break the $4 billion almond industry, by far the state's most valuable agricultural export. The US Department of Agriculture estimates that bees increase national crop values by at least $15 billion every year. Yet despite these pollinator demands, frustrated and disheartened commercial beekeepers continue to hang up their veils – nearly three-quarters have called it quits in the past 15 years. "It depresses the hell out of me," lamented one. In addition to threatening wholesale habitat reorganization, climate change also spurs the growth of weedy plant species that produce allergy-aggravating pollen. Interestingly, locally produced honey naturally alleviates many of these symptoms. Anecdotal evidence shows that as bees collect pollen spores and nectar from the plants that make humans sneeze and wheeze, they transfer small amounts into their honey, which triggers an immunity response, similar to a vaccine, in some sufferers. No bees means more sneeze.

So where to live in this hotter, drier West? Scientists suggest that most of California and the Southwest will suffer from drought, severe high temperatures, and wildfires. Phoenix already endures more than a month's worth of days that exceed 110 °F, and it's going to get hotter. Within the last few years the city has added "haboobs" to the experience of desert living. These ferocious dust storms roar across the Valley of the Sun like a wall of dirt and debris reminiscent of the old Dust Bowl, and reduce visibility to zero. As geography professor Camilo Mora suggested, "if you do not like it hot and do not want to be hit by a hurricane … the best place really is Alaska." Seattle, too, ought to brace for environmental refugees fleeing the heat; in anticipation, Washington state is already vigorously planting vineyards and gearing up to replace Napa Valley as the nation's winery. No matter where we choose to reside, however, the conclusion is the same: we must learn to live differently in the West.

In 2015, August 13 marked "Earth Overshoot Day," the day on which global resource consumption "overshoots" the planet's capacity for production.

Figure E.2 "Earthrise," William Anders' December 24, 1968, iconic photograph of the earth taken from Apollo 8 during the first manned mission to orbit the moon. Nature photographer Galen Rowell has called it "the most influential environmental photograph ever taken." Source: Reproduced with permission of the National Aeronautics and Space Administration (NASA).

It is the earliest on record. In 2014, this measure of humans' Ecological Footprint was four days later: August 17. As recently as 1970, Earth Overshoot Day was December 23. For the United States, the statistics are even more grim; in 2015, the nation overshot its biocapacity on July 14. In other words, just to sate our national demands would require 1.9 earths. We've only got one (see Figure E.2). Clearly, we are moving in the wrong direction.

Yet all is not lost. If collective human action can slow the emission of climate-warming greenhouse gases, the results are hopeful and positive; much like the effects of quitting smoking, the benefits appear almost immediately and improve the longer healthy behavior continues. To that end, in late 2014, the United States and China announced a historic cooperative agreement to combat global climate change by reducing carbon emissions and fossil fuel consumption. In August of 2015, President Barack Obama followed up this promise by announcing the implementation of the Clean Power Plan, designed to reduce greenhouse gas emissions from power producers (especially coal) by more than

30% by 2030, along with a voluntary Clean Energy Incentive Program to encourage the development of renewable energy. If greenhouse gas reductions begin by 2017, for example, the planet can avoid 60% of projected species losses; even if by 2030, losses decrease by about 40%.

Global commitment to sustainability culminated in the 2015 United Nations Climate Change Conference, known as COP21, where 196 countries negotiated the Paris Agreement to limit global warming to less than 2 °C compared to pre-industrial levels. The model for the world? California. A western state with an economy that would make it the eighth-largest on the planet, California is at the vanguard of renewable energy development. "The biggest worry is that curtailing greenhouse emission will have really negative economic effects," said Ann Carlson, co-director of UCLA's Emmett Institute on Climate Change and the Environment. "So far, that has not been true for California." As state Senator Fran Pavley emphasizes, "It has not been the choice between a healthy environmental [*sic*] and a healthy economy. We can do both." As the West seeks a sustainable future, its cities must incentivize green building projects, public transportation, recycling, environmentally appropriate landscaping, wise water use, renewable energy, and citizen education. Voters must demand responsive and responsible local, state, and federal representation that prioritizes environmental health and sustainability. And individuals must strive to reduce their personal ecological footprint by reducing consumption and practicing recycling, composting, and participatory democracy. Simple steps such as supporting local food growers, eliminating plastic bottles and bags, eating less meat, conserving water, and voting with personal spending dollars for sustainably produced items, can produce profound, long-term, positive results. Other possibilities include habitat restoration and preservation. Westerners can protect the birds and the bees by xeriscaping with native plants, providing water and bird nesting boxes, eliminating pesticide use, and keeping cats indoors. Hobby beekeepers are helping sustain hives and pollination activities at the local level, which also creates a closer human bond with the natural environment even in the cities. One practice that must change is commercial pesticide application. Despite beekeeper appeals to the Environmental Protection Agency and several European nations' bans on the use of neonicotinoids because of their detrimental effect on birds and bees, Americans still apply the poisons to nearly all (95%) of their corn and canola oil crops, and to a significant percentage of most other commercially raised agriculture. The cost–benefit analysis here simply doesn't add up.

Climate change will continue to accelerate as the world's population races toward a staggering 9.5 billion or more by 2050. Humans have proved a remarkably successful species. In fact, archeology professor Curtis Marean has called us "the most invasive species of all." We did not reach the 1 billion mark until the early 1800s. The second billion took 120 years. Yet in the past 50 years, we have more than doubled: 3 billion in 1959, 4 billion in 1974, 5 billion in 1987, 6 billion in 1998, 7 billion in 2011. How will we sustain the demands for clean air, clean water, healthy food, automobiles, refrigerators, and cell phones from such burgeoning numbers? Global climate change suggests that we have already overburdened our planet's atmosphere, oceans, and lands. Are we running head-long toward The Great Filter and an unfortunate rendezvous with Fermi's Paradox?

The answer to this question must lie in environmental sustainability, in living within, not in spite of, the carrying capacity of the land. It is our realistic "geography of hope" in the West. For too long we have perfected the "tragedy of the commons." We have exploited and commodified nature in the pursuit of ephemeral economic profits without considering long-term ecological costs. As the writer Wallace Stegner so eloquently observed,

> Something will have gone out of us as a people if we ever let the remaining wilderness be destroyed; if we permit the last virgin forests to be turned into comic books and plastic cigarette cases; if we drive the few remaining members of the wild species into zoos or to extinction; if we pollute the last clear air and dirty the last clean streams and push our paved roads through the last of the silence, so that never again will Americans be free in their own country from the noise, the exhausts, the stinks of human and automotive waste. And so that never again can we have the chance to see ourselves single, separate, vertical and individual in the world, part of the environment of trees and rocks and soil, brother to the other animals, part of the natural world and competent to belong in it.

The broad arc of deep history reveals the evolving relationship between humans and the natural environment in the West over time. As westerners transitioned from subsistence to market economies, and wrestled with frontier and conservation-versus-preservation ideologies, they ultimately arrived at a present characterized by climate change and sustainability challenges. As environmental historian William Cronon has admonished, we are "unlikely to make much progress in solving these problems if we hold up to ourselves as the mirror of nature a wilderness we ourselves cannot inhabit." The complex symbiotic relationship between humans and the environment reveals that there is no "pristine myth" to which we should strive to return; the West as "Eden" has always been a false illusion and it is time to lose it once and for all.

Instead, it is time for a new, collective paradigm – what we might instead call a "triumph of the commons." Just as no one person is responsible for environmental decline, no one person can hope to change the West's – or the planet's – environment. But when each individual acts in the common *good*, rather than in his or her own selfish interest, the results promise extraordinary dividends – what writer Sherwood Anderson has called "a sense of bigness outside ourselves." If it is true that we care about what we know, then the simple question is: what will you do?

Suggested Reading

Dan Baum, "Change of State," *Scientific American*, August 2015, 64–71.

Mike Bostock and Kevin Quealy, "Mapping the Spread of Drought Across the U.S.," *New York Times*, updated weekly. www.nytimes.com/interactive/2014/upshot/mapping-the-spread-of-drought-across-the-us.html?&hp&action=click&pgtype=Homepage&version=HpSumMediumMediaFloated&module=second-column-region&region=top-news&WT.nav=top-news&_r=2&abt=0002&abg=1 (accessed February 8, 2016).

Nick Bostrom, "Where are They? Why I Hope the Search for Extraterrestrial Life Finds Nothing," *MIT Technology Review*, May/June, 2008, 72–77. www.nickbostrom.com/extraterrestrial.pdf (accessed February 8, 2016).

Gabe Bullard, "We've Consumed More than the Earth Can Produce this Year," *National Geographic*, August 13, 2015. http://news.nationalgeographic.com/2015/08/150813-earth-overshoot-day-earlier. See also: www.overshootday.org (accessed February 8, 2016).

The Climate Issue," *National Geographic* Vol. 228, No. 5 (November 2015).

Joel E. Cohen, "Seven Billion," *New York Times*, October 23, 2011.

Ian Crawford, "Where Are They? Maybe We Are Alone in the Galaxy After All," *Scientific American*, Vol. 283, No. 1 (July 2000), 38–43.

William Cronon, "The Trouble with Wilderness; or, Getting Back to the Wrong Nature," in William Cronon, ed., *Uncommon Ground: Rethinking the Human Place in Nature* (New York: W.W. Norton & Co., 1995), 69–90.

William deBuys, "Phoenix in the Climate Crosshairs: We Are Long Past Coal Mine Canaries," *TomDispatch*, March 14, 2013. www.tomdispatch.com/post/175661/tomgram%3A_william_debuys%2C_exodus_from_phoenix/#more (accessed February 8, 2016).

Jared Farmer, "This Was the Place: The Making and Unmaking of Utah," *Utah Historical Quarterly*, Vol. 82, No. 3 (Summer 2014), 185–193. See also: http://heritage.utah.gov/history/farmer (accessed February 8, 2016).

Jennifer A. Kingson, "Portland Will Still Be Cool, but Anchorage May Be the Place to Be," *New York Times*, September 22, 2014.

Leia Larsen, "Bark Beetle Research Shows Future Evolution of Utah Forests," [Ogden] *Standard Examiner*, October 7, 2014.

Daniel deB. Richter, "The Accrual of Land Use History in Utah's Forest Carbon Cycle," *Environmental History*, Vol. 14, No. 3 (July 2009), 527–542.

Sammy Roth, "At Paris Climate Talks, Nations Looking to California," *The Desert Sun*, November 30, 2015. www.desertsun.com/story/news/environment/2015/11/14/paris-climate-talks-nations-look-california/75540806 (accessed Feburary 8, 2016).

Wallace Stegner, "Wilderness Letter," Wallace Stegner to David E. Pesonen, December 3, 1960. http://web.stanford.edu/~cbross/Ecospeak/wildernessletter.html (accessed February 8, 2016).

John D. Sutter, "Climate Change: Why Beef is the new SUV," September 29, 2015. www.cnn.com/2015/09/29/opinions/sutter-beef-suv-cliamte-two-degrees (accessed February 8, 2016).

Tim Urban, "The Fermi Paradox," *Huffington Post*, August 17, 2014. www.huffingtonpost.com/wait-but-why/the-fermi-paradox_b_5489415.html (accessed February 8, 2016).

Bryan Walsh, "The Plight of the Honeybee," *Time*, Vol. 182, No. 8 (August 19, 2013), 24–31.

Richard White, "'Are You an Environmentalist or Do you Work for a Living?': Work and Nature," in William Cronon, ed., *Uncommon Ground: Rethinking the Human Place in Nature* (New York: W.W. Norton & Co., 1995), 171–185.

Michael Wines, "Colorado River Drought Forces a Painful Reckoning for States," *New York Times*, January 5, 2014.

Michael Wines, "States in Parched Southwest Take Steps to Bolster Lake Mead," *New York Times*, December 17, 2014.

Index

Note: Page numbers in **bold** refer to figures.

Losing Eden: An Environmental History of the American West, First Edition. Sara Dant.
© 2017 John Wiley & Sons, Inc. Published 2017 by John Wiley & Sons, Inc.

CPSIA information can be obtained
at www.ICGtesting.com
Printed in the USA
LVHW051154011221
704676LV00002B/43

9 781118 934289